THE
JOHN CHAPPELL
NATURAL PHILOSOPHY
SOCIETY

Papers by the members of the John Chappell Natural Philosophy Society
presented at their annual conference

University of Washington, Seattle, United States 2019

Edited by

DAVID DE HILSTER
ROBERT DE HILSTER

Boca Raton, Florida

John Chappell
Natural Philosophy Society
THE PUBLISHER

2019

Published by the John Chappell Natural Philosophy Society, Boca Raton, Florida.

Library of Congress Cataloging-in-Publication Data:

CNPS 2019 Annual Proceedings / David de Hilster, Bob de Hilster . . . [et al.].
p. cm.-(CNPS series in science annuals)

"CNPS-Publications."
Includes bibliographical references and index.
ISBN 978-0-359-71534-3 (pbk.)
Printed in the United States of America.

10 9 8 7 6 5 4 3 2 1

Table of Contents

An Electric Field Model of the Aether

Musa D. Abdullahi

12 Bujumbura Street, Wuse 2, Abuja, Nigeria, e-mail: musadab@outlook.com

Space contains isolated bodies or matter each composed of equal amounts of positive and negative electric charges as sources of electric fields. The fields exist in space but are balance out exactly everywhere. The strong electrical forces of repulsion and attraction, between the charges in two neutral bodies, proportional to the product of the charges, in accordance with Coulomb's inverse-square law, balance out exactly everywhere and vanish at infinitely long distances from their respective sources. The equivalent pressure, energy density and mass density of the aether, proportional to the sum of squares of the electric fields, remain. The weak gravitational forces of attraction, proportional to the product of squares of the charges, remain and add up, in accordance with Newton's universal law. The universal space, crisscrossed by electric fields from charges in bodies, constituting a medium supporting electromagnetic radiation and gravitation, is proposed to be the aether, as conceived by J. C. Maxwell and others. Electric permittivity and magnetic permeability are properties of electric fields of the aether. A vacuum has no property. Beyond the aether is a vacuum, with no electric field, extending to infinity.

Keywords: Aether, electric charge, electric field, force, gravity, light, mass, matter, radiation, space, speed

1. Introduction

It is reasonable to suppose that there is an absolute medium, filling all space, which supports gravitation and in which light and other electromagnetic waves are propagated. This luminiferous medium is called aether [1, 2, 3], as conceived by Newton [4], Einstein [5] Maxwell [6] and others. The concept of the aether, as a medium uniformly filling the whole of infinite space, is untenable, since nature is not so infinitely extravagant. The only thing that could uniformly fill the whole of infinite space is a vacuum, a void or nothingness or something, like an electric field, a vector quantity vanishing to zero at infinitely long distances from its source. Beyond the aether is a vacuum, a void extending to infinity. A vacuum has no property.

An identification of what really constitutes the aether would go a long way in resolving the difficulty with warping or curvature of four-dimensional space-time continuum of the theory of general relativity [7, 8]. It may lead to the long-awaited unification of electrostatic and gravitational forces [9, 10]. The force of gravity, such a pervasive and persistent force, may have a simple and reasonable explanation, which has, so far, escaped the modern physicists.

What is introduced in this paper is an electric field model of the aether, where the universal space, crisscrossed by electric fields from matter or bodies, constitutes the aether. Therefore, the aether exists wherever there is matter in space. Electric permittivity μ_o and magnetic permeability ε_o are properties of electric fields of the aether.

The electric field model of the aether is simpler, in contrast to the epola (electron-positron lattice) model [11, 12], the Dirac model (infinite sea of particles with negative energy) [13] and other particulate models. The aether is a real thing and fathomable but not so easily perceptible. What-

ever aether model there might be, it must account for the force of attraction due to gravity and supp ort propagation of electromagnetic radiation at the speed of light. Wherever, there is an imbalance of the electric charges in matter a resultant electric field appears. The electric field model of the aether should exhibit frictional motion of electric charges, like an electron, with emission of radiation. The model should allow motion of neutral bodies, like the planets, without friction.

1.1. Speed of light in the aether

James Clerk Maxwell [6], in a significant and epoch-making treatise, showed that the speed c of light, in space, is given by:

$$c = \frac{1}{\sqrt{\mu_o \varepsilon_o}} \qquad (1)$$

where μ_o is the permeability and ε_o the permittivity of electric fields of the aether. It can immediately be seen that the electric field model of the aether supports propagation of electromagnetic waves at the speed of light. What remains is to show that the aether, in the electric field model, has pressure, energy density and mass density, like air in the atmosphere.

1.2. Michelson-Morley experiment

The Michelson-Morley (MM) [14, 15] experiment was performed in 1887 by Albert Michelson and Edward Morley. It was an attempt to detect the existence of a supposed medium permeating all space as the carrier of light waves, like sound waves in the atmosphere. The experiment showed that there was no transit time difference for light, reflected off mirrors, travelling at the same speed and covering the same distance in perpendicular directions. Whereas if the aether carrier existed, light moving in the direction of propagation should take a longer time to cover the same distance compared to light going in the perpendicular direction. The null result of the MM experiment, and that of many subsequent and more refined ones, was considered as evidence that the aether did not exist.

The author [16] showed that the result of the MM experiment should be a null as there was no relative motion between the source of light and the reflecting mirrors or any other part of the apparatus. The aether could exist but might be a different kind of carrier of light.

1.3. Mass-energy equivalence law

The author [17] showed that the mass-energy equivalence law, should be:

$$E = \frac{1}{2}mc^2 \qquad (2)$$

where E is the electrostatic energy or intrinsic energy of a particle of mass m. Equation (2) differs from the relativistic formula by a factor of 1/2.

The intrinsic energy of an electric charge of magnitude Q, in the form of a spherical shell of radius a, is given by the well-known classical formula:

$$E = Q^2/8\pi\varepsilon_o a \qquad (3)$$

In view of equations (1) and (2), equation (3) gives mass m of the charge as:

$$m = \mu_o Q^2/4\pi a \qquad (4)$$

Since mass of a particle can be expressed in terms of its electric charge (equation 4) and charge is supposed to be independent of velocity, so also mass should be independent of velocity. The total energy of a particle of constant mass m moving with velocity v, is the sum of intrinsic energy and kinetic energies, thus:

$$E = \frac{1}{2}(c^2 + v^2) \qquad (5)$$

2. Electric Field Model of the Aether

The aether is proposed to be a crisscross of electric fields emanating from neutral bodies or matter in space. Each neutral body is composed of equal numbers or equal amounts of electric charges. Figure 1 shows two neutral bodies of masses M_1 and M_2 with their centers of gravity at a separation r. Let mass M_1 consist of $N_1/2$ positive charges and $N_1/2$ negative charges, represented as $(-1)^i Q_i, (i = 1, 2, 3...N_1)$. Let M_2 contain $N2/2$ positive charges and $N2/2$ negative charges, put as $(-1)^j Q_j, (j = 1, 2, 3...N2)$. An electric charge $\pm Q_i$ of mass m_i, in M_1, is separated from an electric charge K_j of mass m_j, in M_2, by a distance r_{ij}. The space within and between the masses, in Figure 1, constitutes the aether. The sum of electric charges, in each mass, comes to zero, thus:

$$\sum_{i=1}^{N_1}(-1)^i Q_i = 0$$

$$\sum_{j=1}^{N_2}(-1)^j Q_j = 0$$

Figure 1.   Two Bodies with M_1 and N_1 Charges

where: $(i = 1, 2, 3...N_1)$ and $(j = 1, 2, 3...N_2)$

Figure 1: Two neutral bodies, of mass M_1 consisting of N_1 electric charges $\pm Q_i$ each of mass m_i and mass M_2 containing N_2 electric charges $\pm K_j$ each of masses m_j, with their centers of gravity distance r apart in direction $\hat{u}$.

The aether is characterized, at any point in space, by the charge and field equations:

$$\sum_{i=1}^{N}(-1)^i Q_i = 0 \qquad \sum_{i=1}^{N} Q_i^2 \neq 0 \qquad (6)$$

$$\sum_{i=1}^{N}(-1)^i \mathbf{E}_i = 0 \qquad \sum_{i=1}^{N} E_i^2 \neq 0 \qquad (7)$$

where $i = 1, 2, 3...N$. Q_i is the ith charge and E_i the electric field intensity (a vector) from the ith charge in a body. The number N may be infinitely large.

While the electric charges and fields from a neutral body, being positive and negative, balance or cancel out exactly everywhere, the square of each electric charge (Q_i^2) and square of each electric field (E_i^2) add up to account for the pressure, energy density and mass density of the aether and gravitational force of attraction. The wonder of the square of a negative number being always positive is in manifestation here.

Any imbalance in the electric fields of the aether would cause polarization of the electrical charges in a body and possible flow of charges as an electric current. Indeed, the aether is comparable to air in the atmosphere, with pressure and density and where wind flow takes place as a result of imbalance in pressure.

2.1. Equivalent pressure, energy density and mass density of aether

An electric field E_i exerts equivalent pressure p_i, a scalar quantity, given by:

$$p_i = \varepsilon_o E_i^2$$

The equivalent pressure P of electric fields of the aether, at a point, becomes the sum:

$$p = \sum_{i=1}^{\infty} p_i = \varepsilon_o \sum_{i=1}^{\infty} E_i^2 \neq 0 \qquad (8)$$

The equivalent energy density of an electric field E_i is:

$$w_i = \frac{1}{2}(\varepsilon_o E_i^2)$$

The equivalent energy density (*not mass density*) of the aether, at a point, becomes the sum:

$$W = \frac{1}{2}\left(\varepsilon_o \sum_{i=1}^{\infty} E_i^2\right) = \frac{1}{2}(\rho c^2) \qquad (9)$$

The equivalent mass density (*not energy density*) ρ electric fields of the aether, at a point, becomes the sum:

$$\rho = \mu_o \varepsilon_o \sum_{i=1}^{\infty} E_i^2 \qquad (10)$$

The aether is a medium, like air, water, an elastic solid or a stretched string, supporting propagation of a wave with speed v, given by equations (1), (8) and (10), as:

$$v = \sqrt{\frac{\gamma P}{\rho}} \qquad (11)$$

For the aether $\gamma = 1$, for air $\gamma \approx 1.4$. For an elastic solid the pressure P, is Young's modulus.

2.2. The aether and gravitation

The small force f between two electric charges Q and K, in space, is a combination of electrostatic forces of repulsion or attraction given by Coulomb's law and gravitational force of attraction given by Newton's law. The force of repulsion is:

$$\mathbf{f} = \frac{QK}{4\pi\varepsilon_o r^2}\hat{\mathbf{u}} - G\frac{m_1 m_2}{r^2}\hat{\mathbf{u}} \qquad (12)$$

Substituting for the masses m_1 and m_2 with m_1 proportional to Q^2 and m_2 proportional to K^2, into equation (12), gives the force of repulsion as:

$$\mathbf{f} = \frac{QK}{4\pi\varepsilon_o r^2}\hat{\mathbf{u}} - G\frac{m_1 m_2}{r^2}\hat{\mathbf{u}} = \frac{QK}{4\pi\varepsilon_o r^2}\hat{\mathbf{u}} - \chi\frac{Q^2 K^2}{r^2}\hat{\mathbf{u}} \qquad (13)$$

where $\hat{\mathbf{u}}$ is a unit vector in the direction of force of repulsion and χ is a constant. In equation (13) the force of attraction, where K is negative, is:

$$\mathbf{f} = \frac{QK}{4\pi\varepsilon_o r^2}\hat{\mathbf{u}} - \chi\frac{Q^2 K^2}{r^2}\hat{\mathbf{u}} \qquad (14)$$

The import of equations (13) and (14) is that force of repulsion between two charges is slightly decreased and force of attraction similarly increased. The net force of attraction $\mathbf{f}_G$ is:

$$f_G = -2\chi\frac{Q^2 K^2}{r^2}\hat{\mathbf{u}} \qquad (15)$$

For a body of mass M_1 containing $N_1/2$ positive and N1/2 negative charges each of magnitude Q and another body of mass M_2 containing $N_2/2$ positive and $N_2/2$ negative charges each of magnitude K, separated by a distance Z in space, the force of gravitational attraction comes to:

$$F_G = -G\frac{M_1 M_2}{Z^2}\hat{\mathbf{u}} = -\frac{2\chi}{Z^2}N_1 N_2 Q^2 K^2\hat{\mathbf{u}} \qquad (16)$$

3. Results and Discussion

1. The paper has succeeded in presenting the aether as a balanced electric field medium, which has pressure, energy density and mass density. The medium supports propagation of electromagnetic radiation at the speed of light (equation 1) and accounts for the force of gravity between bodies in space (equation 16). The pressure, like atmospheric pressure, being uniform in all directions at a point, is not perceived, except in isolated or abnormal circumstances.

2. The aether exists as a manifestation of electric fields from electric charges in matter or from bodies in the universal space.

3. The electric field model of the aether is simpler and more useful than the particulate models under discussions by physicists.

4. The electric field model of the aether should put to rest the notion of warping of four-dimensional space-time continuum to make for force of gravity between objects.

4. Conclusion

The universal space, crisscrossed by electric fields emanating from neutral bodies, balancing out exactly everywhere in space and vanishing at infinitely long distance from their respective sources, constitutes the aether, as a physical medium intercon-necting everything and supporting radiation and gravitation.

REFERENCES

1. E. Whitteker (1910): *A History of the Theories of Aether and Elec tricity*. Longmans Green and Co., Dublin.

2. F. Wilczek (1999): "The Persistence of Aether". *Physics Today*. Vol. 52, pp. 11 - 13.

3. http://www.spaceandmotion.com/Physics-Space-Aether-Ether.htm

4. I. Newton (1687): *Mathematical Principles of Natural Philosophy* (Translated by F. Cajori). University of California Press, Berkeley (1964).

5. A. Einstein (1905): "On the Electrodynamics of Moving Bod ies". Ann. Phys., 17.

6. J. Maxwell (1892): *A Treatise on Electricity and Magnetism*. Ox ford, 3rd ed., Part iv, Chap. 2

7. *R. Geroch (1981): General Relativity from A to B. University of Chicago Press. Chicago.*

8. J. Hartle (2003): *Gravity: An Introduction to Einstein's General Relativity*. Addison-Wesley, San Francisco.

9. M. Abdullahi (2017): "The Aether: A balanced Electric Field Medium for Radiation and Gravitation". 3rd CNPS Conference, Vancouver, Canada.

10. M. Abdullahi (2016): "An Explanation of the Cause of Force of Gravity", 2nd CNPS Conference, Boca Raton, FL, USA.

11. M. Simhony (1994): *Invitation to the Natural Physics of Matter, Space and Radiation*. The Hebrew University, Jerusalem.

12. http://www.epola.co.uk/dwnlds/epola%20in%20brief.pdf

13. P. Dirac (1930): "A theory of Electrons and Positrons".
Proc. R. Soc. London. A. 126 (801), 360 - 365.

14. A. Michelson & E. Morley (1887): "On the relative motion of the earth and the luminiferous ether". *Am. J. Science. 34, 333*)

15. Michelson (1904): "Relative Motion of Earth and Aether." *Philosophical Magazine.* (6), 8, 716-719.

16. M. Abdullahi (2014): Available at:
https://www.academia.edu/38044838/
Relativistic_and_Non-relativistic_Explanations_
of_the_Results_of_Michelson-Morley_Rogers_
Bertozzi_Sagnac_

17. M. Abdullahi (2014): Available at:
https://www.academia.edu/7692116/On_the_Energy_
and_Mass_of_Electric_Charges_in_a_Body

Aberration Of Electric Field And Accelerated Motion Of An Electron With Constant Mass

Musa D. Abdullahi

12 Bujumbura Street, Wuse 2, Abuja, Nigeria, e-mail: musadab@outlook.com

An electron of mass m and charge e moving with velocity v at angle θ to the accelerating force, due to an electric field of intensity E, is subject to aberration of electric field. Aberration is due to relativity of velocity $(c - v)$ between the electrical force, transmitted with velocity of light c and the electron moving with velocity v at time t. The accelerating force m(dv/dt) is less than the electrostatic force eE, the difference being radiation reaction force. Energy radiated is the difference between change in potential energy and change in kinetic energy. Motion of the electron with constant mass and its radiation power are treated under acceleration with $\theta = 0$ or deceleration with $\theta = \pi$ radians or at constant speed v, in a circle of radius r, with $\theta = \pi/2$ radians. It is shown that circular revolution of an electron round a central force of attraction, as in the Rutherford's nuclear model of the hydrogen atom, is without radiation and stable outside quantum mechanics, contrary to classical and relativistic electrodynamics.

Keywords: Aberration angle, acceleration, electric field, charge, mass, radiation, special relativity, velocity

1. INTRODUCTION

Aberration of electric field is a phenomenon similar to aberration of light discovered by English astronomer, James Bradley, in 1725 [1]. This discovery, which provided the first direct confirmation of motion of the Earth round the Sun, is one of the most precise and significant findings in science. Bradley made the first determination of the speed of light, in comparison with the speed of revolution of the Earth round the Sun. Aberration of light is a clear demonstration of relativity of speed of light with respect to a moving object, contrary to the theory of special relativity [2, 3]. Aberration of light is now relegated to the background in favour of special relativity. It is hardly mentioned in modern physics, perhaps because it is a contradiction of the cardinal principle of constancy of the speed of light according to the theory of special relativity [4, 5]. Aberration of light is considered as more of a subject in remote astronomy rather than a course in mundane physics. Aberration of electric field is the missing link in modern physics. This paper hopes to bring back to limelight aberrations of light and its twin, aberration of electric field. [6, 7]

Indeed, if the speed of light were that constant for all observers, it could never have been measured, in so far as any measurement is relative to something. The speed of light turned out to be the most measured and most accurately known quantity in the universe.

Electromagnetic radiation, as well as an electrical force, is propagated in space with velocity of light. In the aberration of electric field there is relativity of velocity (c - v) between an electrical force propagated with velocity of light c and an electron moving at velocity v. As such, the electrical force cannot "catch up" and impact on an electron also moving with the velocity of light c. The velocity of light thus becomes the ultimate limit to which an electric field can accelerate an electron with emission of radiation and mass of the particle remaining constant.

With constant mass, the limiting speed of light comes about as a result of emission of radiation. Energy radiated from an electron, accelerated by an electric field, is the difference between change in potential energy and change in kinetic energy. At the speed of light, as a limit, the energy radiated is equal to the potential energy lost in the accelerating field.

As a result of aberration of electric field, for an electron of mass m and charge $-e$ moving at time t with velocity v and acceleration dv/dt in an electric field of intensity E, the accelerating force m(dv/dt) is less than the electrostatic force $-eE$, the difference is the radiation reaction force [6, 7]. The radiation reaction force in rectilinear motion is $-eE\mathbf{v}/c$ and radiation power, the scalar product of radiation force and velocity, becomes eEv^2/c. In circular revolution perpendicular to the electric field, the radiation power is zero. This makes motion of an electron, round a positively charged nucleus, as in the Rutherford's nuclear model of the hydrogen atom without radiation and stable outside Bohr's quantum mechanics [8, 9].

2. ABERRATION ANGLE

Figure 1 depicts an electron of mass m and charge $-e$ moving at a point P with velocity v at an angle θ to the force of attraction due to an electric field of intensity E from a stationary source charge +Q at O. The electron is subjected to aberration of electric field whereby the direction of propagation of the force of attraction, given by velocity vector c, is displaced from the instantaneous line PO through angle of aberration α such that:

$$sin\alpha = \frac{v}{c}sin\theta \qquad (1)$$

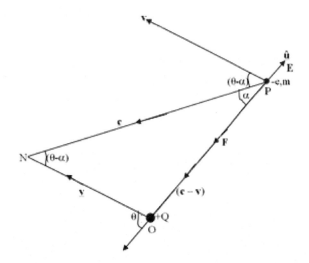

Figure 1. An electron of mass m and charge $-e$ at P moving with velocity v in an electric field of intensity E due to a stationary charge +Q at O.

The astronomer James Bradley first derived equation (1), as given by the sine rule with respect to the triangle PON in Figure 1.

3. VELOCITY OF TRANSMISSION OF ELECTRICAL FORCE

With reference to Figure 1, the vector z = (v - c) is the relative velocity of transmission between the electrical force propagated with velocity of light c and the electron moving with velocity v, thus:

$$\mathbf{z} = (\mathbf{c} - \mathbf{v}) = -\sqrt{c^2 + v^2 - 2cv\cos(\theta - \alpha)}\hat{\mathbf{u}} \quad (2)$$

where $(\theta - \alpha)$ is the angle between the vectors c and v and $\hat{u}$ is a unit vector in the positive direction of the field E. The electron can move with $\theta = 0, \theta = \pi$ radians or $\theta = \pi/2$ radians.

With $\theta = 0$ there is motion in a straight line with acceleration and equations (1) and (2) give the relative speed of transmission of the electrical force as:

$$z = (c - v) \quad (3)$$

Where $\theta = \pi$ radians there is motion in a straight line with deceleration and the relative speed of transmission becomes:

$$z = (c + v) \quad (4)$$

If $\theta = \pi/2$ radians and noting that $sin\alpha = v/c$, there is circular revolution with constant speed v. Equation (1) and (2) give the speed of transmission of the force as:

$$z = \sqrt{c^2 + v^2} \quad (5)$$

Equations (3), (4) and (5) demonstrate the relativity of speed of light with respect to a charged particle moving with speed v.

4. ACCELERATING FORCE

The accelerating force F at time t, in an electric field of magnitude E, is put as:

$$\mathbf{F} = \frac{eE}{c}(\mathbf{c} - \mathbf{v}) = md\mathbf{v}/dt$$

and

$$\mathbf{F} = -\frac{eE}{c}\sqrt{c^2 + v^2 - 2cv\cos(\theta - \alpha)}\hat{\mathbf{u}} = md\mathbf{v}/dt \quad (6)$$

where $\hat{\mathbf{u}}$ is a unit vector in the positive direction of the electric field E. For motion in a straight line under acceleration, with $(\theta = 0$, equations (1) and (6) give the vector equation:

$$\mathbf{F} = -eE(1 - v/c)\hat{\mathbf{u}} = -m\frac{dv}{dt}\hat{\mathbf{u}} \quad (7)$$

The scalar first order differential equation, for an accelerated electron, is:

$$eE(1 - v/c) = m\frac{dv}{dt}\hat{u} \quad (8)$$

The solution of equation (8) for an electron accelerated from zero initial speed, by a uniform electric field of magnitude E, is:

$$\frac{v}{c} = 1 - e^{-(at/c)} \quad (9)$$

where $a = eE/m$ is a constant.

For motion in a straight line under deceleration, with $\theta = \pi$ radians, equations (1) and (6) give the vector equation:

$$\mathbf{F} = -eE(1 + \frac{v}{c})\hat{\mathbf{u}} = m\frac{dv}{dt}\hat{\mathbf{u}} \quad (10)$$

The scalar first order differential equation, for a decelerated electron, is:

$$eE(1 + \frac{v}{c}) = -m\frac{dv}{dt} \quad (11)$$

The solution of equation (11) for an electron decelerated from the speed of light c, by a uniform electric field of magnitude E, is:

$$\frac{v}{c} = 2e^{-(\frac{at}{c})} - 1 \quad (12)$$

Where $\theta = \pi/2$ radians there is motion in a circle of radius r with constant speed v and centripetal acceleration of v^2/r. Noting that $sin\alpha = v/c$, equation (1) and (6) gives the vector:

$$\mathbf{F} = -eE\sqrt{(1 - v^2/c^2)}\hat{\mathbf{u}} = -m\frac{v^2}{r}\hat{\mathbf{u}} = -m_o\frac{v^2}{r}\hat{\mathbf{u}} \quad (13)$$

$$-eE\hat{\mathbf{u}} = -\frac{mv^2}{r\sqrt{(1 - \frac{v^2}{c^2})}}\hat{\mathbf{u}} = -\frac{m_o v^2}{r\sqrt{(1 - \frac{v^2}{c^2})}}\hat{\mathbf{u}} \quad (14)$$

where $m = m_o$, the rest mass.

The theory of special relativity gives the force F on an electron of a rest mass m_o, not equal to the moving mass m, moving in a circle of radius r, in a radial electric field of magnitude E, with constant speed v, as:

$$-eE\hat{\mathbf{u}} = -\frac{mv^2}{r}\hat{\mathbf{u}} = -\gamma\frac{m_o v^2}{r}\hat{\mathbf{u}} \qquad (15)$$

Equation (14) becomes identical to equation (15), if:

$$m = \frac{m_o}{r\sqrt{\left(1 - \frac{v^2}{c^2}\right)}} = \gamma m_o \qquad (16)$$

where the moving mass m is not equal to the rest mass m_o. The Lorentz factor γ (gamma) was introduced by Albert Einstein, in the manner of Lorentz-FitzGerald length contraction, to explain why a charged particle cannot be accelerated beyond the speed of light c.

The relativistic mass-velocity formula (equation 16) is a physical misinterpretation of mathematical equations (13) and (14). It is the accelerating force which decreases with speed, reducing to zero at the speed of light, not the mass that increases with speed to become infinitely large at the speed of light. The relativistic mass m, in equation (16), is the ratio of electrostatic force (-eE) to centripetal acceleration $(-v^2/r)$, for circular revolution, with radius r, of an electron, in a radial electric field of magnitude E, as given by equation (14). Lorentz factor γ urned out, by sheer coincidence or through Einstein's genius, to be the ratio of electrostatic force (-eE) to accelerating force $(-mv^2/r)$ in circular revolution.

It is unfortunate that special relativity chose mass, rather than force, as the variable. It is much easier to deal with zero force at the speed of light than infinite mass at the speed of light. It is wrong to apply equation (16) to rectilinear motion. For rectilinear motions, equations (8), (9), (10), (11) and (12) apply.

5. RADIATION POWER

The difference between the accelerating force F, as given by equation (6), and the electrostatic force or impressed force eE, is the radiation reaction force, a vector Rf given by:

$$\mathbf{R}_f = \frac{eE}{c}(\mathbf{c} - \mathbf{v}) + e\mathbf{E} \qquad (17)$$

The radiation power Rp is the scalar product $\mathbf{v}.\mathbf{R}_f$, thus:

$$R_p = -\mathbf{v}.\mathbf{R}_f = -\frac{eE}{c}(\mathbf{c} - \mathbf{v}).\mathbf{v} + e\mathbf{E}.\mathbf{v} \qquad (18)$$

With reference to Figure 1, radiation power R_p is expressed in terms of the angles θ and α, as:

$$R_p = \frac{eEv^2}{c} - eEv\cos(\theta - \alpha) + eEv\cos(\theta) \qquad (19)$$

Equation (19) shows that the radiation power is eEv^2/c under acceleration with $\theta = 0$ or under deceleration with

$\theta = \pi$ radians. For $\theta = \pi/2$ radians, there is circular revolution, round a central force of attraction, with zero radiation power.

6. RESULTS AND DISCUSSION

1. Equations (3), (4) and (5) show that the speed of light, relative to an observer, can be subtracted from or added to, contrary to the relativistic principle of constancy of the speed of light for all observers, stationary or moving. So, a cardinal principle of the theory of special relativity is being debunked once more.

2. It is shown that Lorentz factor γ in equation (15) has nothing to do with mass, but it is the result of motion of a charged particle perpendicular to an electric field.

3. The relativistic mass-velocity formula (equation 16) is an example of Beckmann's Correspondence Theorem (Petr Beckmann, 1987: Einstein Plus Two. Golem Press), where the desired or expected result is correct but based on the wrong underlying principles.

4. An electron accelerated or decelerated by an electric field, with constant mass, emits radiation such that the energy radiated is the difference between change in potential energy and change in kinetic energy.

5. An important result of this paper is contained in equation (19). Here, if $\theta = \pi/2$ radians, there is circular revolution, round a central force of attraction, with constant speed and zero radiation power. This makes Rutherford's nuclear model of the hydrogen atom inherently stable. Revolution in a circle is at constant radius with constant speed, without any change in potential or kinetic energy. Radiation takes place only where the electron is somehow dislodged from a circular orbit. It then revolves in an unclosed elliptic orbit with radial displacement and change in potential and kinetic energy and emission of radiation at the frequency of revolution, before reverting back to the stable circular orbit.

7. CONCLUSION

The paper has brought out the significance of aberration of electric field as a missing link in modern physics. With aberration of electric field there should be no need for the theory of special relativity to explain the speed of light being an ultimate limit and no need for quantum mechanics to explain the source of radiation from accelerated charged particles.

REFERENCES

1. J. Bradley (1728): Phil. Trans., Royal Soc. 35, 406. Also see: https://en.wikipedia.org/wiki/James_Bradley

2. A. Einstein (1905): "On the Electrodynamics of Moving Bodies", Ann. Phys., 17, 891.

3. A. Einstein; & H.A. Lorentz (1923): The Principles of Relativity, Matheun, London.

4. E. F. Taylor & J. A. (1992): Spacetime Physics: Introduction to Special Relativity. W. H. Freeman, New York.

5. A. Shadowitz (1988): Special relativity (Reprint of 1968 ed.). Corier Dover Publications. pp. 20-22.

6. M.D. Abdullahi (2013): "An Alternative Electrodynamics to the Theory of Special Relativity", 20th NPA
Conference, College Park MD, USA.

7. M.D. Abdullahi (2014): Available at:
https://www.academia.edu/7691834/
Motion_of_an_Electron_in_Classical_
an_Relativistic_Electrodynamics_
and_a_Radiative_Electrodynamics

8. E. Rutherford (1911): "The Scattering of α and β
Particles by Matter and the Structure of the Atom". Phil.
Mag., 21 (1911), 669.

9. N. Bohr (1913): On the Constitution of Atoms and
Molecules, Phil. Mag., Series 6, 26.

Notes on a Uniformitarian Hypothesis of the Microcosm

Jim T. Decandole

19166 130th Ct. NE Bothell, WA, USA, Jimhu@yahoo.com

The problem with mathematical theoretical physics is anthropocentrism. The mental activities of observation, recording, calculation, and manipulation are not relevant in the microcosm. An alternative method of natural philosophy is to neglect the human experience and describe the phenomena of nature from the point of view of the center of a fundamental particle.

The smallest, simplest particle and form of motion, called an oscillon, is assumed here to be the sole constituent of space, matter, light, and neutrinos. The oscillon is visualized as a self-generating, self-measuring, and oscillating physical system of a point of tangency moving relative to a constant center point.

The interactions of pairs of oscillons vary from complex to simple, according to the dimensionality of their relativity. When the spatial relations of interacting oscillons are three-dimensional, they form matter. When their relativity is two-dimensional, they form light. When they interact in one dimension, they form neutrinos.

Keywords: space, matter, light, neutrino

1. Anthropocentrism

Our search for knowledge and understanding about the world and the natural phenomena that we observe is an endeavor that has been made more difficult by our self-awareness. We tend to place ourselves at the center and to believe that our existence and our consciousness are of the greatest importance. This is called anthropocentrism.

This tendency has affected the work of philosophers and scientists since the ancient Greeks and is still doing so today. We have to be aware of the effects of our bias and to struggle to overcome them. Nevertheless, great progress has been made over the centuries, and the pace of new discovery is constantly accelerating.

In the past, anthropocentrism was responsible for the idea that the Sun, Moon, and planets revolve around the Earth. For more than two thousand years, this idea was the prevailing view of astronomers. Together, the European Renaissance, the Copernican revolution, and the invention of the telescope were sufficiently powerful to push the old belief aside.

The old false world-view was geocentric. The new correct understanding was that the Sun is at the center of the solar system, that Earth is a planet, and that planets revolve around the Sun. The heliocentric theory of the motions of the planets was tested and proved, resulting in great advances in the work of astronomers and all those who use the scientific method.

The process of overthrowing a false theory involves several steps. First, all the assumptions of the theory must be identified. Next, each assumption must be examined and tested. If an assumption is found to be inadequate in any way, then alternative assumptions should be proposed. In their turn, the alternative assumptions require study and experiment.

Anthropocentrism manifests itself in other aspects of science. We have a tendency to put matter at the center, thereby neglecting the other forms of motion. Our identification with the three-dimensional world in which we exist results in other possible interactions being ignored. We elevate the properties of matter-such as mass, temperature, charge, gravity, magnetism, density, and chemistry-to the status of fundamentals when they may be mere side effects. We seem to be obsessed with the search for life on other planets and on whether humans are unique.

1.1. Geocentric Theory

The knowledge used by the first natural philosophers to develop their theory of motion was the store of data gathered by their predecessors: time-keepers, astronomers, astrologers, calendar officials, and teachers.

These forerunners had no "geocentric theory"; they just observed, measured, and recorded what they saw in the Solar System. They did not need the "relativity of moving objects" to accomplish their tasks successfully. The more observations they recorded, the more accurately they calculated future events. Their method worked, and it was a functional system of time based on the motion of the Earth, even though the practitioners believed it was the motion of the heavens. Copernicus initiated the scientific revolution in the sixteenth century by overthrowing the assumption that the Earth is stationary at the center of the universe, and by asserting that the Earth is a planet like the others orbiting the Sun. Since then, there have been a series of setbacks of the anthropocentric worldview.

Darwin established in the nineteenth century that humans are animals like the others. Then we learned that the chimpanzee is our closest relative and that we originated in the highlands of East Africa. We had earlier realized that the Sun was a star like the others. The geologists Hutton and Lyell overthrew catastrophism and demonstrated the great age of the Earth and the irrelevance of our species to its history.

2. Uniformitarianism

The modern scientific study of geology got started when Charles Lyell, following the hypothesis of James Hutton, formulated the principle of uniformitarianism. Lyell suggested that the processes of geological change are the same now as they were in the past. He postulated that the entire history of the Earth could be accounted for by the agents of change that we now observe, which include deposition, earthquakes, erosion, floods, glaciation, mountain building, volcanism, weather, and so on.

At the time that Lyell advanced his new principle, the main alternative theory was catastrophism, a concept that derived from Biblical and mythical accounts of the history of the Earth. Its main idea was that periodically devastating floods or earthquakes transformed the surface of the planet. This meant that there was no record in the present of the pre-catastrophic state of affairs.

Catastrophism proposed that geological change was sudden, violent, and global. Uniformitarianism countered that (a) change is gradual, incremental, and local; (b) that geological processes are evolutionary; (c) that the processes occurring currently are the same processes as have always been happening; and (d) that the results of those processes are always the same. Uniformitarianism proposes that all geological formations are caused by physical and chemical processes that have operated continuously and uniformly throughout time.

The question arises whether uniformitarianism is only a geological theory, or can be a theory of nature as a whole. Furthermore, is it only applicable to a particular place and time, or does it explain with equal validity the phenomena of other places and other times? Is it a useful doctrine for the study of both macrocosmic and microcosmic processes? Is it adaptable to the sciences of astronomy and particle physics?

2.1. Fundamental Processes

Microcosmic processes such as combustion, deposition, erosion, evaporation, flow, freezing, growth, melting, and solution are generally unceasing and occur at any time. Macrocosmic processes, such as collisions, eruptions, explosions, and tremors, usually start and stop and are time-specific.

Natural selection, the fundamental process in biological history, is consistent with the uniformitarian principle. A fundamental process such as evolution, the hydrological cycle, plate tectonics, and sedimentation may be interrupted or reoriented by earthquakes, volcanism, asteroid impacts, nuclear winter, and extinction, but will immediately resume unchanged.

2.2. Continuous Motion

The assumption that microcosmic phenomena are uniformitarian is the important idea here. The motion of a particle, its oscillation and interaction, is continuous and cannot be changed or stopped. The particle's measurement of itself and other particles with which it interacts is also continuous, and the method of measurement does not change.

No matter what macrocosmic events occur that may cause changes in larger structures of which the particle is a constituent, the particle remains intact, its motion is the same, and its being after the event is identical to its previous existence.

3. Time

The human experience of time is very much related to its passage. The interaction with our environment that enables us to survive is shaped by the succession of night and day, the yearly seasons of heat and cold and rain and drought, and the times of flowering and fruiting. Our lives are a progression over time from birth and growth to maturity, followed by old age and death. In the course of our lives, we store experience in our brains by means of memory. The elders pass on their accumulated knowledge through their leadership, parenting, teaching, and storytelling. For thousands of generations, this culture of tradition, common sense, lore, and mythology was passed orally from mind to mind as our species thrived and spread across the continents. Human memory is thus a non-technological means of recording experience and retrieving it at a later date when the cycle of life makes it useful. In prehistoric days, we started to record events by means of pictures, such as paintings on rock and carvings on bone. We learned the cycles of movement of the Earth, Sun, Moon, planets, and stars, and used this knowledge to invent calendars.

Subsequently, we made use of monuments, alphabets, ideograms, writing systems, books, libraries, printing, film, photography, audiotape, and videotape as permanent recordings independent of memory.

Our experience of time is dominated by our awareness of the present, past, and future. Our knowledge of the past is entirely dependent on memory and recording, which are products of human consciousness. Without such recording and transmission, the past does not exist.

3.1. Experience of Time

The most anthropocentrically misleading aspect of human behavior is our experience and understanding of time, which are dominated by our recording of it. Our relation to time is fundamentally different from the particle's experience of time. In the microcosm, there are no means of recording, and the only time is now.

The function of time in the microcosm is a quantity of motion. The period of oscillation is the time of the simplest form of motion. When two spatially identical oscillating particles interact, the variables in their temporal relation are duration and phase. Are the periods the same length? Are the points of reflection simultaneous?

3.2. Memory

How is time experienced by a particle without memory? What is motion without memory? Is there a passage of time without memory?

Time is a quantity that relates to change and variation. Period, frequency, and speed are all temporal measurements. Oscillation, a process of change wherein the direction of motion regularly reverses, involves a measurable quantity of time.

3.3. Recording

In nature, time is only duration. In order for the past to exist, there must be a record, and for a record such as memory, writing, film, or tape to exist, there must be a brain.

3.4. Units of Time

Our units of time are based on an arbitrary standard derived from the natural period of terrestrial rotation. The division of that period into a functional minimum unit, the second, is based on the human biorhythm-that is, the heartbeat. Any period of time less than a second is not practical. Nevertheless, it is short enough that at a given order of magnitude, it is within the range of the natural unit of time, which I will discuss at length in Section 14.

3.5. Measurement of Time

What is time without sensing, observing, and analyzing? There is no origin, no past, no memory, no history, and no future.

What is the particle's self-measurement in respect to time? An oscillating particle has a period, frequency, and phase. A particle in motion has distance, direction, and speed.

The devices and techniques used in the measurement of time, including clocks, calendars, stopwatches, carbon dating, dendrochronology (measurement of tree rings), and stratigraphy (study of rock strata) are all artificial. Units of time such as the nanosecond, second, minute, hour, day, week, month, and year are also man-made.

3.6. Now and Then

Nature is all about order, uniformity, symmetry, constancy, and repetition. To the human mind, this is uninteresting, even boring. We prefer the unusual, the sudden, and the unexpected changes, which are more stimulating and entertaining to our senses and mind. However, to experience an event as unusual, one needs memory in order to compare now and then. Nature has no such expectations.

Of course, there is change in nature; otherwise, there would be no universe. Motion is the difference between nothing and something, and all change in nature is a form of motion.

4. Mathematics

Mathematics is a mental, abstract, and artificial activity that requires a means of recording and retrieval. It is a process that uses observations, measurements, and data acquired at intervals of time.

Calculation is a behavior that is not possible for a microcosmic particle. But self-measurement and short-range measurement of other directly interacting particles are within the competence of a particle.

4.1. Nature's Mathematics

When it came to selecting a method of inquiry for this work, by necessity I chose natural philosophy over mathematical physics because my formal training in mathematics ended at high school graduation. Subsequently, I learned that nature's mathematics is exclusively metrical-

that is, about measurement.

Nature is simple and so is geometry. The symbolism of higher mathematics is impossible for a simple, minimal, oscillating particle, whose capabilities are limited to the four measurements of distance, angle, direction, and period.

4.2. Unreasonable Effectiveness

Sometimes the use of mathematics in science is unnatural. That is, it is contrary to nature. It is artificial, forced, and affected.

Many physicists refer to the phrase the unreasonable effectiveness of mathematics. Mathematics can be described as flexible, versatile, conformable, adaptable, facile, contrivable, or handy. An example of this artificiality is "renormalization," a mathematical procedure used in relativistic quantum field theory.

Another case of anthropocentric mathematics in mainstream physics is the use of probability and statistics. This requires many observations over a period of time, the gathering of data about prior and subsequent conditions, and calculations that use sophisticated techniques. This process is unnatural, mental, and artificial. The particle in the microcosm does not have the capability of statistical analysis. Therefore, such work is of dubious value to natural philosophy.

4.3. An Invented Tool

Modern science is extremely dependent on modern mathematics. Newton initiated this fundamental relationship within the scientific method when he demonstrated mathematics' utility in explaining and describing motion. Nowadays, facts and theories cannot be deemed proven unless they include an accepted mathematical description.

However, we must not forget that mathematics is a tool. It is artificial rather than natural. Before the rise of homo sapiens there was no calculating with numbers, but the phenomena of nature were the same as today. In fact, Newton achieved his understanding of motion after he invented the method of calculus.

We invented mathematics because it was useful, just as we made tools because they made our everyday tasks easier. Nature is the source of materials like stone, wood, fiber, clay, and metal. Our counting, observing, and measuring of objects and events in our environment led us to the science of numbers - arithmetic, geometry, algebra, trigonometry, and calculus. So, what are nature's numbers?

4.4. Epicycle and Deferent

In the pre-Copernican period, when it was mistakenly believed that the Sun, Moon and planets revolved around the earth, it was still possible for astronomers and astrologers to predict the movements and positions of these bodies. There was a mathematical foundation for their work, which was based on analysis of long-term observation. Here is a demonstration of the power of human intellect using the tool of calculation to produce practical mathematical analysis and description, despite inaccurate observation, primitive technology and a false set of assumptions.

The epicycle and the deferent were among the mathematical constructions that enabled the ancient astronomers to make sense of the observed retrograde motion of the planets in the course of their annual path through the heavens. The assumption was that a planet's motion had two components - a circular orbit of the earth called the deferent and a smaller circle, called the epicycle, about points on the deferent. To improve the accuracy of the calculations Ptolemy added the equant and the eccentric, both mathematical constructs based on imagined motion. But these devices did not describe anything real and, when the heliocentric theory came to the forefront, they were shown to be inventions of the mind.

In the present age, as investigation of nature extends in scale from the smallest particle to the largest group of galaxies, but direct observation is impossible in either case, scientists have markedly increased their dependence on mathematics. In other words, we already have deficits in observation and technology, so beware false theory, mistaken assumptions, anthropocentrism, misleading analogies and unnatural inventions.

5. Motion

On the planet Earth, a macrocosmic object, we see that processes of change other than voluntary animal locomotion are cyclical. A cycle is a sequence of events or phases that are repetitive, continuous, and connected in a circular way, such that the last is followed by the first. Among such cycles are the hydrological, atmospheric, biological, and tectonic.

Water is the material of the hydrological cycle. It evaporates from the surface of the ocean, rises into the air, and accumulates into clouds. In the clouds, water condenses and forms droplets that precipitate back to the surface as rain, dew, or snow, which flow into the ground, streams, and rivers. Small rivers are tributaries of large rivers that flow downhill until they discharge their water back into the ocean.

The air of the atmosphere is a mixture of several substances. Plants inspire carbon dioxide from the air and through photosynthesis extract the carbon and expire oxygen. Animals breathe in the oxygen and use it as fuel through respiration.

In the biological cycle, molecules of the various elements and compounds found in the atmosphere, hydrosphere, and lithosphere are used in the growth of plants and animals. When a life form dies, its tissues are eaten or otherwise transformed, and its chemicals are returned to the soil. Rock is the material of the tectonic cycle. Heated rock from the mantle layer of the Earth flows to the surface of the lithosphere at the mid-ocean ridges and forms new oceanic crust. It also accumulates in the magma chambers of volcanoes and is erupted as lava, ash, and gas. The oceanic crust and its added layer of sediment are subducted at the continental margins as the less dense oceanic plate descends under the heavier continental crust and is returned to the mantle.

Another cycle is found in the action of wind and water eroding surface rocks into sand, stones, mud, and minerals, which are transported and deposited elsewhere. Surface currents in the ocean move warm water from the tropics toward the poles, while deep currents carry cold water in the opposite direction. Similarly, the movement of air-that is, the weather-results in heating and cooling in different locales, depending on the direction of flow between the equator and the poles. The cycle of seasons-winter, spring, summer, and fall-is determined by the annual orbit of the Earth and its changing orientation toward the Sun.

All these cycles are species of motion-that is, change in the spatial relations of molecules or objects. The cycles are also uniformitarian processes-that is, they are continuous and never stop. And whereas the effects are macrocosmic, the agents are, by and large, microcosmic particles.

5.1. Theory of Motion

A theory of motion is a theory of everything. The final theory will be a correct, complete theory of motion in the microcosm. Every physical thing, object, phenomenon, particle, and form of energy is a species of motion.

A theory of motion is a description of change in spatial relations. All possible arrangements of systems of particles are the stable endpoints of changes in the spatial relations of the members of the system.

5.2. Wave or Particle?

Since the scientific revolution began, there has been debate and confusion about whether a given microcosmic phenomenon is exhibiting wave or particle motion. Particle describes structure and substance more than motion. Wave describes motion while ignoring structure.

Light has historically been deemed to be waves, not particles, and has been described by writers as sunbeams, rays, sunshine, rainbows, shadows, radiation, emanation, flames, lightning, and so on. One former hypothesis was that light is corpuscular-that is, consists of corpuscles. When the hypothesis that light is a wave became ascendant, its motion was described as wave trains and wave fronts. Its wave motion is transverse, not longitudinal.

The light produced in Crooke's Tube was named cathode rays. Subsequently, it turned out to be a stream of electrons, particles of matter.

Radioactivity was determined to be alpha particles (helium nuclei), beta particles (electrons), and gamma rays (high-frequency electromagnetic radiation).

The photon is a calculated quantity of radiation energy, used mathematically as if it were a particle.

Cosmic rays were found to be energetic atoms and protons and are now called cosmic particles. The neutrino began as a quantity of energy that was calculated to be "missing" during certain radioactive transformations. Later, a similar calculation found it to be part of the process of nucleosynthesis in stars. It was calculated to be magnetically neutral and was named the "neutrino," a small neutral particle. The physical hypothesis of the neutrino has always been as a particle. Until now, it has never been described as a wave or a form of radiation. This calculating, hypothesizing, and naming was a process in which anthropocentrism was influential. Having been deemed to be a particle, the neutrino was then assumed to have mass, a property of all particles of matter. Efforts have been made to determine a measurable mass for the neutrino, and some experimenters have claimed success.

However, light is deemed to be massless and chargeless, so little experimental effort has been made to measure its mass.

5.3. Flocking and Schooling

The flocking of birds, the schooling of fish, and the swarming of insects are a familiar type of motion. A large number of animals move as a group, seemingly in unison. How do individuals in the group maintain their position and direction?

These animals have a field of vision that is practically spherical. The sight of an individual animal gives it a constant three-dimensional view of the adjacent members of the group. The eyes are the organ that senses the information needed for measurement. The ones in front of and behind the measuring animal are in its radial dimension, those to the left and right are in its tangential plane, and those above or below are in a parallel plane.

The motion of the animal at the center is defined by its central spherical frame of reference. The spatial relations between the central member and each adjacent member are determined by an external tangential frame of reference. The information obtained by the central member visually enables it to determine whether the other is approaching or receding, turning left or right, or moving up or down. It can then make instantaneous adjustments in its own motion, as necessary, to stay at the same distance and in the same direction as its fellows.

6. Measurement

The only natural part of mathematics is measurement. The rest of mathematics is performed by humans and is artificial, symbolic, and mental. Nature does not calculate. Nature does not record. Nature has no memory.

The explanatory power of mathematics regarding natural phenomena is undoubted. Words, pictures, diagrams, models, and animation are equally powerful. Mathematics is the least realistic method of explanation. Realism requires a moving three-dimensional representation.

Measurement is integral to the interaction of two identical particles. The one has "knowledge" of the other by means of their common frame of reference. Natural measurement is a continuous process. It is an ongoing "estimation" by one of the relativity of the other. Is its distance farther or nearer? Is its angle changing leftward or rightward? Is its direction the same or opposite?

The range of interaction between the two particles is limited in an inverse square relation. The maximum amount of the cause and effect of the interaction occurs at the minimum separation. The four quantities that a particle can measure are distance, angle, direction, and duration. The three spatial dimensions-radial, tangential,

and axial-and the temporal dimension are derived from these measurements. They determine relations and properties of plane, size, volume, separation, phase, symmetry, synchronicity, front/back, up/down, left/right, clockwise/counter clockwise, and same/opposite.

With its internal spherical frame of reference, a particle measures itself. It measures the other with an external frame of reference-the common frame of reference of the two particles. An external frame is tangential; and when the two particles are at minimum separation, the external frame is tetrahedral.

7. The Practice of Physics

The relationship between the phenomena of nature and the mathematical theoretical practice of physics needs to be reassessed. Among the topics to be considered here are:

1. The role of mathematics: calculation vis-Ãă-vis measurement.
2. Awe of mathematical prediction.
3. The baneful effects of anthropocentrism.
4. A suffocating orthodoxy.
5. Denigration of visualization and modeling.
6. Experiments that are manipulative rather than imitative of nature.
7. Theories about the observer.
8. Misconceptions about time.
9. Expensive technology; e.g., the large hadron collider and the space telescope.

7.1. Mathematical Assumptions

James Clerk Maxwell is remembered for his equations. He changed natural philosophy into the mathematical physics that today is the ascendant methodology in the study of nature. He is admired for his successful "prediction" of radio, the long-wave part of the spectrum of radiation. He did not discover radio. That laboratory task was achieved by Heinrich Hertz, two decades later. One could say that Hertz invented radio, since both the transmitter and the receiver were manmade. Natural radio was "discovered" when the study of static interference affecting commercial broadcasters was traced to lightning and the Sun, Jupiter, and the Milky Way.

Prediction is no big thing. Successful discoverers or inventors ask the right questions, make true assumptions, and see the way forward. During the course of their work, most of them have also made wrong assumptions and failed to demonstrate that those assumptions conform to nature. Many other researchers have never succeeded because their speculations, conjectures, assumptions, hypotheses, and theories were not "predictions." Their imaginings did not come true, their ways forward were dead ends, and their hypotheses were falsified, but their work was a necessary part of the process of increasing knowledge of nature.

Sometimes, false assumptions still produce acceptable mathematical results. One such case is the 2,000-year reign of the geocentric Ptolemaic theory of the solar system. In this case, the acceptable results were the calculation of future solar eclipses, the positions of the planets and stars, and the time of the New Moon, upon which the calendar and astrology were founded. In those days, professional mathematicians made a good living as astronomers, astrologers, and calendar officials because their observations and calculations were sufficiently accurate to satisfy their employers. The admiration engendered by their ability to foretell and prophesy future events is still with us.

This sad story of ignorance can largely be attributed to the flexibility of mathematics, its ease of manipulation, and its susceptibility to "renormalization." Mathematics is a tool, an artifice, whose users are adept at inventing and theorizing. In their imaginations, the ancient practitioners of the numerical arts, who were the leading applied mathematicians of their time, found the deferent, the epicycle, the equant, and the eccentric.

The geocentric theory was falsified by the work of Copernicus, Brahe, Kepler, Galileo, and other philosophers and inventors, with the end result being a scientific revolution. The accuracy and quantity of data resulting from Brahe's patient observations, the new technology of the lens maker's magnifying telescope, and the imagination, mathematical skill, and thirst for knowledge of Copernicus, Kepler, and Galileo came together to conceive, express, and find evidence for an alternative hypothesis of the solar system. It was a heliocentric system, which assumed that the Sun was at the center, and the Earth was a planet like the others.

7.2. Maxwell's Equations

Maxwell, who founded the school of mathematical theoretical physics, was a master of applied physics. One of his assumptions was that it was impossible to "know the mechanism of electricity and magnetism." This meant that it didn't matter if his mathematical model of electrical phenomena were based on false or unproven assumptions, so long as the methods, applications, and technologies derived from this model worked in everyday practice.

This puts him in the same category as Ptolemy and other ancient applied astronomers. Their highly successful mathematical method of determining future positions of the heavenly bodies was based on false assumptions about the motions of the Earth, Sun and planets. However, unlike Maxwell, they did not express the pessimistic, unscientific view that the actual motions were unknowable.

7.3. Microcosmic Causes

The microcosm is primary, the macrocosm is secondary. The microcosm is hidden. We cannot see, touch, or sense it, and our instruments cannot detect or measure it. It can only be imagined, assumed, conjectured, visualized, modeled, and hypothesized. Its visible effects can be observed, detected, measured, calculated, and manipulated. Knowledge of these effects leads indirectly to theories about their causes.

For twenty-five centuries, the atomic hypothesis of matter successfully explained every terrestrial phenomenon

that was investigated. However, it remained a theory, unproven according to its doubters. Then, in 1896, radioactivity was discovered. This previously unknown phenomenon, now revealed by nature itself, provided ample evidence of atomic processes, configurations, magnitudes, and properties. This discovery required a revision of the ancient atomic theory to account for the particles that matter and space are made of.

7.4. Imponderable Fluids

Over the centuries, natural philosophers and physicists frequently assumed that the unknown cause of an observed effect was "an imponderable fluid." Phlogiston was involved in combustion. Caloric was the fluid of heat. The phenomenon of electricity was a current (some said two). The medium of light waves was an ether. Vitalism was the force of life.

The mysteries of nature, especially the motion of particles in the microcosm, were deemed to be forever invisible, undetectable, and immeasurable. That kind of assumption is still being used today. "Dark" matter and "dark" energy are postulated to explain mathematical hypotheses and interpretations about space and its contents, gravity, and natural history.

7.5. Atomic Structure

When radioactivity was discovered in 1896, exploration of the microcosm went into top gear. A succession of discoveries using this new tool occurred over the next fifty years. Radioactivity was found to consist of alpha particles, beta particles, and gamma rays. Cathode rays and beta particles were found to be different manifestations of the same phenomenon-free electrons, which were identified as the negatively charged constituents of atoms.

After the atomic nucleus was discovered, its positively charged constituent was named the proton. The hydrogen atom was correctly described as having a nucleus of a proton orbited by an electron. Isotopes of elements were discovered, and the constituent of the atom that is neither negative nor positive was named the neutron-a transformed proton.

Nucleosynthesis, the stellar process whereby hydrogen atoms are transformed by fusion into helium and the other elements, accompanied by the emission of gamma rays and neutrinos, was correctly described. Neutrinos were noted to be the least interactive particle in the microcosm. The shell structure of the electrons and its role in the formation of molecules was understood. We learned that the electron's trajectory was variable, and more than one electron shared the same orbit.

7.6. Natural and Artificial Electricity

Natural electricity is static electricity. It manifests itself as a discharge. A current or flow of electricity in a metal wire is artificial, invented electricity. The electricity of a chemical battery or other storage device is also man-made. The power of an electromagnet or generator is a product of human technology.

The word charge is derived from the Latin carrus, which means "wagon" or "load."

7.7. Observers and Interactors

Theories about or including the observer are common in physics today. This tendency is anthropocentric to the extreme. The observer may be a physicist, philosopher, mathematician, or participant in a thought experiment, who experiences relativity, simultaneity, uncertainty, or some other physical concept deemed to be a mystery of nature. An explanation of the concept is deemed to be necessary for the progress of science.

However, an observer is not relevant to natural phenomena, such as the motion of particles in the microcosm, because an observer is not an interactor. Particles do not sense that they are being observed, and their motion is not affected by the presence of humans. The involvement of a human is not reacted to nor measured. Nature can only be understood by describing its own experience, and the human experience is not pertinent.

Being on a train in a station and glancing out to observe a passing train on an adjacent track is a familiar experience. Which train is moving, or is it both? The immediate visual information is insufficient for a determination and must be supplemented by looking at the ground or sky, so that the observer may sense his own movement or lack thereof.

The relativity of the trains' motion is irrelevant because they are not interacting. Each train, one with an observer, is interacting with the Earth, either in motion in one direction or the opposite, or it is standing still. The motion of each train is not a reaction to the other nor the cause of the other.

7.8. Thought Experiment

Thought experiment is a method of inquiry used by theoretical mathematical physicists. Usually, the subject of the thought is microcosmic motion, which leads to calculations and equations related to the real, natural, and observable consequences of unobserved, unknown fundamental motions. Examples of thought experiments include: a planet's orbit having a perfect circle; Maxwell's demon; blackbody radiation; an observer moving at near-light speed; Schrodinger's cat; and the leap of the electron.

However, frequently the type of imagined motion is physically impossible, improbable, or unnatural. But despite that, it is possible to describe these observable effects mathematically in ways that enable us to make use of them.

The process of thought experiments results in formulas, equations, statistics, and designs that are useful in applied physics and technology. Electrical and electronic engineers are dependent on such mathematics, but many of them have doubts about the assumptions regarding the microcosmic causes of the effects that they make use of.

7.9. Non-Euclidean Geometry

The Cambridge Dictionary of Scientists, in its entry for Euclid, states:

In the 19th century, it was accepted that...the fifth postulate (axiom XI) cannot be deduced from the other axioms.... [There were other] geometries in which this "parallel axiom" is false.... In the 20th century, Einstein found that his relativity theory required that the space of the universe be considered as a non-Euclidean space.

These statements are illustrative of the divergence of mathematics from nature. Euclid's postulates (self-evident axioms) are straightforward statements about measurement and how nature works, derived from his experience, reason, and observations and those of his predecessors. Some mathematicians later challenged Euclid's claim of having proven his "system" of geometry. This constituted a debate about Euclid's method, not his description of reality. Those mathematicians offered the "thought experiment" that Euclid's statement about parallelism is false. However, their assumption was contrary to nature and cannot be depicted or modeled. Einstein proposed the thought experiment that the geometry of space is non-Euclidean. Can a theoretician "require" nature to be something that it is not? No, but mathematicians have been using this method for twenty-five centuries.

7.10. Prediction

A prediction in astronomy is a statement about future events based on existing knowledge. In the case of eclipses, calculations of future events are accurate because the motions of the Sun, the Moon, and the Earth are known to a high degree.

A hypothesis is a statement about the unknown. It may be accurate and correct if it conforms to knowledge acquired in the future.

In the method of mathematical theoretical physics, a mathematical hypothesis is called a prediction. The logical, precise, and elegant mathematics of the hypothesis is deemed to be physical and real, and therefore natural. That is, if, following experiment and observation, the hypothesis turns out to be correct, then the calculations themselves are a kind of pre-existing knowledge that deserves to be called a prediction.

Avogadro's hypothesis was called just that. When Mendeleev wrote about new elements, he did not use the word predict. Maxwell hypothesized that the spectrum of radiation extended beyond infrared to the long waves. His idea was subsequently labeled a prediction.

7.11. Empty Space

The division of the universe into outer and inner space is an example of anthropocentric thought. It obstructs a natural definition of the concept of "space." Outer space is thought of as everything above Earth's atmosphere, or as the "void" between stars, or what sunlight travels through. Inner space is not thought of nearly as often, but it could mean the mind or the internal organs. The term seldom refers to the body's cells, molecules, atoms, protons, electrons, and neutrons.

Our worldview causes us to refer to "empty" space, as if the absence of matter means "nothing." In fact, matter is in space and of space. Whatever space may be, it is what matter is made of.

7.12. Theory of the Universe

Current cosmology is a hypothesis about the macrocosm with which hypotheses about the microcosm are now obliged to be consistent. It should be the other way around:

particle theory should be capable of explaining everything in the universe. Who knows what direction particle physics might have gone if it were not barking up that wrong tree?

The Big Bang is a theory of origins, of possible events in the remote past. It is a throwback to the ancient cosmologies and creation myths. Assuming that the uniformitarian principle governs nature, a theory of the universe should be about current, ongoing, minimal local processes and interactions. The past is not relevant to particles because they have neither memory nor means of recording.

The explosive expansion cosmology is primarily a gravitational theory, but gravity is not a fundamental force. Gravity is the interaction of stars-the largest accumulations in the universe of particles of matter. The weak, electromagnetic, and strong interactions are short-range and fundamental to the motion of particles.

The present state of knowledge about the microcosm means that any theory of nature will be based on a series of interdependent hypotheses, assumptions, and analogies derived from indirect, rather than direct, observation and measurement of particles. Some of the assumptions may not be true.

7.13. The Big Bang

The Big Bang theory of the universe proposes that everything in the cosmos was concentrated in the distant past in an infinitely small volume. Then there was an event that initiated an expansion and transformation that resulted in the universe as it exists today. That unique event is referred to as a singularity.

The Gage Canadian Dictionary defines Big Bang theory as "the scientific theory, now generally accepted, that the universe as we know it began with an enormous explosion" (p. 148). This puts the Big Bang theory in the category of creation theories that offer explanations of the origin of things. A uniformitarian approach to nature seeks to explain processes that operate continuously and uniformly throughout time. It does not seek to describe how processes got started.

7.14. Visualization and Modeling

We cannot directly observe particles and their interactions. Particles are too small, and our instruments are incapable of resolving the details. Optical and electron microscopes have greatly assisted in discoveries of the very small, but their limit is greater than the largest atom. Any possible technology that we might use for this purpose includes the probability that the actions of detecting and measuring will change the particle being observed. A beam of particles reflecting off an object during an experiment can change its motion, direction, speed, or temperature, so that it is no longer in its original state.

Manipulating a particle by grasping has the same effect. Causing a particle to collide with other particles may result in its destruction, and only indirect information can be obtained. Nevertheless, manipulation followed by observation of the consequences has provided much of what we know about the microcosm.

The absence of direct observation of particles necessitates the use of modeling. Assumptions about motion, structure, trajectory, interaction, and relationship are made, and the resulting model is compared to the known facts. The model that best accounts for the evidence will usually be accepted by the scientific community as a basis for further work.

Often a model may be inspired by an analogy with something familiar from another field. An example is the use of the term nucleus to describe the position and arrangement of protons, electrons, and neutrons. The structure of a living cell seen by biochemists is assumed by particle physicists to be similar to the unseen structure of an atom.

Similarly, astronomy provides the analogy of electrons orbiting the nucleus as planets orbit the Sun. Previously, borrowing from cookery, the arrangement of electrons and protons in the atom had been likened to raisins in a bun.

Microcosmic interactions and transformations are described by using words such as emission, absorption, decay, fission, fusion, annihilation, and radiation. From the point of view of the participating particles, a visualization of these processes, which cannot be observed in detail, is possible.

The Heisenberg Uncertainty Principle is relevant here. It is a statement about the impossibility of determining with unlimited accuracy the position and momentum of a particle. If a particle's position is known, then its momentum is uncertain, and when we know its motion, we cannot pinpoint its location.

This principle is not a description of the reality of nature. A particle has a position and momentum that are known to it at all times. The Uncertainty Principle is part of the method used by mathematical theoretical physicists.

7.15. Sense of Sight

The pursuit of science and knowledge about the world is dependent on our interactions with that world. We use our senses to obtain information about our location and what is happening in our environment. Principally, it is our eyesight and our vision system that accomplishes this job. The human vision system evolved over millions of years when our ancestors lived in trees. The arboreal way of life requires a binocular arrangement of the eyes and a high level of focus, acuity, and spatial definition, without which one would fall. In tandem with the evolution of our eyes, the brain developed ways of interpreting and responding to the information received through the eyes.

Human vision has a short range and is sensitive only to visible light, the radiation reaching us from the Sun. It is more than adequate for survival and has successfully adapted to a bipedal way of life and our recent cultural evolution.

The guiding principle of the brain's interpretation of information obtained through the sense of sight is that the image is the object. When our ancestors reached for some fruit or a tree branch, the brain directed our movements to accomplish the desired result. If the perceived location of the object were correct, then it would be grasped successfully.

There are situations arising in everyday life when this guiding principle fails. A reflection from a mirror or a similar surface is only an image. Light reflected from an object under water bends because of the difference in the speed of light in water and in air. A mirage on a desert horizon on a hot day is an example of the optical illusions that the brain has trouble interpreting.

When we look out into interstellar space with our telescopes and other radiation detectors, our vision system must adapt. We must remember that the distance to the source of the observed radiation is immense, as is the time required for the radiation to reach us. Both the source and the observer are in motion and have changed position in that time. Therefore, the image is not the object.

7.16. What Nature Does

Nature is simple. There are only a few constituent fundamental particles, and everything observable is made of them. Nature is economical. Having found the ways that work, there is no need for alternatives.

Nature is constrained by the "laws of physics." This means that every natural phenomenon takes place in three-dimensional space, in an internal spherical frame of reference and an external tangential frame of reference. Only what is possible in these reference frames actually occurs. A division of nature has been revealed by science and technology: (1) what nature does; (2) what nature can do but does not; and (3) what nature cannot do, but humans can. In the first category are the natural phenomena that we are familiar with: stars, planets, light, elements, life, magnetism, lightning, fire, and so on. Electrical current and transuranic elements are examples of what nature can do but does not. Nature produces electrical discharge such as the static caused by friction, but does not have batteries, electromagnets, or generators. In the third category is our description of planetary motion. A planet's orbit is determined by its size, its distance from the Sun, and its gravitational interaction with other bodies of the solar system. This is synodic motion. A planet's sidereal motion, relative to a distant star with which it is not interacting, can only be calculated by a human.

8. My Method

For the past twenty-five centuries, progress in natural philosophy has been hindered by five ongoing problems: false assumptions, insufficient data, inadequate technology, contrived mathematics, and anthropocentrism. In the last five centuries, these difficulties have been significantly overcome by the work of great thinkers, but they are still with us, some as powerful as ever.

An attempt to deal with false assumptions arising from facile mathematics and anthropocentrism is the subject of this work. I wish to study nature by using only nature's numbers, by avoiding calculation and adhering to measurement. I propose to cease being an observer on the outside, and to visualize phenomena from the insider's central point of view.

As a particle, I wish to answer five questions: What am I? What do I do? How do I do it? What could I do, but don't? What can other human beings manipulate me to do?

8.1. Natural Philosophy

This is a work of natural philosophy. It is metaphysical, hypothetical, speculative, and theoretical. It is about nature and our knowledge of it. Thus, it is about science and the observation, measurement, and description of natural phenomena. It is about the practice of physics. It is about cosmology. It is a theory of the universe. It is not a report of experiments or calculations. It is about the microcosm and the macrocosm. It is about particles, motion, interaction, and transformation. It is about matter, radiation, and neutrinos. This work has two parts: (a) a history of our knowledge of the microcosm; and (b) a hypothesis based on alternative assumptions. The history will involve the identification of the facts, assumptions, and interpretations of the current paradigm. It will account for the development of physics over the centuries and the specializations, schools, and models that exist today. The history of natural philosophy divides into four periods: (a) from classical Greece to Copernicus (1534 A.D.); (b) from Copernicus to Lavoisier (1789); (c) from Lavoisier to Becquerel (1896); and (d) from Becquerel to the present.

This work is also about method. It is about the human factor and the role of the observer. It will discuss experiment, calculation, and visualization. It will discuss the difficulties presented by anthropocentrism, careerism, the act of measurement, and dependency on mathematics. It will describe the problems encountered in measuring the very large and the very small. It will discuss the limitations of technology.

In the second part of the work, there will be an attempt to describe nature from the perspective of nature itself, eliminating the observer and the problems of invisibility and immeasurability. Answers will be offered to questions such as: What is a particle? Does a particle have a structure? What does a particle do? What is a particle's frame of reference? What is nature's mathematics?

8.2. Methods of Description

Methods of describing nature include words, numbers, pictures, diagrams, and models. Three-dimensional models and two-dimensional pictures are representational of nature, but they are static.

Motion is a property of every natural phenomenon. In order to describe a change in nature, a difference from one state to another, verbal, mathematical, and diagrammatic tools are used. To describe motion accurately and comprehensively, mathematics is essential.

A law of physics is not a human creation. It describes what nature is doing in its reference frame of three spatial dimensions. Nature is constantly measuring, while constantly changing position relative to a fixed point.

The mathematics of nature is measurement or estimation. In formal and practical mathematics, it is geometry (Earth measure). In a particle's frame of reference, it is autometry (self-measure), or topometry (place measure), or stereometry (three-dimensional measure). The ability to measure-to sense the constantly changing position of another particle-is intrinsic. There is no motion without measurement, because all motion is relative.

A measuring particle uses units based on itself. Its radius is the distance-unit, and its period of oscillation is the time-unit. A complete description of motion can be provided with a distance and a period, plus an angle that is either a fraction or a multiple of pi, and a direction that is either positive or negative.

From these measurements, the triangle, sphere, and tetrahedron can be constructed; and the line, plane, vertex, angle, perpendicular, and parallel can be defined. These are all the "mathematics" that nature needs.

8.3. Assumptions

The consistent application of the uniformitarian principle leads to insights of great utility:

1. The microcosm is primary and fundamental, whereas the macrocosm is secondary and consequential.

2. For a particle, time is merely the present, while the past exists by means of recording and recall.

3. Biological natural selection is a trial-and-error process of variation in spatial relations.

4. Ordinary Euclidean solid geometry is sufficient for a full mathematical description of natural phenomena.

5. Natural phenomena involve motion, since they are all interactions between two oscillating particles. The "output" of one interacting particle is the "input" of the other. The motion of each particle is both a cause and an effect.

6. A natural philosophy should be a process of putting questions, uncovering assumptions, and exploring alternative assumptions, hypotheses, and theories of nature in a non-exclusive fashion unrestricted by orthodoxy.

8.4. An Alternative Method

My method is:

1. To ignore human experience completely in order to avoid anthropocentrism, the greatest obstacle to natural knowledge.

2. To be a visualizer and modeler and to abandon the role of observer, quantifier, and manipulator.

3. To follow Ernest Rutherford, who said that he asked himself, "What would I do if I was one of those little buggers?" and Linus Pauling, who expressed a similar thought process.

4. To remove myself from the situation by pretending to be a particle.

5. To write a description of the universe from the point of view of a particle.

6. To use ordinary Euclidean three-dimensional solid geometry.

7. To adhere strictly to simplicity and minimalism as fundamental to nature.

8. To apply the uniformitarian principle universally.

9. To deem the macrocosm as non-fundamental and consequential.

10. To use mathematics in the same way that nature does, without recording.

11. To position myself in the schools of Copernicus, Kepler, Galileo, Newton, Boscovich, Lavoisier, Dalton, Faraday, Mendeleev, and Rutherford.

12. To distance myself from theoretical mathematical physics, Big Bang cosmology, quantum mechanics, and Einstein's theory of relativity.

13. To ignore questions of origin, creation, history, the past, and the future.

14. To apply the following assumptions:

    (a) Stable interactions consist of identical particles that are face-to-face and move in opposite directions.

    (b) Nature is binary: constant/varying, odd/even, positive/negative, right/left, and clockwise/counterclockwise.

    (c) Trajectories are finite: that is, motion is oscillatory, reflective, and cyclic.

    (d) The universe is a system in which all phenomena are interactive and interdependent, and feedback is always present.

    (e) Motion is relative: that is, for every moving part there is a constant unmoving center.

    (f) Fundamental interactions are stable: therefore, collapses, collisions, impacts, contacts, ejections, explosions, punctuated equilibria, and catastrophes are not fundamental.

    (g) Interacting particles are not contiguous but at a distance.

9. The Smallest, Simplest Particle

Since the invention of electrical current, more than two centuries ago, investigation of matter and radiation has revealed that nature is simple. The constituent particles are few and infinitesimal. From the stable fundamental microcosmic particles, a macrocosm of astonishing complexity has been constructed by means of a multitude of spatial interactions.

A proton and an electron arrange themselves in an atom of hydrogen. In stars, hydrogen atoms transform and fuse into the other elements, which combine to form the myriad material molecules of the terrestrial world. From an ancient, microscopic, single-celled creature evolved the diverse species of viruses, bacteria, plants, and animals.

In 1758, Roger Joseph Boscovich published A Theory of Natural Philosophy, in which he made an early attempt to model the atom, visualizing the particle as a point. That concept has been useful ever since, because neither the atom nor any other particle has been directly observed and measured, although a great deal has been learned indirectly. In the full range of physical things, the point is the smallest object observable or imaginable. In geometry, the point is defined as having position but no extent.

Following Boscovich, a hypothesis of the smallest, simplest particle as a microcosmic base of the stable fundamental particles suggests a system of two points at minimum separation, one of which is a constant center point, and the other is a varying point of tangency. For convenience, this hypothetical two-point minimal oscillating particle is named the oscillon (see Figure 1, below).

Figure 1. The Oscillon, Its Frame of Reference, and the Trajectory and Direction of Its Motion

The variation of the position of the point of tangency relative to the center is an oscillation through an angle of pi (180°). Its trajectory, which is a semicircle, terminates at two points of reflection. The direction of motion at one point of reflection is positive, and at the other is negative. The period of the oscillon is the time between reflections, and two periods constitute a cycle.

Measurement is an integral part of motion and interaction. Nature demonstrates this fact in the inverse square relation that determines the motion of a planet orbiting a star. In the microcosm, there are no "observers"; therefore, the process is one of self-measurement by the oscillon. Measurement is the quantification of spatial and temporal relations. In order to measure, the oscillon uses the spherical frame of reference based on its center point.

The oscillon has the ability to measure four quantities: distance, angle, direction, and period. These are sufficient for its purpose. A line from the center to the point of tangency is a radius, and the particle, its oscillation, and its frame of reference are based on the radial dimension. A line through the moving point of tangency, at right angles to the radius and in the direction of its motion, is a tangent, which defines the tangential dimension. Together, the radial and tangential dimensions define the plane of the oscillon. A line through the center at right angles to the plane is the axis, which locates the axial dimension. The three dimensions jointly determine the structure, frame of reference, and motion of the oscillon.

It is worth noting that the tangential dimension does not pass through the center. It is the external dimension, while there is an orthogonal line through the center that is parallel to the tangent. Nature here demonstrates its beautiful symmetry, in that the radial dimension passes through both the center and the point of tangency, the tangential dimension only passes through the tangent point, and the axial dimension only passes through the center.

The units of measurement used by the oscillon are self-referential. Its radius is the unit of distance. The angle between the points of reflection is pi. The direction of motion from a point of reflection is either of two opposites: positive and negative or clockwise and counterclockwise. The oscillon's period of motion from one point of reflection to the other is the unit of time. The system of numbers used by the oscillon is probably not the decimal system, which was derived from the number of human fingers and toes. A reasonable conjecture is that the numbers 0, 1, 2, and 3 fulfill all its functions.

9.1. An Ur-Particle

Is there an elementary particle that is the building block of all the stable elementary particles? Is a small, simple particle all that is needed to construct the known particles? Do such minimal particles interact, combine, and transform in ever more complex relations to form neutrinos, radiation, and matter? Is there an ur-particle-the original, most primitive form of motion in the universe?

If so, what would the smallest, simplest particle be like? There is nothing smaller physically than a point, described by Euclid as having place but no extent. The universe is well defined as the infinity of points.

A particle is a quantity of space that is physically separate from and particular from all other quantities. It has an interior and an exterior. It is three-dimensional. The possession of a center distinguishes one particle from all others because no object has two centers, nor does one thing have the same center as another.

9.2. Nature's Economy

We know that matter (hydrogen, atoms, elements, molecules, and chemicals) is made of only two particles: the proton and the electron. We know that plants and animals, from the smallest viruses and bacteria to the largest whales and redwoods, are made of cells. We understand that nature tends to stick to the tried and true. Having found a way that works, nature does not need an alternative.

Is it logical to assume that all of nature, including space, is made of a single foundational form of motion, and that the complexity that we observe is merely a variation in the dimensionality of the interactions of ur-particles?

10. Frame of Reference

What is the meaning of frame of reference? Grammatically, frame is a noun; and refer, the root of reference, is a verb. A noun represents a thing, object, or entity, and a verb represents an action, experience, or phenomenon. Thus, when describing a frame, object-words like base, figure, line, plane, point, space, and vertex are used.

When describing a reference, action-words like differ, measure, oppose, pass, process, project, relate, start, use, and view are used. Also used are words that describe quantities, such as angle, distance, radian, ratio, separation, and unit, as well as numbers such as 0, 1, 2, π, and $\pi/3$. Relations and qualities are described by using words such as axial, constant, dimensional, directional, external, internal, invariable, minimal, natural, physical, radial, real, straight, and tangential.

The oscillon, a system of two points in a spherical frame of reference, has self-knowledge and a capability of measuring both itself and beyond. It has the means of sensing its surroundings and the potential of interacting with other such systems.

10.1. Continuous Measurement

The measuring done by interacting particles in the microcosm is similar to that of birds in a flock, or fish in a school, or NASCAR drivers in a race. It is dependent on a continuous feed of information about the adjacent members of the group in all directions. The members achieve an optimum distance between individuals by maintaining a balanced separation from their immediate neighbors.

They do not "record" the precise numerical length of a measurement. Because each individual is moving relative to the combined trajectory of the group, the distance from each other is subject to variation at any time. This necessitates continuous comparison and continuous response. Of course, that is what an interaction is-a process of feedback whereby every action is a reaction, and one's output is another's input.

The process of interaction involves more estimation than measurement. The question is not so much "How far away is the other?" as "Is its distance changing?" This involves an assessment of ratios that relate to directions of movement. The measurer responds with actions and changes, such as: accelerating, getting closer, going down, moving up, pitching, rolling, slowing, turning left, turning right, yawing, and so on. Measurements like this are valid only in the present, to be redone over and over, in a process that needs no recording.

10.2. The Self's Point of View

There are two views of a phenomenon: (1) the view from the center, called the internal viewpoint or the self's view; and (2) the view from an infinite number of surrounding points, called the external viewpoint or the observer's view.

The centers of interacting oscillons, by a process akin to natural selection, determine the distinction between front and back, left and right, up and down, in and out, forward and reverse, and clockwise and counterclockwise. It is the orientation of structure and the alignment of motion of one to the other within their common frame of reference that enables them to specify the various different or opposite directions that each is experiencing.

10.3. Absolute Space and Time

There has been a debate in natural philosophy since the time of Newton about whether there is such a thing as absolute space or absolute time. The question, which relates to motion, measurement, frame of reference, and units to be used, is asked from the point of view of an observer-measurer.

I have assumed that the observer is irrelevant to a description of nature, and that the central point of view is paramount. A particle has a center and a frame of reference that are constant, unchanging, and therefore absolute. Each particle has a unique center and its own frame of reference.

For a self-measuring oscillon, there is an absolute space and time, defined by its own frame of reference and by units based on itself and its motion. Thus, a particle's absolute space is not the same as that of any other particle. But since all oscillons are identical, the process and method of self-measurement are the same. The distance-unit and time-unit of nature are absolute.

10.4. The Purpose of Senses

Biochemical evolution has produced animal senses of great diversity and acuity. Our senses operate at all scales-from very large, such as touch and gravity, to very small, such as light waves and pheromones. However, the purpose of these senses is the same as the "senses" of the oscillon: namely, to provide a frame of reference for internal and external measurement and for effective interaction with the environment.

Vision is the most useful human sense because of its range: near to far, large to small, dark to bright. It is light-dependent, and direct and reflected light are ubiquitous in our environment.

10.5. Are There More Than Five Senses?

Reference is often made to the five senses of hearing, sight, smell, taste, and touch. Listing only five is meaningful if we are talking about what our conscious mind is ordinarily aware of. However, there are other senses that operate at a more unconscious level, such as:

1. Sense of gravity (up and down)
2. Sense of balance (vertical and horizontal)
3. Sense of time (fast and slow)
4. Sense of distance (near and far)
5. Sense of temperature (hot and cold)
6. Sense of pressure (soft and hard)
7. Sense of moisture (dry and wet)
8. Sense of weight (light and heavy)
9. Sense of identity (self and other)
10. Sense of change (constant and variable)

11. Oscillation, Interaction, Locomotion, and Wave Motion

Is it a universal characteristic of motion to be two-stroke? Is every type of motion a back-and-forth cycle? Is there a power stroke followed by a return stroke? Does every trajectory lead to a return to an earlier position? Is there always reflection and repetition? Is there motion in one direction followed by motion in the opposite direction? Both oscillation and rotation exhibit this characteristic.

A piston moves "down" on the power stroke and "up" on the exhaust stroke. Humans move with bipedal locomotion: when one extended leg plants on the ground and thrusts forward, the other leg bends in the air and swings back through the same angle and distance. While the body travels relative to the ground, the legs oscillate relative to the torso.

11.1. Synodic Motion

Synodic is a good word to describe the interaction of particles. The Gage Canadian Dictionary gives the Greek origin of the word as syn- "together" + hodos "going." The synodic period of one planet relative to another is the time between their nearest approaches to each other when their gravitational interactions are greatest. A planet's synodic motion is the orbital trajectory determined by its varying gravitational interaction with the other bodies of the solar system. The interaction of particles results in motion that is synodic. Microcosmic input/output and action/reaction processes are continuous and uniform. Synodic motion is natural motion.

11.2. Motion in the Plane

All trajectories have a center; all trajectories are planar; all trajectories are cyclic. A trajectory is the path taken by a moving point in relation to a constant point. The constant point is the center of the frame of reference containing the two points. A trajectory is the time-related change in the direction, angle, and distance of the moving point relative to the fixed point.

Only two-dimensional trajectories are possible in nature's three-dimensional space. All trajectories are in the plane that contains the center and all possible positions of the moving point. Planar trajectories may be rectilinear or curvilinear and may have the shape of a line, spiral, circle, ellipse, parabola, or hyperbola. Trajectories are finite in distance and continuous in time.

Nature imposes the limits of a minimum and a maximum on motion. These are manifested in the oscillon. The distance between the varying point and the constant point is the minimum. The distance between the points of reflection of the varying point is the maximum. The radius of the oscillon is a minimum, and the semicircular trajectory is a maximum.

11.3. No Nature Without Motion

So far as we know, everything in the universe is in motion. Nothing is at rest. Motion never stops. When a person is unconscious, the lungs breathe, the heart beats, the nerves fire, and the Earth rotates and revolves in a rotating galaxy. Every form of energy, work, force, power, or change involves motion.

There are two types of motion: oscillation and locomotion. When a particle oscillates, part of it changes position relative to its center, but the whole stays in the same place. When a body is in locomotion, its center moves relative to another center, and the whole moves from one place to another.

11.4. Repetitive Motion

In common practice, the word oscillation is used synonymously with vibration, swing, and wave to describe the repetitive motion of objects that return to their start-

ing positions. Familiar examples are sound waves, seismic waves, ocean waves, ripples on a pond, and vibrating strings. In these cases, there is a material medium through which energy propagates after the application of a force. The oscillatory movement of the air, earth, water, or fiber continues as long as the force is applied, and then, as the energy dissipates, the medium returns to its original state. The movement of a pendulum is an oscillation. The Gage Canadian Dictionary defines pendulum as "a body or mass hung from a fixed point so as to move to and fro under the forces of gravity and momentum" (p. 1089). The period of a pendulum is the time taken to swing from one limit to the other, and the cycle is the time of a to-and-fro motion. The angle of swing is the amplitude. The frequency of a regularly repeating motion is the number of cycles completed in a given time. To discuss the oscillation of a solitary particle in an imaginary empty universe, I find the analogy of the pendulum most helpful, since I am looking for a regularly repeating motion, self-generated, free not forced, and to and fro, with a curvilinear trajectory. However, rather than having a continuous spinning or rotating trajectory, the motion reaches a certain point, reflects without stopping, and continues in the opposite direction to the starting point.

11.5. Attractive Interaction

Regarding the self-generating, self-measuring, oscillating particle and a second identical particle, there are an infinite number of possible spatial and temporal relationships. If their positions are within range-that is, if their external frames of reference overlap-then interaction may occur. Two of these interactions are meaningful, but only one results in stability.

The spatial relation of identical particles is symmetrical if they are in the same plane, and if their points of reflection are co-linear. Their temporal relation is synchronized if their periods are in phase. If their directions of motion are opposite, one clockwise and the other counterclockwise, then the interaction is attractive. If they are oscillating in the same direction, both clockwise or counterclockwise, they repel each other.

11.6. A Solitary Particle

How should a particle be defined? Is it the smallest division of space? Is it the minimum volume? Is it the smallest quantity of motion? Does it have the shortest radius? Is it a quantity of one? A natural object or phenomenon may be defined in terms of its properties, which are determined by observing it, measuring it, breaking it, and causing it to interact with other objects. To answer the question of what a particle is, we can imagine a time and a place in which there is only one particle. Since there is nothing external to such a particle, and it is not interacting with any other particles, the only view of its existence is from within. That view is of the properties of the particle in and of itself, its being, its reality, and its physicality.

11.7. Natural Selection

Natural selection, the felicitous phrase introduced by Charles Darwin, is the way nature deals with alternative spatial relations. Is it possible for particles to interact in a way that is different from the existing arrangement? Can the same particles interact in more than one spatial configuration?

The more complex the particle, the more alternatives are possible. Particles of matter form complex molecules, or chains of atoms. An atom of carbon can combine with atoms of other elements in a seemingly limitless number of ways.

Over time, all alternative spatial configurations may occur by chance. Nature "tries" to see if an alternative works or results in "error." If the alternative is a stable interaction, harmonious with existing nature, then it may be selected and become common.

The history of the universe is a process of successive natural selections. The first natural selection occurred when two identical points in space differentiated into a constant point and a varying point, and motion began. Next, there was a choice of positive or negative, and the direction of motion was selected. Then a point of reflection was chosen, and the trajectory of motion was selected.

11.8. Wave Motion Is an Optical Illusion

All the familiar terrestrial waves occur in a material medium. Ripples in a pond and whitecaps on a lake occur in water; sound is a movement of air; and seismic waves are a quaking of the ground. The molecules of the medium oscillate in place. Water waves and ground tremors are transverse waves, meaning that the motion of the particles is at right angles to what we perceive as the direction of the wave. In air, the motion is longitudinal-that is, the molecules are oscillating in the same direction that the sound wave is propagating. These familiar waves are caused by macrocosmic events such as a golf ball landing in a pond, the wind interacting with the surface of the ocean, or a sudden slip of two plates of the Earth's crust along a fault line. What we experience as a wave-that is, a horizontal movement of the medium from the originating phenomenon to another location-is an illusion. The real motion is a sequence, over time, of microcosmic particles oscillating relative to a constant center and interacting with adjacent particles. The brain, receiving information through the visual sense, interprets the observations by using its experience of time-that is, memory-so that it seems like something is moving from place to place.

The illusion becomes obvious when we observe the actual motion of a medium of macrocosmic particles oscillating in sequence, creating what is called a stadium wave, also known as a Mexican or audience wave. Here the particles are human bodies, and the oscillation is a vertical movement by each person from the sitting to the standing position with an extension of the arms over the head, followed by a return to the seated position. It appears to our brain that something is moving around the oval stadium in an up-and-down fashion, and that that movement has the shape of a wave.

The participating individuals in the audience, facing inward, interact with their neighbors on one side by means

of vision and create the wave by moving in an orderly, regular, and uniform sequence. This is metachronal motion (from the Greek meta-, "before," and chron-, "time")-that is, motion produced by sequential action.

A diagram of wave motion is also illusory. It is a curved line of crests and troughs relative to a baseline, indicating a trajectory or direction of motion. In fact, the motion is of particles oscillating transversely to the baseline, and there is no physical connection between the particles other than their interaction in a common frame of reference.

11.9. The Medium of Light

Light and the other frequencies of electromagnetic radiation are also transverse wave motions. Light is emitted by stars and propagates through space in all directions. Some of it is absorbed or reflected by material bodies. Scientists generally have accepted that starlight is a wave, but there is no consensus about the medium through which it is propagating.

Is space the medium? If so, what is space made of? Is it ether? That is a hypothesis based on the assumption that the medium of light is made of matter. However, no experimental evidence of an ether has ever been demonstrated, which indicates that the medium is not material. Other hypotheses about space and the medium of light have been proposed, but the debate continues. Experiments using stadium waves could demonstrate the different frequencies and wavelengths of the motion of interacting particles. The motion of particles when waves intersect could be investigated. Various periods of oscillation and intervals of interaction could be researched.

11.10. The Model of an Oscillon

An oscillon is a system of two points. One of the points is a constant, invariable center. The center is zero: a point of reference, a viewpoint, a base, and an origin. The other point is a variable, moving point of tangency. The oscillon is a binary system made of points, of which there are two; they are separate and different, one constant and the other in motion. The center point and the point of tangency are real, physical, and natural.

An oscillon has identity, dimensionality, size, and shape. It has an interior and an exterior. The oscillon has a frame of reference, which is a process of measurement of distance, angle, direction, and shape (see Figure 1, above). The process makes use of lines, figures, planes, intersections, angles, and numbers, which are not physical. A frame of reference is not physical, but the act of referring is real.

The distance between the oscillon's center and point of tangency is a radius that is constant. The straight line between the center and the initial position of the point of tangency is the baseline of the frame of reference. The radius, which passes through both the center and the point of tangency, defines the radial dimension of the oscillon. The distance between the points is the minimum physically possible separation, whose length is one distance-unit.

The numerical name of the center is zero (0) and of the point of tangency is one (1). A radius has two directions:

outward from the center to the point of tangency $(0 \rightarrow 1)$ or $(1 \leftarrow 0)$, and inward from the point of tangency to the center $(1 \rightarrow 0)$ or $(0 \leftarrow 1)$. Conventionally, the outward direction is frontward and positive, and the inward direction is backward and negative.

There is an extension of the baseline from the center in the negative direction. On this line, at 1 distance-unit from the center, is the opposite point of tangency-that is, the point of reflection. The distance between the starting point and the point of reflection is 2 distance-units. The line between them is a diameter, and each of its segments is a radius. The number of the opposite point of tangency is 2.

The space between the baseline and any other line through the center, and the difference in their directions, is an angle. The center-that is, the point of intersection of such lines-is the vertex of the angle. One such line is the co-linear extension of the baseline radius, and the measure of the angle between the radius and the extension is pi. The angular measure is the same, regardless of the direction of measuring. Pi is a number. The equivalent of an angular measure of pi is 180 degrees.

A line through the point of tangency at an angle of 90°to the radius is a tangent. The tangent, which passes only through the point of tangency, defines the tangential dimension of the frame of reference. The radius and the tangent together establish the plane. The tangent has two directions-of which, conventionally, one is right and positive, and the other is left and negative.

A line through the center at an angle of 90°to the plane is an axis. The angle is constant. An angle of 90°is a right angle, and the relation of the axis and plane is perpendicular or orthogonal. The axis, which passes only through the center, defines the axial dimension of the frame of reference. It has two directions: conventionally, one is up and positive, and the opposite is down and negative. The radius, tangent, and axis are all perpendicular to each other, and this relation is constant.

An oscillon is a fundamental particle with an oscillating point of tangency. Any line through the center in the oscillon's plane is a radius. There is a point of tangency on such a radius at 1 distance-unit from the center. Thus, in relation to the baseline of the frame of reference, a radius and tangent, moving in tandem in the plane, have angular variability. Tangents in the plane at opposite points of tangency are parallel to each other. The difference between the directions of any radius in the plane and the baseline of the frame of reference is an angular measure that varies from zero to pi. The direction of the angle from the baseline is either positive or negative.

The internal frame of reference of an oscillon is based on two physical points: the center point and the point of tangency. The frame has three dimensions: the first is radial, the second is tangential, and the third is axial. The separation of the points and the angular relation of the dimensions are constant. The shape of the frame of reference is spherical.

11.11. The External, Tangential Frame of Reference

The common center of two oscillons is the point of intersection of their common tangents. That is the center of tangency, and it is co-linear with and equidistant from the centers of the particles. It defines their common frame of reference and lies on their common radius (see Figure 2, next page).

The angle of intersection of pairs of common tangents depends on the distance between the oscillons. When the separation is zero, the particles are tangent to each other, and the angle is zero. The common tangents coincide, and the particles are touching.

The oscillons also have common tangents that are co-linear. Their angle of intersection is 180°. Such tangents are parallel to each other and to the common radius.

When the interaction of two oscillons is stable, their separation is minimal and non-contiguous. Their centers and the center of tangency form a common radius. Their common tangents intersect at supplementary angles of 60°and 120°.

The acute angle between the tangents is 60°, and the angle between a tangent and the common radius is also 60°. This special intersection is equiangular-that is, all six angles between the tangents and radius are 60°.

11.12. The Tetrahedral Frame of Reference

A 60°angle is special because it is the angle of the equiangular, equilateral triangle, the simplest two-dimensional plane figure, or polygon. Similarly, it is the angle of the tetrahedron, the simplest three-dimensional "solid" figure, or polyhedron. The Greek roots of these words are: tri- "three," tetra- "four," poly- "many," -gonia "angle" or "corner," -hedra "side," "face," or "plane," as well as stereo- "solid" or "three-dimensional." A tetrahedron has four vertices, six edges, and four planes or faces, each of which is an equiangular triangle. Three edges intersect at each vertex at an angle of 60°, and two planes meet at each edge at a dihedral angle of 71.529°.

Thus, the common frame of reference of such stable interacting oscillons is tetrahedral. The center of tangency, where the tangents intersect, is both a vertex of a tetrahedron and the base of this frame of reference. An edge of a tetrahedron is a segment of a tangent. The rest of the frame is a continuous array of co-vertical tetrahedra derived from this starting point. None of these lines, points, and figures are physical, but they make up a real frame of reference that is indispensable to the measurement that relative motion requires (see Figure 3, below).

The tetrahedra connected to each other at their vertices enclose a space with the figure of a truncated tetrahedron. The edges of the tetrahedra form the eighteen edges of the truncated tetrahedron, which also has twelve vertices and eight planes. This frame of reference is also referred to as the space-filling combination of tetrahedra and truncated tetrahedra.

A regular polyhedron, such as a tetrahedron or truncated tetrahedron, is the locus of spheres (see Figure 4, below): the circumsphere passes through the vertices, the insphere

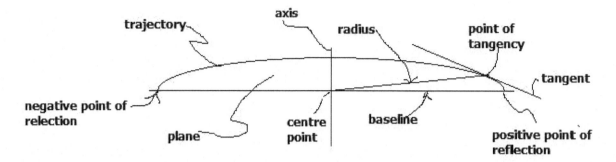

Figure 2.   Diagram of Center of Tangency and Center of the Common Frame of Reference of Two Interacting Oscillons

The array of co-vertical tetrahedra; the vertices of each tetrahedron labeled 0, 1, 2, 3;

A pair of opposite co-vertical tetrahedra, one positive and one negative: the co-planar edges (01, 10, 12, 21, 20, 02) drawn in thin solid line; the background edges (03, 13, 23) in dotted line; the foreground edges (30, 31, 32) in thick solid line.

A central tetrahedron and its four opposite co-vertical tetrahedra; the plane, background and foreground edges drawn as above; the edges (01, 12, 23, 30) of the tetrahedron in the exteme foreground opposite to the edges (10, 21, 32, 03) of the central tetrahedron behind it.

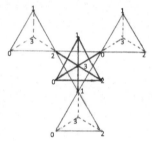

Figure 3.   Diagram of Co-Vertical Tetrahedra

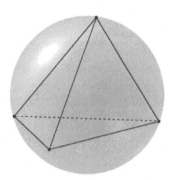

Figure 4.   The Spheres of a Tetrahedron: Circumsphere (top), Insphere (middle), Midsphere (bottom)

is tangential to the planes, and the midsphere is tangential to the edges. In the external frame of reference, the spherical internal frame of reference of each interacting oscillon coincides with a midsphere of a truncated tetrahedron.

11.13. The Midsphere of the Truncated Tetrahedron

This tetrahedral array is an external tangential frame of reference of a spherical frame of reference. The midsphere of a truncated tetrahedron is the locus of an oscillon and its internal frame of reference. None of the components of the frames-the baselines, edges, faces, planes, spheres, tetrahedra, triangles, truncated tetrahedra, and vertices-are physical objects. The array exhibits symmetry in four planes.

The common vertex of a pair of co-vertical truncated tetrahedra is the common center of the midspheres of the pair of truncated tetrahedra. In a tetrahedral frame of

reference, the center of tangency of two co-planar oscillons coincides with the common center of such spheres. The angle between intersecting tangents is 60°, and the angle between such tangents and the radius of the pair is also 60°. The angle between the common radius and the point of tangency, at the center of an oscillon, is 30°.

If the radius of an oscillon is 1 unit, then, calculating from the geometric relation between sides and angles in a 90-60-30 right triangle, the distance from the center of the oscillon to the common center of the pair is $2 \div \sqrt{3}$ units (1.154). The length of an intersecting tangent segment is $1 \div \sqrt{3}$ units (0.577). The length of an edge of a tetrahedron is also $1 \div \sqrt{3}$ units.

11.14. The 30-60-90 Triangle

The Pythagorean Theorem states that in a right triangle, the square of the length of the hypotenuse equals the sum of the squares of the lengths of the legs. The 30-60-90 triangle is a special right triangle and is half an equiangular, equilateral triangle. Triangle QPR, below, is a 30-60-90 triangle, and the following is the proof that the length of the hypotenuse is twice the length of the shorter leg, and the length of the longer leg is $\sqrt{3}$ times the length of the shorter leg.

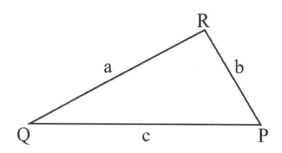

Angle QRP = 90°
Angle RPQ = 60°
Angle PQR = 30°
$RP = shorter leg = b$
$QP = hypotenuse = 2(RP) = c = 2b$
$QR = longer leg = \sqrt{3}(RP) = a$
Since $c^2 = b^2 + a^2$
And $a^2 = c^2 - b^2$
$a^2 = (2b)^2 - b^2$
$a^2 = 4b^2 - b^2$
$a^2 = 3b^2$
And $a = \sqrt{3}b$
$b = a \div \sqrt{3}$
$c = 2a \div \sqrt{3}$

Let triangle QPR be the base of the tetrahedral external frame of reference of a pair of interacting oscillons. Then:

Q = center of an oscillon
R = point of tangency of an oscillon
P = common center of interacting oscillons
QR = longer leg = radius of the oscillon
RP = shorter leg = tangent segment of the oscillon
QP = hypotenuse = common radius of the pair of oscillons

Then $QR (radius) = a = 1$
And $RP (tangent) = b = 1 \div \sqrt{3} = 0.577350269$
And $QP (radius of the pair) = c = 2 \div \sqrt{3} = 1.154600538$

11.15. Tangential Relations

An oscillon also has an external frame of reference. This is the common frame of reference of two oscillons or, more specifically, of two centers. Thus, it is also the frame of reference of two spherical internal frames of reference. The part of the internal frame that is external to a particle is the tangent. The frame of reference of two interacting particles is defined by the spatial relation of their tangents.

The external frame of reference is tangential and has no physical center. The center of the frame is the point of intersection of the common, shared tangents of the interacting particles. The center of the frame is also the midpoint of the line that joins the centers of the two oscillons.

11.16. An Array of Co-Vertical Tetrahedra

The tetrahedral frame of reference is an array of co-vertical tetrahedra; each tetrahedron shares a vertex with four other tetrahedra (see Figure 5, below). The spaces between the tetrahedra are truncated tetrahedra. The combination of tetrahedra and truncated tetrahedra is space-

filling. The array of tetrahedra is three-dimensional and continuous, and has four planes of symmetry.

Figure 5. Model of the Array of Co-Vertical Tetrahedra Made of Paper Clip Wires and Translucent Tape

11.17. The Space Filling Combination of Tetrahedra and Truncated Tetrahedra

This construction is a model (see Figure 6, below), built of paperclip wires, transparent tape, and balloons, of:

1. An array of co-vertical tetrahedra.

2. The tetrahedral frame of reference of two interacting stable fundamental particles at minimum separation.

3. The space filling combination of tetrahedra and truncated tetrahedra.

4. The common tangential frame of reference of a pair of spherical frames of reference.

5. A description of the linear, planar, perpendicular, parallel, and symmetrical relations of the polyhedra.

6. An illustration of a variant sphere packing, that is, the linear, perpendicular, parallel, and layered relations, of non-contiguous midspheres.

7. A representation of the direction of the ordering of the vertices, by means of labeling the vertices with the numbers 0, 1, 2, and 3.

In Figure 6, the balloons represent the midspheres of truncated tetrahedra. The midspheres are separated by a truncated tetrahedron occupied by segments of four midspheres. A balloon is missing from the central truncated tetrahedron because of difficulty of access. This arrangement of seven non-contiguous midspheres is a close sphere packing.

12. Interaction of Two Oscillons

Regarding the self-generating, self-measuring oscillon and a second identical particle, there are an infinite number of spatial and temporal relationships. If their positions are within range and their external frames of reference

Figure 6. Model of the Space-Filling Combination of Tetrahedra and Truncated Tetrahedra

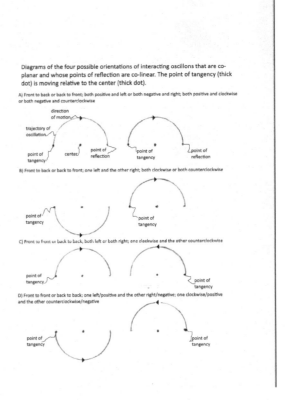

Figure 7. The Four Possible Orientations of Interacting Oscillons That Are Co-Planar and Whose Points of Reflection Are Co-Linear

overlap, then interaction may occur. The spatial relation of identical oscillons is symmetrical if they are in the same plane, and if their points of reflection are co-linear. Their temporal relation is synchronized if their periods are in phase (see Figure 7, below).

In pairings A and B, the motion of both oscillons is either clockwise or counterclockwise. In pairings C and D, the motion of one oscillon is clockwise, while the other is counterclockwise. In pairings A and C, the motion of both oscillons is either to the left or to the right. In pairings B and D, the motion of one oscillon is to the right, while the other is to the left. The two oscillons in C and D are front to front-that is, their moving points of tangency meet at adjacent points of reflection. When interacting oscillons are back to front, as in A and B, the moving points do not confront each other.

The interaction illustrated in pairing D is attractive and stable. The combined motion of the two oscillons resembles wave motion. The motion illustrated in A, B, and C is not connected in a symmetrical, synchronous, and comprehensive fashion and does not have the shape and order of waves. Therefore, the orientation of the pairs of oscillons in A, B, and C does not result in attractive, stable interaction.

The diagrams are drawn from the external point of view, and the motion is described as seen by an observer. This means that the sense of a left or a right direction is that of the observer and applies to both oscillons. However, the view from the center of an oscillon, when it is interacting front to front with another oscillon, is such that its sense of positive and negative, or of left and right, is opposite to the other's sense and applies only to itself.

12.1. The Cycle of Oscillation

The cycle of oscillation of a pair of oscillons can be demonstrated, in the absence of animation, by the dia-

grams in Figure 8, below.

Legend:

circle = spherical frame of reference of an oscillon
straight line = tangent segment of an oscillon
intersection of line and circle = moving point of tangency
1/8 = fraction of cycle of oscillation

Eight positions of the moving point of tangency are shown, and between each position the point moves through an arc of one-eighth of a circle.

At the initial position (0/8 cycle), the point of tangency and one of the two points of reflection coincide. Halfway through the cycle (4/8), the moving points encounter each other at the opposite point of reflection. After reflecting, the points return through an angle of 180° to their original positions (8/8), and the cycle is complete. Another reflection initiates a new cycle.

13. Action at a Distance

What is the range of the oscillon's external frame of reference? To what distance from the oscillon's center does its capability of measuring extend? At what maximum separation does the oscillation of one particle affect the motion of another such that they interact attractively? I have assumed that "action at a distance" is a definitive principle of natural phenomena. Particles are not contiguous. The

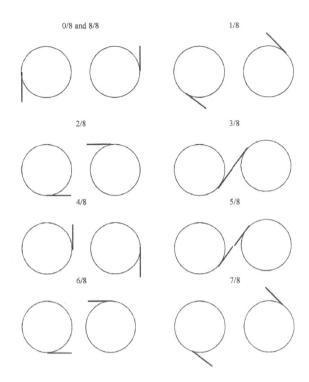

Figure 8. Cycle of Eight Positions of a Pair of Interacting Oscillons (one clockwise, the other counterclockwise)

oscillons' moving points of tangency have separate trajectories that do not coincide. Their internal spherical frames of reference do not overlap. They never touch.

However, the tangential dimension is external to both the oscillon and its frame of reference, except at the oscillating point of tangency where a tangent intersects a radius. The length of the such tangent is indefinite, but we can assume that a segment is at least as long as a radius, i.e. one distance-unit in each direction.

When oscillons are interacting stably and their common frame of reference is tetrahedral, a pair of 30-60-90 triangles are formed by their co-linear tangents, their parallel radii and the line joining their centers (see Figure 2). Assuming that the length of a radius is 1 unit, then the length of a co-linear tangent segment is $1 \div \sqrt{3}$ units = 0.577. The length of the hypotenuse of the triangle, from an oscillon's center to the common center, is $2 \div \sqrt{3}$ units = 1.154, and the distance between their centers is $4 \div \sqrt{3}$ units = 2.309.

The length of the moving point's trajectory between points of reflection is π units = 3.1416. The length of the segment of the moving point's curved trajectory, from the point where a radius and tangent intersect to the line joining the centers, is $\pi/6$ units = 0.5236.

All these natural values are derived from the internal and external frames of reference, and the length of the trajectory, 3.1416 units, is the longest. If, for example, the length of the tangent segment were 3.1416 units, then the angle of intersection of co-linear tangents with the common radius would be approximately 18°, and the distance

between the centers would be about 6.6 units. Therefore, the range of interaction and measurement, the extent of the external tangential frame of reference, is within the limits of a maximum length and minimum angle of the intersecting tangents.

14. Natural Units of Measurement

The oscillon is a self-measuring oscillating particle, whose center, radius, period, and trajectory are constant. The path of the oscillon's motion is semicircular like a pendulum. This means that the distance of its oscillation and the speed of its motion are also constant. Its units of measurement are self-referential. The natural distance unit is the radius of the oscillon, and the natural time unit is its period.

Using the formula c (circumference) = $2\pi r$ (radius), and, giving the radius a value of 1, we calculate that the variable point of tangency of the oscillon moves π distance-units, and its speed is π distance-units per time-unit. For the oscillon, since it does not calculate or use formulas, π is a measurement like the other natural units.

The oscillon is the smallest, simplest, and most fundamental quantity of space and motion. The separation of its center and point of tangency is the least possible distance given by a natural differentiation of one part of space from another and is therefore a minimum. Since its radius is a minimum distance, it follows that its oscillation is a maximum distance, and its rate of motion is a maximum speed.

14.1. The Speed of Light

The speed of light is a fundamental quantity of nature. It has been measured at 299,792,458 meters per second. Its symbol is c. All frequencies in the spectrum of radiation-including gamma rays, x-rays, ultraviolet light, visible light, infrared light, microwaves, and radio waves-travel at this speed. It is also the speed of electricity, and is assumed to be the speed of neutrinos.

Speed, a ratio of two measurements, is a quantification of motion. Usually it is an expression of distance per time, such as 60 kilometers per hour. Or it can be time per distance, as in, "It takes about five hours to fly from Toronto to Vancouver." Direction is the third measurement implied by speed. The scientific term for speed with a specified direction is velocity, but the two words are often used interchangeably.

In interstellar space, light travels at a constant speed. When propagating from one material medium (such as air) to another (such as water or glass), the speed diminishes. C is a maximum speed. No object, particle, ray, or wave can travel faster than c.

The constant and maximum properties of the speed of light need to be explained. What do those properties mean in relation to the motions and interactions of microcosmic particles? What is revealed by the numerical value of 299,792,458, a measurement in the decimal system of numbers and the metric system of units? Why that number and not some other?

The speed of light can be expressed in different systems of measurement, as indicated in Table 1, below:

Unit	Value
Inches per second	1.18028 x 1010
Feet per second	0.983571 x 109
Yards per second	3.27857 x 108
Meters per second	2.99792458 x 108
Kilometers per second	2.99792458 x 105
Miles per second	1.86282397 x 105
Leagues per second	0.62093 x 104

14.2. The Metric System

Measurement requires a specification of units, and the SystÃÍme Internationale (SI) is the standard used in science, commerce, construction, transport, and other activities. In this system, the basic unit of distance is the meter and of time, the second. Both of those man-made quantities were originally derived from measurements of the planet Earth. The polar circumference is the base for distance, and the period of rotation is the base for time.

The rotation period of a day was divided into hours, minutes, and seconds. The numerical value of those units was based on the system of angular measurement, already in use, of the circle divided into 360 degrees, which in turn was loosely based on the number of days per year. That resulted in a day of 24 hours, an hour of 60 minutes, and a minute of 60 seconds.

The shortest unit, the second, is conveniently close to the normal cadence of counting and to the human heartbeat. The day is equal to 86,400 seconds (24 x 60 x 60), and the second is equal to 1.1574 x 10-5 (1/86,400) times the length of the day. The scale of these artificial time units extends to shorter or longer time periods, such as milliseconds or millennia, of any order of magnitude.

When the metric system of measurement was devised in France after the revolution of 1789, the new standard unit of distance was based on the supposedly measured and calculated distance from the North Pole to the equator through the meridian of Paris. This quantity, which was defined as the meter, was recorded on a platinum bar by marks separated by one 10-millionth of the measurement. The length was similar to previous units based on a man's pace or an archer's arrow.

For distances greater or less than a meter, the metric system uses the orders of magnitude of the decimal system of numbers. Commonly used distances, such as the nanometer (10-9 meter) and the kilometer (103 meter), are named, and prefixes have been derived for the others. The megameter is usually written 103 kilometers.

14.3. The Ratio $\frac{c}{\pi}$

A comparison of the speed of light and the speed of the oscillon, both of which are constant and maximum, shows that their numerical values ($c = 299792458$ and $\pi = 314159265$, respectively) are similar in a significant

way. The ratio $\frac{c}{\pi}$ of the two quantities is 0.95426903. Is this proximity a coincidence, or is it a clue to the mysteries of nature? Is it possible that the natural distance-unit, the radius of the oscillon, equals $0.954269 \times 10^{-?}$ meters, the order of magnitude being uncertain.

The size of a hydrogen atom is $1x10^{-10}$ meters, and the size of a proton is $0.84184x10^{-15}$ meters. The proton-to-electron mass ratio is 1,836 to 1. The highest frequency gamma ray has a wavelength in the range of 10^{-13} meters-some scientists say 10^{-15}. The size of a neutrino is unknown. The oscillon, postulated to be the precursor particle of these microcosmic phenomena, must be smaller than any of them and have an order of magnitude in the range of 10-16 to 10-18.

14.4. The Oscillon Hypothesis

This section is an account of how the oscillon hypothesis describes and explains the known universe. It outlines the essentials of the alternative assumptions of a uniformitarian hypothesis of the microcosm. Alternative assumptions will be elaborated in subsequent chapters. The oscillon hypothesis is a theory of the universe. It is specifically a theory of the microcosm and the fundamentals. It is a particle theory about protons, electrons, light, neutrinos, and space. It is a theory of motion regarding oscillation, interaction, and transformation. The oscillon is the simplest, smallest kind of particle and motion. It is a system of two physical points, one of which oscillates relative to its constant center. The oscillation is self-generated, and the relativity is self-measured.

The whole of space, of matter, of light and neutrinos, of the macrocosm and the microcosm-of everything, in fact, that exists and moves-is made of oscillons. Each phenomenon of nature is one of the different interactions that oscillons are capable of.

14.5. A Difference of Dimensional Relativity

Oscillons can interact with each other in one dimension, two dimensions, or three dimensions. When oscillons interact in one dimension, we call them neutrinos. When their interaction is two-dimensional, we experience light. When oscillons interact three-dimensionally, they do so as matter.

Oscillons can transform the dimensionality of their interactions. Nuclear fusion in stars is a change of the three-dimensional interaction of matter into the two-dimensional interaction of light. The emission of neutrinos in nuclear fusion is a transformation from motion in three dimensions to motion in one dimension. The absorption of radiation by matter is a change from two-dimensional to three-dimensional interaction.

In the oscillon hypothesis, there are three additional transformations, for a total of six. A change from two to three dimensions of interaction is the process of formation of protons, in addition to being the absorption of light by matter. When the dimensionality of interacting oscillons changes from that of a line to that of a sphere, in the presence of a proton, an electron is produced. When oscillons transform from one- to two-dimensional interaction, the phenomena change from neutrinos to light. The sixth transformation, from two dimensions to one, does not appear to be necessary. Such transformations do not alter the oscillon in any way. Nuclear fusion is the stellar process whereby hydrogen atoms combine to form helium. The unstated assumption underlying the standard account of this phenomenon is that the helium atoms, the light, and the neutrinos produced are innovations. The oscillon hypothesis is based on an alternative assumption-namely, that the light and the neutrinos are not novelties, but are reproductions of the sources, the precursors, of the proton and electron union.

14.6. The Medium of Light and Neutrinos

The oscillon hypothesis postulates that all of nature is made of an ur-particle, the oscillon. This means that space consists of oscillons and that oscillons are the medium through which both light and neutrinos propagate. In this hypothesis, neutrinos are a kind of radiation and are not independent particles. The phenomenon of light is the interaction of the particles of the medium in two dimensions. The phenomenon of neutrinos is the interaction of the medium in one dimension. The oscillon hypothesis is a steady state cosmology, like that proposed by W. D. MacMillan. It assumes that there is an ongoing process of the formation of protons and electrons. It is not a hypothesis of the origin or history of the universe, because it deems the past to be irrelevant. Nor is it a hypothesis based on gravity, because it holds that the gravitational interaction is not fundamental.

14.7. From Simple to Complex

The oscillon hypothesis of variation of dimensionality conforms to the observed order of natural phenomena from simple to complex. The motion of neutrinos is the least interactive phenomenon. Neutrinos rarely interact with matter, and it is unlikely that there is any interaction between them and light. The interaction of oscillons solely in the radial dimension is simple. The interaction of light out of matter is emission, and the interaction of light into matter is absorption. There is a spectrum of frequencies of electromagnetic radiation, of which visible light is the central component. The spectrum extends from high-frequency gamma rays to low-frequency radio waves. Light is the interaction of oscillons in both the radial and tangential dimensions. Its properties are considerably more complicated than those of neutrinos. The most complex phenomenon with the greatest set of properties is matter. This is because, compared to a linear or planar interaction, the interaction of oscillons in three dimensions allows an unlimited variety of spatial arrangements. A three-dimensional interaction is in the radial, tangential, and axial dimensions. The internal motion of oscillons is always in a plane. When oscillons interact three-dimensionally, they are in the same or a parallel plane, and their axes are either co-linear or parallel.

14.8. Formation of Hydrogen

The transformation of the interaction of oscillons from two dimensions to three is a process of self-assembly into a ring of 6 oscillons (see Figure 13). The ring has a toroidal shape with an empty center. Self-assembly continues until there is a complete proton that consists of 612 oscillons arranged in 102 rings, which are arranged in layers and shells (see Figure 11). There are 11 layers parallel to the plane of the oscillons' motion, arranged from top to bottom in layers of 7, 8, 9, 10, 11, 12, 11, 10, 9, 8, and 7 rings. There are 6 concentric shells, arranged from inner to outer shells of 2, 8, 14, 20, 26, and 32 rings (see Figure 15). This arrangement of layers and shells also has the shape of a torus. The arrangement of oscillons in a proton is derived from the number 1,836. One of the fundamental relations revealed by nature is that the mass of the proton is 1,836 times the mass of the electron.

The electron is a an oscillon that transforms from one-dimensional to three-dimensional interaction when it passes through the central hole of a toroidal proton. The oscillon's motion changes from an oscillation of 180° to a rotation of 360°. The association of a proton and an electron in a hydrogen atom is a union, and the members of the pair cannot exist without each other. The hole in the torus is the opening through which the electron orbits the proton.

An electron passing through the hole in the proton is rotating and orbiting in the plane at right angles to the plane of motion of the oscillons of the proton. This difference of plane is the spatial relation that accounts for charge. Charge is a property of matter that derives from the relativity of the interaction between the proton and its electron. The proton is described as having a positive charge, the electron as having a negative charge, and the charges are described as opposite.

According to the oscillon hypothesis, because there is a third charge-namely, the neutral charge of the neutron-the variation in charge is best described as different rather than opposite. The different neutral charge of the neutron is a consequence of the spatial relation of its interaction with the proton and the electron in an atom. The neutron is a proton whose internal motion is in the plane at right angles to the planes of the proton and the electron (see Figure 20, below).

14.9. Formation of Helium

An atom of hydrogen is a union of a proton and an electron. The next more complex and heavier element is helium. An atom of helium is a combination of two protons, two electrons, and two neutrons. The oscillon hypothesis theorizes that the interaction of these constituent particles takes place in a three-planed configuration. The protons are side by side in one plane. The electrons are in an orthogonal plane and share an orbit that passes through the centers of the protons. The plane of the two neutrons is at right angles to that of the protons, and the electrons also pass through the holes of the neutrons (see Figure 19).

The electron has a number of properties, including: bound, co-orbital, excited, flowing, free, grounded, ionized, leaping, and shared. The oscillon hypothesis suggests that changes in the trajectory of the electron's orbital motion account for these properties. An electron has a variable trajectory because its center, or focus, is not fixed. The proton's center is a vertex of the electron's orbit and is constant. The orbit may be circular, elliptical, parabolic, or hyperbolic; its radius may vary from a minimum to a molecular distance; and its vertices may be the centers of protons in separate atoms. Change in an electron's orbit takes place when the electron is at the vertex in the hole of its proton. (see Figure 18).

14.10. A Disk of Protons

The oscillon hypothesis proposes that the nucleus of an element is a disk of protons assembled into a close sphere packing, known as a Groemer packing. The sequence of numbers 2, 8, 14, 20, 26, and 32, the sum of which is 102, is a clue to the periodic arrangement of protons in the elements. The noble gases-helium, neon, argon, krypton, xenon, and radon-sit at the end of each row of the periodic table. Their atomic numbers, the number of their protons, are 2, 10, 18, 36, 54, and 86. The number of protons added to each element in this sequence is 8, 8, 18, 18, and 32. This is indicative of a planar arrangement in a sphere packing to a base of two.

Thus, the atom, the torus-shaped protons, and the vibrating oscillons are all in the same plane. The plane of the neutrons is at right angles to the plane of the disk of protons. In the atoms of the heavier elements, the neutrons form two layers, one above and one below the disk of protons. The number of neutrons in an element or isotope is always less than twice the number of protons. (see Figure 19).

14.11. The Location of Proton Formation

Central to the oscillon hypothesis is the uniformitarian assumption that protons, electrons, and hydrogen atoms are now being made somewhere in nature. Since stars are made of hydrogen, it seems likely that hydrogen is formed within a galaxy, the location of stars and star formation. Emissions of radiation, such as quasars, gamma ray bursts, and fast radio bursts, have been observed that are different from those of stars. The oscillon hypothesis assumes that the sources of these emissions are not material objects, so they are good candidates for the location of proton formation.

The proton is an extremely stable particle, and the oscillon hypothesis implies that there are more protons now than there once were. Stellar nuclear fusion produces gamma rays and neutrinos, while the protons and electrons of the original atoms of hydrogen remain intact. Thus, the gamma rays and neutrinos are surplus quantities of motion or energy that a star, with its immense size, pressure, and temperature, is capable of generating. This is an increase of motion and radiation that leads to an increase in the amount of matter.

The oscillon hypothesis assumes that while the weak nuclear, the electromagnetic, and the strong nuclear interactions are fundamental, the gravitational interaction is not. Gravity is too weak to operate at the scale of the particle. Gravity is the consequence of the accumulation of great amounts of atoms in clouds of molecular hydrogen, which then grow into stars. It is a three-dimensional interaction and, as a consequence, its range is immense, leading to huge galactic assemblies of gravitationally interacting stars.

14.12. Nature's Numbers

The oscillon hypothesis suggests that the number system of nature is the base four system of numbers. The decimal system (0, 1, 2, 3, 4, 5, 6, 7, 8, 9, 10...) is an anthropocentric invention based on the number of fingers on a pair of human hands. A natural number system should be simple, for which an even numbered base is necessary. The binary system (0, 1, 10...) seems awkward. The next simplest system is the base four or quaternary system (0, 1, 2, 3, 10...). The first five numbers of the base four system include the first three prime numbers, the first square, pi, the simplest plane figure (the triangle), and an optimal order of magnitude. The base four system encompasses the three planes of the sphere, the four planes of the tetrahedron, and the range of measurements of the spherical and tetrahedral frames of reference. The genetic code of the biosphere uses a base four number system. A more appropriate name for the base four system is "two-squared," since the word decimal (which also applies to the base four system) is already in use (referring to the base ten number system), and there is no four, 4, or quater in it.

15. Dimensionality

Matter, light, and neutrinos are the three distinctly different phenomena of nature that must be described and explained by a scientific philosophy. A uniformitarian hypothesis of nature assumes that motion is the physical property of the phenomena that differs in a simple way. The hypothesis assumes that all phenomena-the different frequencies of the spectrum of radiation; the varying properties, structures, and chemistry of elements; or the countless diverse molecules of organic life-are explainable by simple variation in spatial relations of interaction. The oscillon hypothesis of the microcosm assumes that the three different types of motion are the result of a difference in the dimensionality of oscillons' interactions.

Why are there three such phenomena of nature, and not two or four? The oscillon hypothesis suggests that it is because space has three dimensions. Relative motion and its inherent property of self-measurement take place in a frame of reference that has radial, tangential, and axial dimensions. The relativity of motion is not necessarily three-dimensional. The assumption that two-dimensional and one-dimensional relativity of motion also occur is the foundation of the alternative view of nature in the oscillon hypothesis. The essence of this theory is that the most logical explanation of the co-existence of matter, light, and neutrinos is the variation in relativity that three dimensions enable.

It is indisputable that matter is a three-dimensional relative motion. The hydrogen atom, the simplest and most common form of matter, is made of the union of two very different particles, the proton and the electron. Matter has a set of complex properties and is capable of combining in the astonishing variety of elements and objects that constitute the macrocosm. Humans are made of matter, so our experience of relativity is exclusively three-dimensional.

When the relativity of oscillons' motion is three-dimensional, their interaction is not just linear or planar but omnidirectional. The field of interaction is not limited to those oscillons whose motion is in the same relative line or the same relative plane, but encompasses a sphere of relativity.

15.1. Linear, Planar, and Spherical Relativity

The stable interaction of a pair of oscillons discussed in Section 13 is one-dimensional. The oscillons are either front-to-front or back-to-back, their centers are co-linear, and their oscillations are in phase. In the same way, an oscillon interacts with more than one other oscillon, the one in front and the one behind. Thus, a linear chain of oscillons could extend indefinitely, and the sequence of their oscillations would have the appearance of wave motion in both directions. Oscillons interacting with those in front of and behind them are in the radial dimension only, and their relativity is linear.

When oscillons interact in two dimensions, they interact with particles whose oscillation is in the same plane as their own. They interact with the particles beside them, on the left and right, in addition to those in front and behind. The field of interaction is formed by the radial and tangential dimensions, and the relativity is planar.

An oscillon that interacts in three dimensions interacts with those in front, back, left, and right, plus those above and below-that is, oscillons whose motion is in a parallel plane. Their relativity is spherical and omnidirectional, and the field of interaction is formed by the radial, tangential, and axial dimensions.

15.2. Transformation

Transformation is the phenomenon of oscillons changing the dimensionality of their interactions. Six such transformations are possible in three-dimensional space. The emission of light by material objects, the absorption of light by matter, and the emission of neutrinos by stars are transformations of this type, according to the oscillon hypothesis. These phenomena account for transformations from three to two, from three to one, and from two to three dimensions. The other three transformations have not been observed in nature. The change of dimensionality from two to three occurs when protons are formed. This is the same transformation as the absorption of light in photosynthesis, in photoelectric cells, and in the rise in temperature when the Earth faces the Sun.

At the same time that a proton is formed, a change from one to three dimensions occurs when an electron is formed, which unites with a proton to make hydrogen. The location of this transformation is the hole in the torus of the proton. It takes place at the same time as the formation of a proton and results in a hydrogen atom-that is, the proton-electron union that constitutes 80 percent of matter in nature and is the building block of the other elements. A transformation from one to two dimensions is the change from the motion of neutrinos to the motion of light. The transformation from two dimensions to one is not needed in order to account for the known phenomena of nature.

These five transformations constitute the interconnected creation of every natural phenomenon by means of the varying interaction of oscillons, the fundamental universal ur-particle. The conjecture that six transformations are connected as a set of uniform processes means that the transformations from three dimensions to two or to one-that is, the emission of light or of neutrinos-are replications of precursor interactions. Thus, the oscillon hypothesis disagrees with the unstated assumption of the current explanation of these emissions that light and neutrinos are new or innovative phenomena.

15.3. Emission and Absorption

A hypothesis of the microcosm needs to describe and explain the phenomena of transformation of motion. Three such transformations are currently known.

The motion of matter transforms into the motion of light in stellar nuclear fusion, radioactivity, lightning, and the incandescent lamp. The motion of matter transforms into the motion of neutrinos in nuclear fusion and certain radioactive processes. The motion of light transforms into the motion of matter in the absorption of radiation as heat, photosynthesis, vision, and the photoelectric effect.

The fact that the transformation involving matter and light works both ways is highly significant. Atomic motion becomes radiant motion, and the propagation of light becomes the flow of electricity.

The neutron is a transformed proton. The neutron exists naturally only in association with the proton-electron pair. Outside the nucleus, a neutron decays into a proton. But how does a proton become a neutron? The spatial arrangement of these three particles in an atom-that is, the dimensional relation of their individual motions-is the key to understanding the different charges of neutrons, electrons, and protons.

Figure 9, below, is a representation of the set of transformations of nature and their relation to each other. At the top is the oscillon, the particle that constitutes space. Neutrinos, which are referred to here as a form of radiation, are the one-dimensional interaction of oscillons. Light, or electromagnetic (EM) radiation, is the phenomenon of two-dimensional interactions of oscillons. The hypothetical location and process of formation of light from neutrinos is indicated by the arrows of combination and transformation connecting them.

The process of formation of protons from light, and the process of formation of electrons from neutrinos-that is, the change of the interaction of oscillons from two to three dimensions and from one to three dimensions, respectively-are indicated by the arrows of combination and transformation connecting them. A proton and an electron unite in an atom of hydrogen, and hydrogen atoms then accumulate to form molecules and stars.

In stars, hydrogen atoms combine through nuclear fusion and nucleosynthesis to form helium and other elements. In the process, two protons transform into neutrons by interacting with the remaining protons in the plane at right angles to the base plane of the helium atom. Consequent to this process of fusion and synthesis is the release of two electrons and the change of some of the original internal motion of the hydrogen atoms into radiant light and neutrinos. The interaction of oscillons as three-dimensional matter transforms by emission into the interaction of two-dimensional light and one-dimensional neutrinos. This replication of precursors and the closed interconnection of the set of transformations are represented by the arrows connecting light to light and neutrinos to neutrinos.

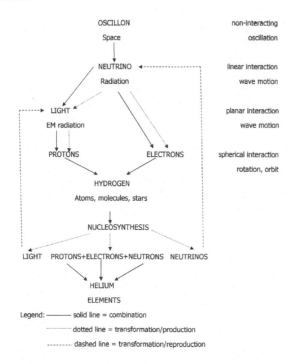

Figure 9. Schematic Diagram of the Processes of Combination and Transformation of All Three Forms of Motion in the Microcosm

16. Space and Ether

The words space, universe, nature, particle, motion, and phenomenon all have connotations of each other. The whole is described by the first three words, and the parts by the other three. Everything in nature is made of particles, and every particle is a form of motion. Does it make sense to divide nature into matter and space? To separate and isolate matter in that way is an anthropocentric concept. Matter is in space and of space. Only an infinitesimal fraction of space is occupied by matter.

Is space empty? In the parts of space not occupied by matter, there are light and neutrinos propagating from every direction. There is motion and there are phenomena. Are there particles? For a long time, space was hypothe-

sized to be the medium through which the wave motion of light propagates. The medium was an elastic, invisible substance called ether. This hypothesis was based on the assumption that a medium was necessarily some form of matter, based on the analogy of water waves and sound waves.

Subsequently, it was demonstrated that space was not made of matter and that the material ether does not exist. However, the idea of space as a medium persists because it is counterintuitive to assume that space is empty.

It is their different motion that distinguishes matter, light, and neutrinos. Each interacts with others of its own kind in a stable, synchronized, symmetrical, and constant spatial relationship. It is the dimensionality of their interaction-that is, of that spatial relationship-that varies. A different dimensionality could be described as a different spacetime, or perhaps as a different topochron-from the Greek topos ("place") and chronos ("time").

17. Matter, Light, and Neutrinos

What has happened to the radiation and neutrinos emitted by all the stars in all of time?

Do neutrinos have a destination?

Does radiation have a function?

Certainly, the function of our sun's radiation is not to provide heat and light to other material bodies. Only a tiny fraction of the sun's output is intercepted by the planets and moons (to say nothing of their occupants). Furthermore, the function of the sun's radiation is not to reveal the sun's presence. An even tinier part of a star's light is detected by an observing eye or camera. Has this prodigious amount of energy been wasted? Do these emissions propagate eternally, never to transform, accumulate, or cycle?

Is the universe a system in which all things are connected through interdependent processes? Are all the forms of motion, matter, radiation, and neutrinos derived from a common source, having transformed in stages from simple to complex, from weakly interacting to strongly, from having few properties to many? What is the fundamental physical property that distinguishes the three types of motion?

The transformations that we are aware of may provide answers to some of these questions. In particular, the emission of gamma rays and neutrinos by atoms in the process of stellar fusion is a good place to start. One underlying assumption of the current theory of the universe is that the products of fusion are novel-that is, the heavy elements, radiation, and neutrinos produced in nucleosynthesis and supernovÃę from atoms of hydrogen are something new under the sun. There is an anthropocentric assumption that the complex atoms and molecules that are the building blocks of planets and life forms really matter, whereas the motions of radiation and neutrinos are incidental byproducts.

17.1. Reproduction of Precursors

Instead, let us assume that light and neutrinos are reproductions of the precursors of protons and electrons. Furthermore, let us assume that the dimensionality of interaction with its own kind distinguishes one form of motion from another. Also, let us assume that neutrinos are a one-dimensional interaction, light is a two-dimensional interaction, and matter is a three-dimensional interaction.

These assumptions mean that a necessary part of nature is a process whereby protons and electrons are currently and constantly being formed from their precursor particles. Needless to say, that phenomenon has not been observed. However, this conjecture is not new. It is the basic assumption of steady state cosmology, which contradicts the idea that all matter was formed in the explosive expansion of the Big Bang. It is possible that, while the formation of hydrogen atoms is hidden from us, the raw materials of that phenomenon are very much in evidence. A process of formation of a complex particle from simpler precursor particles implies that the precursors accumulate at a given location, and their combination results in a transformation into something different.

17.2. Dimensionality and Complexity

Judging from the number of interactions that these forms of motion are involved in, it is evident that matter is the most complex form of motion in nature and that neutrinos are the least complex, with radiation in between. Presumably, neutrinos are interacting with each other as they stream outward from the Sun. When they reach Earth, most of them pass through the planet as if it were transparent, while a few may interact with atoms and thereby reveal themselves to our detectors. It is not known whether there is any interaction between radiation and neutrinos. Matter, which is the three-dimensional interaction of protons, electrons, and neutrons, has a large suite of complex properties, arrangements, and behaviors. A partial list of these would include:

absolute zero, acid, air, alpha particle, aluminum, animal, atom, ash, beta particle, brain, carbon, charge, chemistry, cloud, comet, continent, cosmic ray, density, dust, electricity, element, fission, fusion, galaxy, gas, glacier, glass, gravity, heat, helium, hydrogen, ion, iron, isotope, life, liquid, machine, magnetism, mass, metal, mineral, molecule, moon, nitrogen, nucleosynthesis, ocean, organism, oxygen, planet, plant, plate tectonics, polarity, pottery, pressure, rain, salt, sand, silicon, solar system, solid, spectroscopy, star, technology, temperature, volcanism, water, and weight.

Radiation arrives at Earth from the Sun in the form of wave trains and wave fronts. Some of it is reflected, and the rest is absorbed by matter. Light is also produced in natural phenomena such as aurora, bioluminescence, chemistry, combustion, fluorescence, heat, lightning, phosphorescence, radioactivity, sparks, and static electricity. Numerous artificial devices also emit light.

Radiation interacts with the chlorophyll of plant cells in the process of photosynthesis. The motion of sunlight transforms into the motion of electricity in solar cells. There is a spectrum of frequencies of radiation, the so-called electromagnetic spectrum (see Figure 10, below), from high-frequency gamma rays and x-rays, to ultraviolet, visible, and infrared light, to microwaves and low-frequency radio waves.

17.3. The Hidden Microcosm

The microcosm is the world of protons, electrons, light, and neutrinos. It is the realm of matter, radiation, and neutrinos. It is the universe of stable, elementary particles. Its scale is the very small, the minimal, and the infinitesimal.

The microcosm is a hidden world that has never been seen by human eyes. It has been visualized over the centuries by philosophers and scientists. It has been observed and measured, both directly and indirectly, by technological means. Using these measurements, mathematicians have calculated and quantified the motions of matter, radiation, and neutrinos.

17.4. Classification of Phenomena

Is it possible to arrange the stable particles in order from simple to complex? Is there a hierarchy of the forms of motion? The factors to be considered include a particle's interaction with its own kind, its interactions with other particles, and the variations in its properties. A simple particle is one with a dynamically straightforward relationship with its twins, the lowest number and fewest kinds of interactions with alien particles, and the lowest number of variables in structure and behavior. Conversely, a complex particle is one with a full range of interactions with different particles, great variability in structure, properties, and behavior, and a complicated spatial relation of its constituents.

The neutrino seems to be the simplest natural type of motion. Neutrinos are emitted by stars as a product of nuclear fusion, but they rarely interact with matter. Presumably, they interact with each other, perhaps in a train. They seem to be massless and chargeless.

Matter is at the opposite position in the hierarchy. An atom of hydrogen is the union of a proton and an electron, two very different particles. The proton can change into a neutron and vice versa. The electron can change the trajectory of its motion-for example, from circular to elliptical, or vice versa.

Protons, electrons, and neutrons combine to form the ninety-two natural elements, each with a unique set of properties. Different elements combine to form the host of substances that make up the lithosphere, hydrosphere, atmosphere, and biosphere of Earth.

Hydrogen is involved in processes that produce light and other forms of radiation, neutrinos, and cosmic rays. It accumulates into molecules, clouds, stars, and galaxies. Stars age and change into supernovæ, which produce the heaviest elements.

In the middle of the hierarchy sits radiation. Its motion varies in frequency and wave length, which is manifest in the electromagnetic spectrum. Its velocity and trajectory in space are constant. Radiation is massless and chargeless.

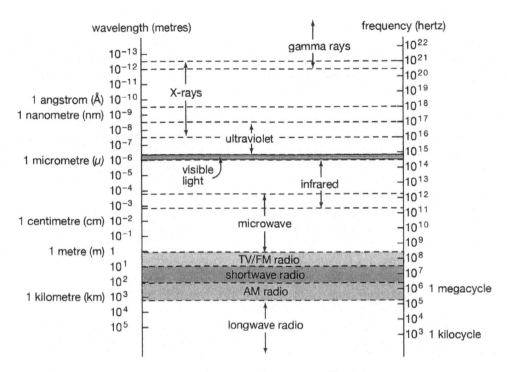

Figure 10. The Spectrum of Frequency of Radiation

The motion of radiation is described as wave trains and wave fronts. Radiation is absorbed, reflected, and emitted by matter. It is a product of nuclear fusion and radioactivity. It is produced by static electricity, combustion, bioluminescence, and other natural phenomena. When the light from one star intersects with the light from another, it does not reflect, collide, combine, or change in any way. Radiation and neutrinos are propagating through space, even occupying the same space without the slightest interaction with each other.

18. Gravity

The mainstream theory of the universe assumes that there are four fundamental forces: gravity, the strong nuclear force, the electromagnetic force, and the weak nuclear force. These phenomena are also referred to as the fundamental interactions: gravitational, strong nuclear, electromagnetic, and weak nuclear.

The word force is misleading in this context because it implies only causative action. That is, it implies that the cause can be separated from its effect, that the cause of the force can be ignored, and that the cause is somehow optional rather than mechanical and automatic. But as the classic phrase says, for every action there is a reaction. In the microcosm, every action is a reaction and vice versa. In the realm of particles, there are only interactions-that is, a succession of motions that are both actions and reactions.

Why should the inclusion of the gravitational interaction in this list of fundamentals be questioned? The most revealing difference between it and the other three is that the strong, electromagnetic, and weak interactions are nu-

clear interactions between individual particles of matter, whereas the gravitational interaction is between accumulations of atoms. In other words, the first three interactions are fundamental in the microcosm, whereas gravity is operational, applicable, and determinant in macrocosmic interactions and dominates at the largest scales. This difference may be restated by noting that physicists use quantum theory as a means to understand the strong nuclear, electromagnetic, and weak nuclear interactions, while using continuum theory to describe gravity. According to the Oxford Astronomy Encyclopedia, "Attempts have been made to quantize gravity but with little success.... No quantum theory of gravity has been found, and the mathematics describing the fundamental forces disallow this unification."

18.1. Is Gravity a Fundamental Interaction?

The view that gravity is fundamentally the same as the other forces is anthropocentric. Gravity is central to our existence; our sense of gravity is operating constantly. A human being, an accumulation of matter at the interface between the ground and the air, interacts with the Earth, also a material body.

The three microcosmic interactions have become known only recently. The microcosmic phenomena in our bodies-electrical signals in the nervous system, the extraction of oxygen in respiration, the absorption of nutrients in digestion, the regulation of temperature, etc.-are within the realm of the unconscious. The locomotion of a macrocosmic terrestrial life form is dominated by gravity. We have been reluctant to downgrade the status of the gravitational interaction and to recognize that it is profoundly different from the microcosmic interactions

According to the Oxford Astronomy Encyclopedia, "the weakest of the four fundamental forces dominates the evolution of the universe." There are anthropocentric views of nature expressed in this statement. The cosmology of astronomers focuses on the macrocosm of accumulations of hydrogen, stars, and galaxies, and the universe as a whole. In fact, the microcosm, where the basic fundamental processes of nature take place, is dominant in determining the contents, motions, and phenomena of the world.

If the gravitational interaction is not fundamental and does not operate at the microcosmic scale, how is it to be accounted for? In the oscillon hypothesis, gravity is the result of the accumulation of numerous hydrogen atoms in clouds and stars. It is a cumulative effect of the strong nuclear interaction of the proton-electron union, as these basic units of matter assemble into macrocosmic bodies. Both the strong nuclear interaction and gravitational interaction are three-dimensional, whereas the weak nuclear interaction is one-dimensional, and the electromagnetic interaction is two-dimensional. This three-dimensional property explains the immense range of gravity and the fact that it is always attractive.

18.2. Causative or Consequential

Fundamental is necessarily a description of the microcosm. Causes are the exclusive realm of particles. Everything in the macrocosm is an effect rather than a cause. Gravitational interaction is a phenomenon of the whole, not the parts. It is the consequence of the accumulation of atoms into stars and galaxies.

19. Mass

The Gage Canadian Dictionary defines mass as "a measure of the amount of matter that a body contains." It is a measurement of size or quantity. It is a count or enumeration of the parts of the whole. The thing being measured is a material body made of protons, electrons, and neutrons. The volume, or amount of space, of an object of known measurements, such as a ball or box, can be determined by using a formula that results in a three-dimensional quantity expressed in cubic units. Density is a ratio of the quantity of matter in a particular unit of volume. The property of density relates to the separation, or amount of space, between the constituent particles of a material body. Weight is a measurement of the mass, or heaviness, of an object that is interacting gravitationally with the Earth.

In order to measure an object's mass, a balance or scale is required that compares the object to another object of known mass. This process yields the weight of the object. Everybody knows his or her own weight, but how many people know their volume? The mass of a body such as a moon or a comet can be calculated relative to the known mass of a planet or star with which it is gravitationally interacting.

In the microcosm, there is no such thing as a balance, nor the builder and operator of a balance, nor a calculator. The microcosm is the world of autometric oscillating interactors having the ability to measure-which ability is limited to distance, angle, direction, and period. The oscillon also has a sense of self or oneness. It is a quantity of one, and its size is the unit of mass.

19.1. Measurement of Mass

Mass is a quantification of the amount of matter. It is a measurement of the whole, the sum of the parts. For the self-measuring oscillon, the unit of mass is the self, and the act of measuring mass involves counting the number of interacting oscillons. Mass, matter, gravity, and three dimensions are inseparably connected.

The gravitational interaction is a form of relative motion that incorporates an act of measurement. Because it is three-dimensional, its range is limited only by the size of the largest material object, a star, and the largest accumulation of such objects, a galaxy.

If every natural phenomenon is an interaction of oscillons, the process of counting the number of oscillons participating in the phenomenon involves determining the number of identical selves. In three dimensions, one oscillon is interacting with all oscillons. Thus, a star is an accumulation of oscillons that have accumulated into protons and electrons that have accumulated into molecules of hydrogen.

An oscillon is a quantity of space defined by its spherical frame of reference, which has a size, extent, or volume determined by its radius. The radius of the sphere is constant, and the amount of space occupied by the oscillon is constant. There is space between each non-contiguous interacting oscillon, and in stable interactions such space is minimal and constant.

19.2. Masslessness

Mass is a measurement of a property of matter. It relates to the size of material bodies made of protons, electrons, and neutrons that vary in scale from a single hydrogen atom to the accumulation of hydrogen atoms in a giant star.

However, light does not have the property of mass, so the photons of electromagnetic radiation are deemed to be massless. "Indeed," writes Roger Penrose, "the mass of the photon, if non-zero, would have to be less than 10-20 of an electron's mass for good observational reasons. Moreover, the photon appears to be clearly singled out, among all the bosons in the theory, by being a massless particle."

The oscillon hypothesis assumes that neutrinos are massless. The neutrino, writes Penrose, "can be treated as a massless particle. (Its mass is, in any case, extremely tiny in relation to the mass of an electron, and certainly not more than 6 x 10-6 of the electron's mass.)" Physicists have determined that space is not material and is therefore massless. A form of motion or a type of particle that lacks the property of mass is not a form of matter, nor is it a form of three-dimensional interaction.

20. The Sphere-Packing Hypothesis

The ratio of a proton's mass to an electron's mass is a fundamental quantity of the microcosm. The mass of a proton is 1836.153503 times that of an electron. Although a proton's mass is not an even multiple of an electron's mass, the number 1836 is a very interesting number, which warrants close investigation. The questions arise, "Why that number and not some other?" and "Is it a clue to the composition, arrangement, motion, and interaction of these particles?"

The prime factors of 1836 are 1, 2, 2, 3, 3, 3, and 17. One of the combinations of these factors is 18 x 102; 18 is the product of 1 x 2 x 3 x 3, and 102 equals 2 x 3 x 17.

The number 102, a very interesting number (see Figure 11, below), is the sum of 2 + 8 + 14 + 20 + 26 + 32. Each number is 6 more than the previous one. The sequence 2, 8, 14, 20, 26, and 32 represents the number of spheres in the "layers" or "rings" of a sphere packing. This is a Groemer packing, whose base is two spheres rather than one. Any number of spheres from 2 to 102 can be assembled into a disk or layer of minimal area that, for larger numbers, always has a hexagonal shape.

20.1. Groemer Packing

Each circle in Figure 11, like those dealt with by Groemer packing, represents a proton-that is, its toroidal shape and spherical frame of reference-as seen from above or below. Whereas in a Groemer packing the circles are contiguous, the uniformitarian hypothesis assumes that protons are not touching, but share a common tangent at 60°to the line joining their centers. The uniformitarian hypothesis further modifies the assumptions of Groemer packing by stipulating that the number of protons in the base is 2, rather than 1. This assumption is derived from the following clues: (a) the atomic numbers of the noble gases; (b) the electron shell structure; (c) the alpha particle; (d) the cosmic abundance of the elements; and (e) the proton-to-electron mass ratio of 1836 to 1.

Groemer packing is used with the objective of minimizing the area of the convex hull containing the circles. To that end, when there are alternative choices, nature selects the packing with the smallest number of larger edge holes and the biggest number of smaller central holes (the fewest circles in the perimeter). Nature also selects the arrangement that is as hexagonal as possible, since six sides are better than five or four for minimizing area.

The adaptation of the rules of Groemer packing to questions of atomic structure results in the minimization of the area of the disk of protons while promoting symmetry, balance, and harmonious motion. Therefore, when there are two alternative arrangements, nature selects the one with greater symmetry about both axes. Nature also chooses to complete filling the inner layer before starting the next one.

20.2. The Periodic Table of Elements

The periodic table of elements is a fundamental quantification of nature (see Figure 12, below) The table is an arrangement of the ninety-two naturally occurring elements according to their number of protons-that is, the atomic number of the element. The rows and columns of the table reveal the similarities and differences of the elements.

One such column is the noble gases, so-called because they are inert and seldom combine with other elements.

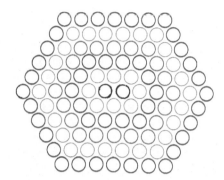

Figure 11. Diagram of a Packing of 102 Non-Contiguous, Co-Tangential Spheres (circles of the same shadings are in one of six hexagonal layers)

These elements and their atomic numbers are: helium, 2; neon, 10; argon, 18; krypton, 36; xenon, 54; and radon, 86. The differences in their atomic numbers, and the number of elements in the corresponding rows of the periodic table, are 8, 8, 18, 18, and 32.

There is a hypothesis of the structure of the atom in which the electrons orbit the nucleus in shells that vary in distance from the nucleus. The electrons in each shell share an orbit-that is, the electrons are co-orbital. There is a limit to the number of electrons that can share an orbit, with the more distant shells having a greater capacity. The sequence of numbers of such limits is also 2, 8, 8, 18, 18, 32.

There is a correspondence between the latter sequence of numbers and that of a packing of 102 spheres. The first, second, and sixth layers are identical. This may not be a perfect match, but neither is it a coincidence.

The microcosm has been stingy in revealing numerical clues, despite our assuming that nature is mathematical. The familiar numerical demonstrations are Euclidean solid geometry; the spherical frame of reference; the tangential frame of reference; the periodic table of elements; the speed of light; and the relative size of the proton and the electron. These are a set of natural, fundamental measurements that reveal much about the relativity, motion, interaction, transformation, and accumulation of minimal, self-generating, self-measuring oscillating particles.

20.3. The Periodicity of Protons in Atoms

Figure 12, below, is a representation of the order of self-assembly of protons in atoms. Based on the sphere-packing hypothesis of formation of atoms, it is an alternative to the familiar periodic table of the elements. Each sphere is labeled with an atomic number from 1 to 86 and the symbol of the name of the atom. There are 16 gaps in the order where no atom is located.

At the center of the figure are the pair, hydrogen (1) and helium (2). The groups of elements in the columns of the periodic table are represented here in lines radiating from the central pair. The rows of elements of the periodic table are shown in the hexagonal rings surrounding the central pair.

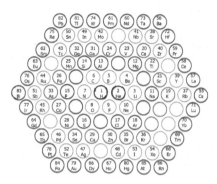

Figure 12. Diagram of the Periodicity of Protons in Atoms According to the Sphere-Packing Hypothesis (Not Including Numbers 87 to 92)

Thus, the diagonal ray down and right from He is that of the other noble gases, 10, 18, 36, 54, and 86. The horizontal ray to the right of He is the group of 3, 11, 19, 37, and 55. Continuing in the counterclockwise direction are the lines of the other groups, each of five atoms: 4, 12, 20, 38, 56; 5, 13, 31, 49, 81; 6, 14, 32, 50, 82; 7, 15, 33, 51, 83; 8, 16, 34, 52, 84; and 9, 17, 35, 53, 85.

Then there are the groups of three atoms shown in lines radiating from the gaps in the second ring. Starting from the gap between 11 and 12, the line horizontally to the right is the group of 21, 39, and 57. Continuing in the counterclockwise direction are the lines of the remaining groups, each of three: 22, 40, 72; 23, 41, 73; 24, 42, 74; 25, 43, 75; 26, 44, 76; 27, 45, 77; 28, 46, 78; 29, 47, 79; and 30, 48, 80.

The final group of fourteen atoms radiate singly from the gaps in the fourth ring. Their atomic numbers are 58, 59, 60, 61, 62, 63, 64, 65, 66, 67, 68, 69, 70, 71.

Surrounding the central pair of H and He is the six-sided ring of the group of 3, 4, 5, 6, 7, 8, 9, and 10. The next ring, where a gap is symbolized by ( ), is the group of 11, ( ), 12, ( ), 13, 14, ( ), 15, ( ), 16, ( ), 17, 18, ( ). The third ring is the non-sequential group of 19, 21, 22, 20, 23, 24, 31, 32, 25, 26, 33, 27, 28, 34, 29, 30, 35, 36, ( ), ( ). The fourth ring is 37, 39, ( ), 40, 38, 41, ( ), 42, 49, 50, 43, ( ), 44, 51, 45, ( ), 46, 52, 47, ( ), 48, 53, 54, ( ), ( ), ( ). The outer ring is 55, 57, 58, 59, 72, 56, 73, 60, 61, 74, 81, 82, 75, 62, 63, 76, 83, 77, 64, 65, 78, 84, 79, 66, 67, 80, 85, 86, 68, 69, 70, 71. The atoms numbered 87, 88, 89, 90, 91, and 92 presumably are grouped in the next ring possibly in line with numbers 55, 56, 57, 58, 59, and 60.

The sixteen gaps are grouped in the six segments of the hexagonal arrangement as follows: in the lower-right segment, a triangular group of 6 gaps, and in each of the other five segments a linear group of 2 gaps.

21. Proton and Electron Formation

The following description of the composition, arrangement, structure, and internal motion of a proton is the most speculative part of the oscillon hypothesis. It derives from the assumptions that the proton is made of oscillons, arranged in a sphere packing, shaped like a torus and, like the quark hypothesis, divided sixfold.

When oscillons transform from two-dimensional to three-dimensional interactions, they assemble into a ring of six oscillons in the shape of a torus, which has a hole at the center of the ring (see Figure 13, below). Additional rings of six oscillons assemble concentrically to the axis of the initial ring and parallel to its plane. A complete proton consists of 102 rings and 612 oscillons.

Figure 14, above, shows a cross-section of the central plane and hole of the proton. Each circle represents the internal spherical frame of reference of an oscillon. Each of the six spokes of the proton consists of 102 oscillons arranged vertically in a sphere packing. There are 12 oscillons in the layer of the packing, coinciding with the plane of the proton. Adjacent layers on each side have 11, 10, 9, 8, and 7 oscillons for a total of 102.

Each circle (in Figure 15, above) represents the internal spherical frame of reference of an oscillon. Each spoke is a sphere packing of oscillons in a hexagonal arrangement. The packing of 102 oscillons has a base of 2 oscillons, and rings of 8, 14, 20, 26, and 32 oscillons surrounding the base. Between the two spokes is the hole in the proton.

The assembled oscillons continue to oscillate. The oscillations of adjacent members of each ring are synchronous, and so are those of the oscillons of each concentric and parallel ring. Their combined motion, a resonant synodic sequence of oscillations, has the appearance of a wave. The transformation of an oscillon from one-dimensional to three-dimensional interactions takes place in the hole of the proton, resulting in a particle whose point of tangency, rather than oscillating, rotates relative to its constant center point. The new particle is an electron. The center of the proton is a vertex of the electron's trajectory relative to the proton. The proton and the electron form a stable union, and the electron's motion is fundamentally dependent on its proton.

22. Hydrogen and Helium

The constituent particles of atoms are distinguished by having different charges. The proton has a positive charge, and the electron has a negative charge. The neutron, which is a transformed proton, has no charge or a neutral charge. The effects of charge are observed when these particles pass through an electromagnetic field that deflects their motion. The proton is attracted to the negative electrode, and the electron to the positive, while the neutron's motion is not affected.

The charge of an intact atom is neutral, since the equal charges of the proton and electron cancel each other. When the proton and electron separate, in the process of ionization or radioactivity, they are described as charged particles and as positive or negative ions. What is charge? What is magnetism, electricity, and the electromagnetic interaction? Why are light and neutrinos chargeless, whereas the particles of matter possess charge? Why are there three

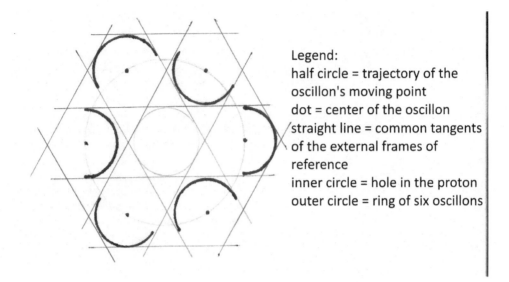

Figure 13.   Innermost Ring of Six Oscillons of a Proton

Figure 14.   Horizontal Cross-Section of a Proton

charges?

The oscillon hypothesis assumes that the observed phenomena are solely determined by variations of the spatial relations, the relativity of the particles, and their motion.

22.1. A Torus-Shaped Proton

Since Ernest Rutherford and other physicists discovered the structure of the hydrogen atom, the proton has provisionally been depicted as a sphere, similar to a billiard ball, suggesting solidity and opacity. In this picture, there is no designation of the proton's plane and axis, nor any indication of motion. Neutrons are depicted as spheres of a different color. The protons and neutrons are grouped randomly into a spherical nucleus. Mathematical physicists are content to leave this analogy unchanged because their scientific method is by calculation rather than visualization, by equation rather than model, by algebra rather than geometry.

The proton does have a plane, an axis, a motion, and a direction that can be described by geometry. In the oscillon hypothesis, the proton has the shape of a torus. The internal frame of reference of an object of this shape is immediately

apparent. The oscillation of its constituent particles defines the plane of the proton. In this hypothesis, each of the three differently charged particles moves in its own plane.

Torus is defined as a shape generated by the rotation, in space, of a circle about an axis in its plane but not cutting the circle. Familiar objects that have this shape are donuts, Lifesavers candy, rings, inner tubes, life belts, and chain links. The formula for the volume of a torus is $2\pi^2 K r^2$ as shown in Figure 16, below.

A torus has a hole at its center. Its plane and axis are constant. A proton of this shape has an empty center of minimal radius, which is conveniently available for the passage of an electron in the course of its orbital motion. Thus, the vertex of the electron's trajectory is fixed at the proton's center, and the center or focus of the trajectory is variable, as depicted in Figure 17, below.

22.2. The Vertex of the Electron's Trajectory

The variable trajectories of the electron are the curves, circle, ellipse, parabola, and hyperbola, which are collectively known as conics. The vertex of the curve is fixed at the center of the proton, and the axis of the proton is the line that determines the shape of the curve. The center or focus of the curvilinear trajectory lies in the plane of the proton. The distance between the vertex and the focus of the curve is variable.

The relation of (a) the distance of the electron from the focus or foci and (b) the perpendicular distance between the electron and a line parallel to the axis of the proton determines whether the trajectory is a hyperbola, parabola, or ellipse. The relations of distance may be constant sum (ellipse), equal (parabola), or constant difference (hyperbola), as depicted in Figure 18, below.

22.3. The Three-Planed Arrangement of Protons, Electrons, and Neutrons

A helium atom consists of two protons, two electrons, and two neutrons. The protons are co-planar, and they form

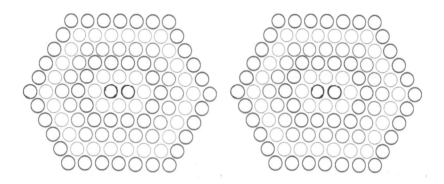

Figure 15. Vertical Cross-Section of a Pair of Spokes of a Proton Showing the Overall Toroidal Shape

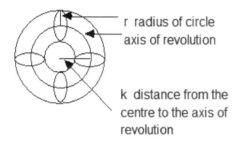

r radius of circle

axis of revolution

k distance from the centre to the axis of revolution

Figure 16. Schematic Diagram of a Torus (the arrows are pointing to the nearest line)

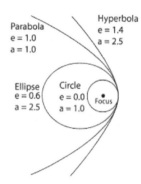

Figure 18. Variations with the Same Vertex of the Trajectory of an Electron

Figure 17. Diagram of the Interaction of a Proton and an Electron

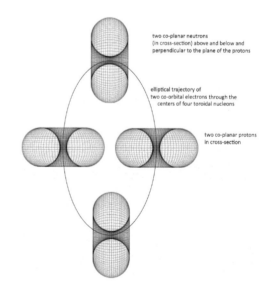

two co-planar neutrons (in cross-section) above and below and perpendicular to the plane of the protons

elliptical trajectory of two co-orbital electrons through the centers of four toroidal nucleons

two co-planar protons in cross-section

Figure 19. Cross-Section of a Helium Atom: The Interaction of 2 Protons, 2 Electrons, and 2 Neutrons

the plane of the atom. The directions of their internal motions are opposite, one clockwise and the other counter-clockwise. The electrons are, both passing through the centers of the protons, and the angle between them is pi. The neutrons are co-planar in the third plane, one above and the other below the plane of the protons, and their centers coincide with the electrons' trajectory.

The distance between a proton's center and the center of the atom is 1.1547 proton radii, the minimum allowed in their common tetrahedral frame of reference. The distance between a neutron's center and the center of the atom is 2 proton radii. The electrons' trajectory is elliptical. The distance between the centers of the protons and between the centers of a proton and a neutron is 2.3094 proton radii. The distance between the centers of the neutrons is 4 proton radii. (See Figure 19, below.)

22.4. The Relation of the Frames of Reference of Sub-Atomic Particles

The plane of the electron's motion is at right angles to the plane of the proton's internal motion. This leaves the other plane of three dimensions available for a neutron, with its internal motion at right angles to the planes of motion of both the proton and the electron. From the point of view of the center of a proton, an electron, or a neutron, each has a frame of reference and an internal motion that defines its radial, tangential, and axial dimensions. Because the motion of each is in a different plane, their planes do not coincide, nor do their dimensions. For example, whereas the proton and the electron have the same radial dimension, the proton's tangential dimension corresponds with the electron's axial dimension, and the proton's axial dimension corresponds with the electron's tangential dimension. Similarly, the electron and neutron share the same axial dimension, but their radial and tangential dimensions are interchanged. Also, the tangential dimensions of the proton and neutron correspond.

The correspondence of the internal dimensions of a proton, electron, and neutron in a three-planed atom is represented in Table 2, below:

Table 2: The Correspondence of the Dimensions in a Three-Planed Atom

Dimensions of proton	Electron-to-proton
Radial	Radial
Tangential	Axial
Axial	Tangential

Table 2: Continued

Neutron-to-proton	Electron-to-neutron
Axial	Tangential
Tangential	Axial
Radial	Radial

The fact that the atoms of most elements contain more neutrons than protons but never attain twice as many suggests layering. A disk of protons forms the base of the atom, and above and below this middle layer are layers of neutrons (see Figure 20, below).

Figure 20. Model of the Disk of Eight Protons in the Nucleus of an Oxygen Atom

22.5. Elements, Isotopes, Reactivity, and Radioactivity

The interaction of protons, electrons, and neutrons is the process that produces the atoms, elements, molecules, and compounds that make up the material part of nature. There are 92 different microcosmic atoms in nature, each consisting of from one to ninety-two protons, the atomic number. The macrocosmic substance made of such an atom is called an element. The different atoms also contain neutrons in numbers varying from 0 (hydrogen) to 146 (uranium). An atom of the same element with different numbers of neutrons is called an isotope. The stability of an isotope depends on its number of neutrons, and the most common isotope of an element in nature is the stablest one. Some elements and most isotopes are unstable and are therefore subject to the transformative process called radioactivity. In other words, all unstable elements and isotopes are radioactive.

The ability to form stable atoms is determined by the spatial relations of the protons, electrons, and neutrons-that is, the relativity of their angles, external trajectories (elliptical, parabolic, or hyperbolic), internal motions (clockwise or counterclockwise), numbers, parallelism, perpendicularity, planes, and the tangential frames of reference of two or more than two. The same variations in relativity determine the atoms' ability to form stable molecules and compounds and to participate in chemical reactions.

The scale of combinations and permutations of such varying relativity is immense, manifesting itself in the complexity of the macrocosm. The oscillon hypothesis proposes that the arrangement of protons in an atom is a disk of Groemer-style sphere-packing, in which the spheres are co-tangential rather than contiguous. Such a packing, which usually has a hexagonal shape, has a minimal area. The base of this packing is two protons, and additional protons are arranged in rings of 8, 14, 20, 26, and 32 protons. The total number of protons in such a packing is 102, which leaves unanswered the question of why only 92 atoms in nature are stable.

Usually, the shape of this packing is fixed, but in the elements that have low atomic numbers, such as carbon (6), the arrangement of their protons may vary in shape to produce different allotropes-in this case, diamond and graphite.

Some questions are unanswered at the present time and require further research. For example, are the internal oscillations of the protons in any atom all moving in the same direction, whether clockwise or counterclockwise, or are the directions opposite-and, if so, in what ratio or sequence? The oscillon hypothesis suggests that the plane of the neutrons is perpendicular to the plane of the protons, but are the neutrons arranged in pairs, are their planes parallel, and are their oscillations in the same direction?

The variable trajectory of an electron is the key to forming chemical bonds between atoms to produce molecules, metals, minerals, acids, bases, inorganic compounds, organic compounds, and so on. An electron is united with a proton due to the vertex of the electron's trajectory coinciding with the proton's center. Again, many questions remain unanswered at the present time. For example, what is the function of co-orbital electrons? When is a trajectory internal or external? When is the direction negative or positive? When is the path an ellipse, a parabola, or a hyperbola? Can electrons share the same vertex? How are their phases related? What effect, if any, does asymmetry in the disc of protons have? The circumstances of such varying relativity are yet to be determined.

22.6. Polarity and Planarity

Opposite, when used to describe charge, implies a linearity or polarity in the relation of positive and negative electrical and magnetic phenomena. This is a misleading assumption that arises from the directionality of attraction and repulsion observed in the magnetic fields of the Earth or an iron bar.

Assuming that the directional difference between positive and negative charges is not linear, then the correspondence of three types of charge and three dimensions is apparent. The positive, negative, and neutral charges of the subatomic particles are determined by their relativity, which is planar. Thus, an electron's charge is neither the same as nor opposite to a proton's charge, but the difference is perpendicularity.

22.7. The Union of Proton and Electron

Niels Bohr proposed his model of the atom soon after Rutherford discovered the nucleus. That model has since been modified but not replaced. It introduced the useful ideas of co-orbital electrons and varying electron trajectories referred to above, along with shells of electrons and wave functions. The model also contained the doubtful assumption of an electron leap or jump, a solar system analogy, and an implication that the arrangement of protons is determined by the arrangement of electrons. Bohr's theory omitted, and has not since produced, a model of the form and constitution of the proton, an ordered spatial arrangement of protons and neutrons, and a spatial explanation of charge.

The emphasis on the motion and interaction of the electron and the corresponding neglect of the proton led to the misleading assumption that atomic structure and interaction are largely dependent on the behavior of the electron. This view prompts the image of the tail wagging the dog. It is an idea that contradicts the fact that the proton is 1,836 times larger the electron. This disparity in size means that whatever the relativity of the electron and proton, the proton is dominant in their interaction. The proton is the "headquarters," and the electron is the "agent in the field."

In every atom, there is always one proton per electron. A proton can handle only one electron, and their union is necessary and complete. The passage of the electron through the proton's central hole in every orbit illustrates their close, dependent interaction. When the electron is in the hole at the vertex of its path, it is constantly linked to its proton, despite the variation that may take place in its trajectory, whether from ellipse to parabola or from near-centered to far-focused.

The assumption of an electron leaping from one orbit to another can only be described as unnatural. Such a trajectory does not seem possible in a mechanistic universe where processes are continuous. Only the voluntary action of a terrestrial animal fits this kind of motion. Nevertheless, the electron has a variety of behaviors that are determined by (a) the electron's relativity within its atom or to other atoms and (b) the different trajectories of motion and interaction that such spatial arrangements permit. This hypothesis suggests that a stable electron and an electron in the ground state have circular orbits. An excited, active, or variable electron has an elliptical orbit. A shared or bound electron is in a parabolic orbit. Free electrons, flowing electrons, and negative ions have hyperbolic trajectories.

When an electron changes its motion, the atom experiences a transformation, which may involve the emission of light or neutrinos. Or the change may initiate a radioactive process. Or the atom may interact with other atoms of the same element or of different elements to form molecules of increasing complexity. The stability of such molecules depends on bonds formed by electrons in the required trajectory.

Having a proton shaped like a torus provides a place where this change of motion can plausibly occur. When the electron is in the proton's hole, the distance between the two particles is minimal, and the "influence" of the proton is greatest. If this process involves a transfer of energy from one to the other, caused by a change of the proton's motion, their proximity facilitates it. The electron enters the hole from its old trajectory and emerges in a new one. The coincidence of the vertex of the electron's trajectory with the central hole of the proton permits the electron's motion to be as flexible as necessary, while keeping it linked to and controlled by the proton. Bohr's assumed leap of the electron can be rejected. The analogies of the solar system and billiard ball are discarded, and a chain link analogy is introduced.

23. Alternative Cosmological Assumptions

According to big bang cosmology, the universe is expanding. Spacetime itself is expanding in volume and carrying its contents along for the ride. By analogy this is visualized as an inflating balloon with points on its surface moving apart. Thus, it is said that there is a mutual recession of galaxies.

The theory of general relativity and other mathematical theories of the universe that preceded the acceptance of the big bang theory also suggested that there is an expansion of the universe. But does expansion necessarily mean an increase in volume?

The oscillon hypothesis assumes that there is an increase in the total energy of the universe-namely, that there are processes taking place within nature that result in more energy, motion, and interaction than previously existed.

Is this conjecture, that the expansion is an increase in

energy, a violation of the law of conservation of energy? It would seem that the answer is yes, in that we are talking about the "creation" of energy. But our universe is full of energy, which must have been "created." The uniformitarian hypothesis of the microcosm seeks to understand the processes that are needed to account for all the objects, forms, and phenomena of nature.

It would seem that the processes of nucleosynthesis are the best candidates for this possible process. That would make stars the locus of the expansion of energy. This seems reasonable when we consider that over its period of existence a star emits prodigious quantities of light and neutrinos, while the numbers of its protons and its electrons remain the same.

In a star, hydrogen atoms transform into more complex combinations of protons, electrons, and neutrons, but no new stable particles are produced. The proposed processes of transformation, whereby the interaction of oscillons varies in dimensionality, result in the disappearance of the precursor particles and the appearance of the novel successor particles. When a hydrogen atom emits light and neutrinos, it is reproducing its precursor particles while remaining entirely intact.

The protons and electrons of the hydrogen atom do not transform into some novel, higher, and more complex form of energy. A microcosm of three spatial dimensions is the end of the line. There is no next dimensional universe.

23.1. Nucleosynthesis

The interior of a star is a radically different environment from the conditions experienced by the precursors of the hydrogen atoms. The immense pressures and temperatures at the core, the proximity of atoms, their minimal relative velocity, their numerous properties of unlimited variability, and their omni-directional interactions are undoubtedly "something new under the Sun."

Nucleosynthesis is a feedback process. The universe and the phenomena of nature are a system of continuous cyclical processes. The oscillons-the smallest, simplest, most primitive and fundamental quantities of space and motion, by means of their oscillation, interaction, and transformation of dimensionality-eventually make stars, which in turn make more star-making oscillons. This is a reproductive process that results in an increase in the total energy and an expansion of the universe.

23.2. Conservation of Energy

The law of conservation of energy states that energy can be neither created nor destroyed. Energy may be transformed-for example, from thermal to mechanical, as in a steam engine-but the quantity of energy is the same after transformation as before. Motion never stops.

The first part of the law implies an anthropocentric assumption. Because humans cannot create energy, nor can any terrestrial macrocosmic process, therefore energy is not being created. In fact, nature has created energy. The essence of nature is motion. According to the oscillon hypothesis that natural processes are uniformitarian, nature can still produce energy-and, in fact, is now doing so.

The current cosmological theory flows from one observation and a mathematical hypothesis. The observation is the universal redshift of the light of distant galaxies. The calculation hypothesizes that the universe is expanding. Another observation, the cosmic background radiation, has been used to confirm this cosmology. The universal redshift is interpreted as a mutual recession of the galaxies and an expansion of the space occupied by the galaxies. The oscillon hypothesis alternatively assumes that the emission of light and neutrinos in nucleosynthesis is a reproduction of precursors, and the continued integrity of the protons and electrons of the emitting hydrogen atoms indicates a closed constructive process rather than destruction. An expansion of energy-an increase of motion-is being described. Restating the hypothesis as a law, energy exists and cannot be caused to stop existing. Create is a loaded word best avoided.

23.3. The Doppler Effect

Is the Doppler effect an acoustic illusion? The production and emission of the sound does not change in any way. Its frequency, wavelength, and volume are the same, but the distance and direction of the moving source and the stationary listener change.

The effect is a change in perception-a misinterpretation by the brain of the vibrations of the organs of hearing. A change in the way a constant sound is heard cannot be deemed to be caused by a property of the source of the sound.

23.4. Sources of Radiation

Advances in astronomy using detectors other than visible light telescopes have revealed other sources of radiation in addition to those from stars. Those sources include quasars, gamma ray bursters, and fast radio bursts. They are invariably assumed to be material objects, much larger than stars, and are usually assumed to be outside the Milky Way, and caused by catastrophes.

The oscillon hypothesis alternatively assumes that some sources of radiation may not be material objects, but instead may simply be accumulations of radiation. The hypothesis seeks to explain these sources as parts of a uniformitarian system, suggesting that stars are the largest material objects in nature. If there are objects made of matter larger or more powerfully energetic than stars, then, in an ancient universe, there should be as many of them as the stars.

Cosmic rays, originally identified as a form of radiation, are now known to be particles of matter, mainly protons. The early theorists of the steady state universe considered cosmic rays to be strong candidates for the products of a proton-forming process in interstellar space. But the source of cosmic ray particles is an ongoing mystery.

24. Acknowledgments

These notes, which were originally intended for personal use, have been selected from notebooks made during thirty years of research into the microcosm, and are arranged here in a more or less logical order. Doubts about mainstream cosmology and the conviction that all natural phenomena are uniformitarian were the impetus for that research. I would like to thank Paul Weisser, Ph.D., for his invaluable editorial assistance in preparing these notes for publication.

The Particle Model Circuit Theory with a Supporting Experiment

Robert de Hilster

23344 Carolwood Ln #6409, Boca Raton, FL 33428, robert@dehilster.com

The Particle Model is a physical model of the universe. That is, all areas of physics can be explained using physical interactions of particles. Gravity, light, magnetism, electrostatics, circuits, and even chemistry can all be explained using particles. In the case of a circuit, the battery uses chemical reactions to emit G1 particles (also known as electrons, but with no charge). The G1 particles move through the circuit at speed 'c'. The G1 particle either passes straight through, or hits an atom and scatters, or it gets trapped as a G1 orbital. Using this concept, this paper describes how the circuit works; predicts a specific result; and then uses a series of 15 three-resistor circuits to show that the measurements support the Particle Model with a 70 to 80 percent correlation.

Keywords: Particle Model, Experiment, G1 Particle, Volts per G1, Interaction Factor

1. Standard Model

Figure 1 is a drawing of a circuit with a 9 Volt battery and three resistors in series.

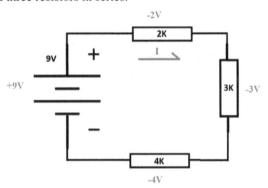

Figure 1.   Standard Model Using Current Flow

With a 9 Volt battery and a total of 9K Ohms in series, Ohm's law would indicate that there is a current of 1 mili-amp at all points in the circuit. The voltage drop across the 4K resistor is 4 Volts, the 3K will drop 3 Volts, and the 2K will drop 2 Volts. This satisfies Kirchhoff's law that the sum of the voltages around the circuit must add up to zero.

2. Particle Model Interactions

In the Particle Model, the G1 particle is used:
1. In gravity as the particle that pushes objects.
2. In the atom and replaces the electron.
3. In light as a stream of G1s with a repetitive pattern.
4. In the magnetic field as a stream of G1s orbiting around and through the magnet.

The G1 particle interacts the same way in all these cases As it enters an object:
1. Most of the G1s pass straight through
2. A few of them will hit the object and bounce off.
3. Some can be trapped as an orbital of an atom or molecule.

The Particle Model uses these interactions for gravity, light, magnetics, electrostatics, circuits and chemistry. All of these can be explained using the Particle Model which is a **mechanical model**.

3. Using the Particle Model

3.1. G1 Particle Equations

Figure 2 is the same circuit as Figure 1, but shows the flow of G1s through the circuit instead of current or electron flow.

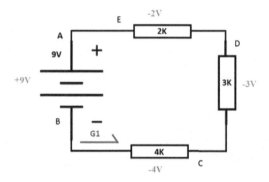

Figure 2.   Flow of G1s in a Circuit

B is the number of G1 particles leaving the battery. As the G1 stream of particles they enter the 4K resistor where it will interact with the resistor according to the the three ways described above. Figure 3 is a diagram of the three possible interactions.

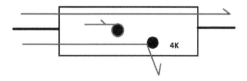

Figure 3.   Flow of G1s Through a Resistor

The top path shows the G1 passing through; the bottom path shows the G1 hitting and bouncing off; and the middle path shows the G1 getting trapped as an orbital. Being trapped is a necessary property for electrostatics.

G1s Lost and Voltage Drop

If there were 1000 G1 particles entering the 4K resistor and some of them were scattered and lost, then there would be fewer G1 particles leaving the resistor. **A loss of G1 particles looks exactly like a voltage drop**. This suggests that there is a direct correlation with the number of G1s lost and the amount of the voltage drop. A direct correlation! Amazing!

Assumption: The number of G1s lost is proportional to the number entering times the value of the resistor.

$$N_L \propto B_i * 4K \qquad (1)$$

To get an equation, add a constant of proportionality I_f, called the Interaction Factor.

$$N_L = B_i * I_f * 4K \qquad (2)$$

A future experiment is planned to determine the value of I_f.

Assumption: Assign a value of voltage (V_{G1}) for the G1 particle . The equation for voltage drop in the 4K resistor is:

$$V_{4K} = B_i * I_f * 4K * V_{G1} \qquad (3)$$

This does not mean there is a physical property that makes the G1 particle a voltage particle. The G1 has no physical property for charge or voltage. But based on the standards set (ohms and voltage) and the instruments used, we can assign the particle a voltage value. Scientist and engineers assign these values, nature does not.

The two constants (I_f and V_{G1}) used in these equations can be calculated by performing a different experiment. The measurements have been made, the calculation is on-going.

Current

As stated earlier, the Standard value for current in this circuit is 1 mili-amp anywhere in the circuit. The TPM model indicates that the current is higher at Point B and gets smaller as you move around and back to the battery. If this difference could be measured, it would show the possibility that the reduction of current is caused by the loss of G1s.

G1s Added and Voltage Gain

Kirchhoff's law indicates that the sum of voltages around the circuit must add up to zero. To match this, the sum of the G1s lost and gained must also equal zero. To have a stable circuit, the loss of G1s through the resistors must be matched by a gain of G1s through the battery. The battery adds the same amount of G1s in each interval of time. The number of G1s lost by the resistors depends on how many enter. If the number entering is too high, then too many are lost. This reduces the number entering the

battery causing the battery to emit fewer G1s. This continues until the number lost by the resistors match the number added by the battery and the circuit is stable.

The reverse works in a similar way. If the number of G1s entering the resistors are too low, then fewer G1s are lost. Which means more G1s enter the battery. This increases the output of the battery until the loss through the resistors match the gain through the battery. Once the circuit is stable, there can be incidental increases and decreases in the Number of G1s flowing through the circuit, but the overall average is as expected.

Chemical Equations

There is a chemical reaction in the battery. The chemical equation shows the release of electrons.

$$Zn \rightarrow Zn^2 + 2e^-; \;\; Cu^2 + 2e^- \rightarrow Cu \qquad (4)$$

These electrons were orbitals of the zinc and copper atoms. As an orbital they move at very high speed, probably 'c'. They will randomly exit the battery unless pushed in the direction of the negative electrode. It is the internal G2 gravity field that moves many of the electrons in that direction.

The standard explanation states that the electron drifts from hole to hole at 3.2 m/s. While the current or signals move from 50% to 99% of the speed of light. That does not make sense. It makes more sense to have the G1 move around the circuit at speed 'c'.

Equations for A through E

Equations for A through E can also be generated. The Value for 'C' is equal to the value of 'B' minus the loss through the 4K resistor.

$$C = B - B(I_f * 4K) = B(1 - I_f * 4K) \qquad (5)$$

$$D = C - C(I_f * 3K) = C(1 - I_f * 3K) \qquad (6)$$

$$E = D - D(I_f * 2K) = D(1 - I_f * 2K) \qquad (7)$$

$$B = A + V_B / V_{G1} \qquad (8)$$

Where V_B is the battery voltage and V_{G1} is the volts per G1 particle.

From these four equations it can be seen that the number of G1 particles is reduced as you go through the circuit until you get to to the battery. The combined equation for E is:

$$E = B(1 - I_f * 4K)(1 - I_f * 3K)(1 - I_f * 2K) \qquad (9)$$

The number of G1 particles leaving the 2K resistor 'E' is a function of the number 'B' entering the 4K resistor and the loss of G1s through all three resistors. This compounding effect adds a fractional amount of loss of G1s to the circuit that is greater than the individual losses.

3.2. Expected Values of A-E

Figure 4 shows the G1 particles flowing through the circuit and shows the values that might be expected. Assume that 1000 G1s enter the battery, Point A. If V_{G1} is set to

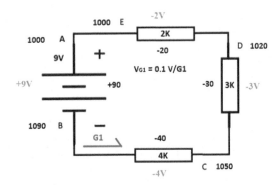

Figure 4.　Setting the Values

0.1 Volts/G1, the 9 Volt battery will add 90 G1s and emit a total of 1090 G1s.

In Figure 4, each connection point is given a letter label. The letter 'A' is the input to the battery and its value is the number G1s flowing into the battery. The output of the battery is 'B'. Then there's 'C' through 'E' where 'E' is the same as 'A'.

The 4K resistor should drop 4 Volts and hence must lose 40 G1s. Point C should have a value of 1050. The 3K loses 30, the 2K loses 20, and E ends up with a value of 1000. When this happens the circuit has stabilized.

3.3. Calculation Using a Spreadsheet

Figure 5 is a partial view of the spreadsheet analysis for the circuit in Figure 4. V_{G1} was set at 0.1 V/G1 and I_f was set at $1x10^{-5}$.

	4K	3K	2K
Voltage-TPM	4.117862	2.964861	1.917277
STD	4.000000	3.000000	2.000000
Delta	0.117862	(0.035139)	(0.082723)
Current-TPM	0.001029	0.000988	0.000959
STD	0.001000	0.001000	0.001000
Delta	0.000029	(0.000012)	(0.000041)

Figure 5.　Comparing Values

The top line is the value of voltage calculated by the TPM equations using the assumed values for I_f and V_{G1}. The second line is the value of voltage expected when using the standard equations. The third line is the difference and clearly shows the 4K loss is high while the 3K and 2K are low.

In order to stabilize, the output of the battery must have a slightly higher value than expected so that the net loss through the three resistors reaches 90 G1s.

Look at the values of TPM current as you move from 4K through to 2K. It decreases. What does that tell you?

4. The Experiment

Fifteen sets of three resistors each were selected to provide fifteen results. Each set was used twice. The first measurement was set up like Figure 4, a large resistor, then

a medium resistor, and finally a small resistor. The second measurement reversed the large and small resistors.

It was expected that the voltage drop on the 4K, when in the first position, would be larger than the 4k when in the third position. Further, is was expected that the voltage loss of the 2K, when in the first position, would be larger than when in the third position.

Accurate Voltmeter

In my experience in working with gravity (TPM gravity equation has an I_f term), and with my circuit design experience, that a very accurate meter was required. The accuracy needed was critical. A 6 1/2 digit digital multimeter was rented.

Pictures of the experiment are shown below.

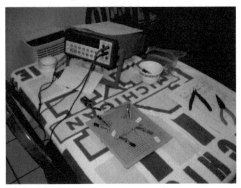

Figure 6.　6 1/2 DMM and Test Board

Results - Large and Small Resistor

See Figure 8 and 9.

The first column is the list of 15 sets of three resistors (C1-C15). The next two columns are the measured values of the voltages when in the first and then the last position. It is expected that the difference will be a positive number. The last three columns are the "TPM calculated" values using the TPM equations. Only the value of resistances and the battery voltage were used.

Large R		Measured voltage drop			Calculated using TPM		
		VR1(N)	VR3(Rv)	Pos	VR1(N)	VR3(Rv)	Dif
	C1	8.0920	8.0924	-0.0004	8.094296	8.093268	0.001028
73.33%	C2	5.5937	5.5919	0.0018	5.596269	5.595116	0.001153
	C3	5.1797	5.1790	0.0007	5.181772	5.181488	0.000284
	C4	4.4691	4.4687	0.0004	4.471195	4.470896	0.000299
	C5	8.0647	8.0627	0.0020	8.072498	8.070715	0.001783
	C6	6.5894	6.5873	0.0021	6.600121	6.600073	0.000048
	C7	6.4353	6.4359	-0.0006	6.449092	6.449534	-0.000442
	C8	7.6274	7.6273	0.0001	7.654331	7.654167	0.000164
	C9	7.4798	7.4797	0.0001	7.515479	7.515301	0.000178
	C10	7.8228	7.8228	0.0000	7.870569	7.870405	0.000164
	C11	4.4471	4.4465	0.0006	4.455539	4.452632	0.002907
	C12	4.4133	4.4140	-0.0007	4.422304	4.422327	-0.000023
	C13	4.5636	4.5655	-0.0019	4.577748	4.578955	-0.001207
	C14	4.4765	4.4761	0.0004	4.494824	4.493735	0.001089
	C15	4.7192	4.7192	0.0000	4.746125	4.745468	0.000657

Figure 7.   9 Volt battery and three resistors

Small R		Measured voltage drop			Calculated using TPM		
		VR1(R)	VR3(N)	POS?	VR1(R)	VR3(N)	Dif
	C1	0.079245	0.079267	-0.000022	0.079299	0.079291	0.000008
	C2	0.538500	0.555140	-0.016640	0.554888	0.555137	-0.000249
86.67%	C3	1.270100	1.270500	-0.000400	1.270212	1.270795	-0.000583
	C4	1.464600	1.464900	-0.000300	1.464843	1.465451	-0.000608
	C5	0.079500	0.079556	-0.000056	0.079496	0.079583	-0.000087
	C6	0.419680	0.419790	-0.000110	0.419821	0.420034	-0.000213
	C7	0.520210	0.523400	-0.003190	0.520510	0.520658	-0.000148
	C8	0.193330	0.193410	-0.000080	0.193458	0.193567	-0.000109
	C9	0.169620	0.169700	-0.000080	0.169732	0.169803	-0.000071
	C10	0.124080	0.124140	-0.000060	0.124192	0.124259	-0.000067
	C11	1.511100	1.511500	-0.000400	1.512055	1.513462	-0.001407
	C12	1.133940	1.133860	0.000080	1.134711	1.134926	-0.000215
	C13	0.880560	0.880380	0.000180	0.881541	0.881540	0.000001
	C14	0.805480	0.805570	-0.000090	0.806644	0.806797	-0.000153
	C15	0.694610	0.694780	-0.000170	0.695627	0.696055	-0.000428

Figure 8.   9 Volt battery and three resistors

Review of Figure 8

The difference in the measured values were calculated by subtracting the voltage loss in the third position (R3) from the voltage lost when in the first position (R1). the values should be positive. Four of the fifteen were negative. That gave a correlation of 73.33%.

A closer examination shows that C7, C12, and C13 were actually predicted by the TPM calculation to be negative, not positive. It seems that the results of the calculation depend on the specific values of the three resistors.

The C1 set of resistors is clearly and error. C1 and C15 gave a zero difference and could be considered an error. The conservative estimate would be 73.33% correlation.

Review of Figure 9

It was a surprise to find that the measured values of the small resistor showed 13 of the 15 were negative not positive. However, the TPM calculated values were also negative.

C12 and C13 were marked as incorrect because they did not meet positive prediction. That gave a correlation of 86.67%. However, C1 and C13 were predicted by the TPM calculation to be positive, not negative. Still, C1 and C12 do not match. 86.67% still holds.

Wrong Prediction for the Small Resistor?

In section 3.2, the expected value for the difference of the small resistor were supposed to be positive. A close look at the spreadsheet calculation for the small resistor indicated that the B value was smaller than the B value for the large resistor.

When the small resistor is first, it required a smaller value for B so that the loss through the 2K and 3K was smaller when it entered the 4K. By doing this the circuit was able to get a loss of 90 G1s in the resistors to match the 90 G1s added by the battery.

5. Conclusion

Does this prove that the Particle Model is the right explanation for an electrical circuit? NO! There is no direct evidence that there is a G1 particle flowing through the circuit as described in this paper.

Nature does not define the circuit as electrical. The standards for voltage and resistance are defined by engineers and scientist. Instruments are developed to measure voltage and resistance based on these standards. It's electrical because we define it that way.

The Particle Model suggests that circuits could actually function as a mechanical process, not electrical. This paper describes a way to define the circuit interactions in mechanical terms and develop appropriate equations. Then two constants are suggested that help relate the mechanical equations to the electrical standards.

This results in the ability to suggest experiments that show the mechanical (TPM) equations can predict the values of voltage and current more accurately than existing electrical equations.

This is not proof that the model is the right model, but it does support the possibility that the TPM model and its equations could be the correct physical description of electrical circuits.

To put things in perspective. I designed circuits for 40 years. If you ask me to design a circuit today, I would use the standard equations. They are clearly easier to use and give reasonable results. But for science, the TPM provides a better explanation and gives better results when needed.

The Particle Model Explains Parallel Resistors

Robert de Hilster

23344 Carolwood Ln #6409, Boca Raton, FL 33428, robert@dehilster.com

The equation for parallel resistors is well known, at least by scientists and engineers. Look up parallel resistors on the internet and you will get an equation that works. You an even find out how to develop the equation from existing equations. What is not known is how each resistor seems to know what the value of the other resistor is and adjust the flow of current properly. This paper describes how the circuit works using the concepts developed in the Particle Model. It's the Gravity 2 field that surrounds the two resistors and controls the flow of current such that each resistor gets the right amount of current.

Keywords: G1 particle, G2 particle, G2 gravity

1. Standard Model

Figure 1 is a drawing of a circuit with a 9 Volt battery and four resistors.

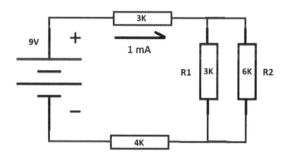

Figure 1. Standard Model Using Current Flow

The 3K and 6K resistors are parallel and results in a 2K resistance. With a 9 Volt battery and a total of 9K Ohms in series, Ohm's law would indicate that there is a current of 1 mili-amp at all points in the circuit. The voltage drop across the 4K resistor is 4 Volts, the 3K in parallel with the 6k will drop 2 Volts, and the 3K will drop 3 Volts. This satisfies Kirchhoff's law that the sum of the voltages around the circuit must add up to zero.

Parallel Resistor Equation

The standard equation for parallel resistors is:

$$R_T = \frac{R1*R2}{R1+R2} = \frac{3K*6K}{3K+6K} = 2K \qquad (1)$$

Try to find a physical explanation of how parallel resistors work. You find this equation all over the place, but no physical explanation.

Current Through Each Resistor

Since the voltage drop across the two resistors is 2 Volts, then the current through the 3K is $2V/3K = 2/3mA$ and for the 6K is $2V/6K = 1/3mA$.

2. Particle Model

The Particle model suggests that there is an G1 particle (like an electron but with no charge) flowing out of the negative end of the battery and moving at speed 'c'. See Figure 2.

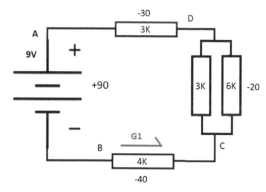

Figure 2. Particle Model using G1 Flow

2.1. The G1 and G2 Particle

The G1 Particle

In the Particle Model, the G1 particle is used:

1. In gravity, it's the particle that pushes objects.
2. In the atom, the G1 replaces the electron.
3. In light, the G1 forms a stream of G1s with a repetitive pattern.
4. In the magnetic field, the G1 is a stream of G1s orbiting around and through the magnet.

The G2 Particle

The G2 particle is is the orbital of a lower level atom (smaller than the atoms in the Periodic Table). As such it is very small and very fast, approximately c^2.

The G2 particle forms a gravitational field around all objects just like the G1 particle that forms Newtonian gravity. When light (G1 stream of particles) approaches a prism, the G2 gravity field causes the light to change directions. It is G2 gravity that causes the G1 particle in the circuit to change directions. See Appendix A for more on the G2 Particle.

Particle Interactions

The G1 particle interacts the same way in all these cases. As it enters an object:

1. Most of the G1s pass straight through.
2. A few of them will hit the object and bounce off.
3. Some can be trapped as an orbital of an atom or molecule.

G1s Lost Through a Resistor

Figure 3 shows the three interactions of the G1 with a resistor.

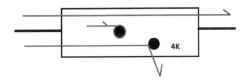

Figure 3. Flow of G1s Through a Resistor

When I first applied these interactions to a resistor I found that the loss of G1 had a direct correlation to the loss of voltage. WOW! This was amazing!

G1s Added by a Battery

If there is loss of G1s through a resistor, then there must be G1s added by the battery. Losing electrons in a resistor and gaining electrons in a battery is not part of the standard explanation. It turns out that the sum of G1s around the circuit is like the sum of voltages and must be equal to zero.

Figure 2 has the battery adding 90 G1s, while the resistors lose a total of 90 G1s. Yes, these are fake numbers, made up to show how the circuit works.

2.2. 3K & 6K Surrounded by G2 Gravity

Figure 4 shows the 3K and 6K resistors of Figure 2 with the G2 force filed surrounding both resistors.

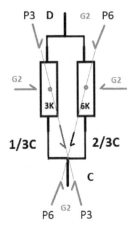

Figure 4. First Analysis is Wrong

In order for the parallel resistors to work correctly, the G1s must split at the 'Y' connection after passing through the 4K resistor. The number of G1s entering the 'Y' is 'C' as shown in Figures 2 and 4. It should split such that the number of G1s entering the 3K is 2/3C and the number entering the 6K is 1/3C.

Analyzing the G2 Forces

The force of G2 gravity is primarily based on the number of G1s in each part of the system. Intuition seemed to indicate that the 6K resistor would have a greater number of G1s than the 3K resistor. But that generates the wrong force.

In Figure 4, the blue arrows surrounding the resistors represents the number of G2 particles directed at the center of the mass of each resistor. Two of these streams, P3 and P6, point at the 'Y' connection after going though the center of mass. There is some loss of G2s as they pass though the 3K, shown as a long arrow, while there is more loss as they pass through the 6K. shorter arrow. The two opposing steams of G2s at the 'Y" connection, set up a net force on the flow of G1s as they enter the 'Y'. The P3 path has a weaker net force than the two opposing streams of the P6 path. This is exactly the opposite of what is needed.

Hacking the Resistor

Since that didn't work, it was necessary to find out more detail about how resistors are made.

In an article from Explain Stuff, there is an equation for the dimensions of a resistor. [1]

$$R = \rho L/A \qquad (2)$$

Equation 2 calculates the value of the resistor using its length 'L' and its cross sectional area 'A'. Figure 5 shows the physical size and the resistance values of the two parallel resistors.

Figure 5. First Analysis is Wrong

In simple words, the resistance (R) of a material increases as its length increases (so longer wires offer more resistance) and increases as its area decreases (thinner wires offer more resistance). The resistance is also related to the type of material from which a resistor is made, and that's indicated in this equation by the symbol ρ, which is called the resistivity, and measured in units of Ωm (ohm meters).

Conclusion: The 3K resistor has a larger physical size an therefore the larger number of G1s. The 6K resistor has a smaller physical size and therefore has a smaller number of G1s. It is the 3K resistor with a larger physical size that causes the greater amount of G2 loss. When analyzing many different situations, it always indicated that the strength of the G2 force was based on the number of G1s in each part.

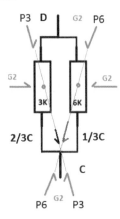

Figure 6. The Correct Forces

Figure 6 shows the 3K causing twice the loss of G2 particles than the 6K and giving twice the net force to the 'Y". The 6K has half the G2 loss than the 3K and hence has half the net force towards the 'Y'. This is the exact split that is needed to make circuit work properly.

Once the G1s start flowing through the circuit, the ratio of the forces remain the same, because of the G1s in the resistors themselves **and** the flow of G1s.

3. The Experiment

This section proposes an experiment to show that the G2 force field, which decreases inversely to the square of the distance, will affect the circuit response as the parallel resistors are moved apart. The test will be done in four or more steps.

Step 1. Place the resistors 0.5 cm apart and measure the time for the circuit to stabilize.

Step 2. Place the resistors 1 cm apart and measure the time for the circuit to stabilize.

Step 3. Place the resistors 2 cm apart and measure the time for the circuit to stabilize.

Step 4. Place the resistors 4 cm apart and measure the time for the circuit to stabilize.

Compare the time delay between steps 1 and 2 to the time delay of steps 2 and 3. Then compare 2-3 to 3-4. Since the spacing has doubled, the time time difference should increase by a factor of 4. Even though the resistors are further apart and the strength of G2 gravity is weaker, the G2 force still has the proper ratio.

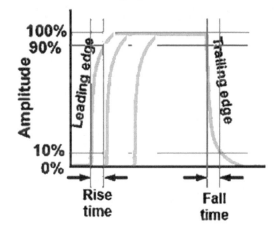

Figure 7. Time Delay between Steps

It might be interesting, but not conclusive, that the rise time and time delay of the circuit will be affected when a magnet is placed on the two resistors. The current might not split the right way.

Appendix and References: Next Page

APPENDIX

A. More about G2 Gravity

G2 gravity was postulated when the Particle Model for light was applied to refraction. There are two videos published that helps explain the origin of G2 gravity.

"EM Radiation" – [https://youtu.be/wzhF8Web_co]
This video describes light as a stream of G1 particles with a repetitive pattern.

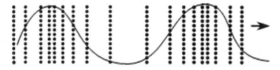

Figure 8.   Light as a Stream of G1 Particles

"Two Gravities" – [https://youtu.be/RxD7ZM1g-So]
G2 gravity was discovered when analyzing the forces required to bend the G1 stream of light as it entered a prism. Figure 5 compares the G1 forces around the earth to the G2 forces around the prism.

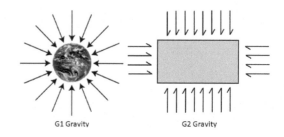

G1 Gravity   G2 Gravity

Figure 9.   Comparing G1 and G2 Gravity Fields

After working with G2 gravity for two years, the main cause of G2 gravity comes from the G1 particle density of the object, that is G1 particles in the earth, the prism, and even the resistors. There may be other factors, but that won't be known until more detailed testing is done. There needs to be a standard for G2 mass just like there is a standard for G1 mass (the 1Kg standard).

REFERENCES

1. explainthatstuff.com
    URL: https://www.explainthatstuff.com/resistors.html

Over 400 Years of Model Revolution

David de Hilster

22936 Ironwedge Dr, Boca Raton FL, 33433 USA, david@dehilste.com

In Thomas Kuhn's book "Structure of Scientific Revolution"[4], he describes a time where there is enough new data that allows for theories to compete to be the next paradigm shift. A model for the universe and physics itself has been in model revolution for over 400 years.

Keywords: Kuhn, Paradigm Shift, Scientific Revolution

A. Introduction

To the science woke, the signs are clear: we are in the middle of a scientific revolution. And there are two very clear signs of this revolution:

- Mainstream science has become unbelievable and religious like with all attempts to criticize it met with immediate rejection
- There are lots of new theories and models from critical thinkers outside the mainstream that greatly improve upon current theory

What may not be clear, is that we have been in this revolution for over 400 years.

B. Scientific Revolution in Science

Signs of the revolution are everywhere with Big Science headlines often bordering on the ridiculous. We see titles that often make us wonder if scientists have gone mad and if anyone but ourselves is noticing the madness. The good news is that your reaction is spot on and that indeed, the headlines we read reflect a crisis in modern science. Here are just some of the more recent headlines:

- How the Quantum Eraser Rewrites the Past | Space Time[1] - Quantum eraser experiments state that a photon of light billions of years ago travels in a certain direction because of the collective consciousness of beings billions of years AFTER the fact. Don't even try to understand this. This headline is public service brought to you by the folks at PBS who are doing their best to explain the inexplicable. String Theory May Create Far Fewer Universes Than Thought
- String Theory May Create Far Fewer Universes Than Thought[2] - String theory was invented as a mathematical excetuar to try to invent one particle upon which we could construct the entire universe. Some of the original creators of this exercise are horrified even to this day that it is taken seriously. Like Big Science today, the theoreticians have created a bubble around themselves taking in the tongues of 11-19 dimensions while using a model of pure invention and mathematics that have little to do with the physical world.
- An Exceptionally Simple Theory of Everything[3] - One new theory that has gotten attention in the mass media is from a surfer dude with a supposedly exceptionally simple theory of everything. Judge for yourself just how simple: "A non-compact real form of the E8 Lie algebra has G2 and F4 subalgebras which break down to strong su(3), electroweak su(2) x u(1), gravitational so(3,1), the frame-Higgs, and three generations of fermions related by triality. The interactions and dynamics of these 1-form and Grassmann valued parts of an E8 superconnection are described by the curvature and action over a four dimensional base manifold."

The here point is simple: Big Science has is lost and the craziness that fills the news today shows just how lost it is. And yes, you are not crazy or alone for thinking this.

C. Reinterpreting the Modern Kuhn Cycle

In 1962, an American physicist, historian, and philosopher wrote one of the most cited books in all of science: "The Structure of Scientific Revolution"[4]. In it, he outlines a cycle of how science goes through a scientific revolution.

Kuhn gives examples of various scientific revolutions from the past:

- **Copernican Revolution:** Moving the earth from the center of the universe to the center of the solar system
- **Chemical revolution:** chemical reactions and atoms
- **Relativity revolution:** Einstein

The major difference between Kuhn and the science woke (SW) community of critical thinkers is that the "relativity revolution" was not the end of a paradigm shift, but the beginning. Today, over 100 years later, Big Science is still stuck in the 3rd and 4th stages of 5 in Khun's cycle of scientific revolution.

Here is the "Kuhn Cycle" as currently seen by the many in the science woke community: The Kuhn Cycle according many in the science woke community.

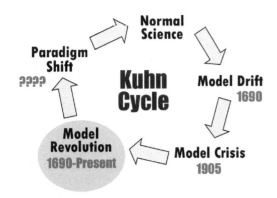

Figure 1.   Modern Kuhnian Cycle

D. Normal Science

Normal Science simply means that mainstream science is in stable time where the current model is working well with little complaints. Between Newton and Einstein, the model for science was Newton's classical mechanics and included the industrial revolution which yielded great technological advances, many of which are still used today.

But soon after Newton, the model began to drift and Newton himself was part of this. Model Drift

In the early 18th century, Newton himself began to suggest a shift in the classical mechanical model of the universe to one that would give physical substance to light and gravity. He and his contemporaries were the first to suggest that light and gravity had "mediums" and that force was transmitted by what they called a luminiferous aether.

This idea for luminiferous aether or graviton particles to transmit light and gravity signaled the start of a model revolution that continues to this day. Unfortunately, no one in Newton's time nor in the hundreds of year after, could come up with a universally accepted physical model for gravity or light.

In an earnest pursuit of a physical model for light, scientists in the 19th century were in search of an "aether" medium through waves of light would travel, much like waves of sound travel through the air. Michelson and Morley famously tried to find this aether but their results showed nothing.

It would take a young upstart scientist to kick us into model crisis and eventually usher us into full model revolution. Model Crisis

Here is where those outside mainstream science interpret Thomas Kuhn's paradigm shift cycle differently from Kuhn himself. As we said earlier, Thomas Kuhn considered relativity a moment where the paradigm of Newton switched to a paradigm of Einstein. But critical thinkers and the science woke consider this the start of model crisis. If Einstein's theories were correct, then a paradigm shift did indeed happen with the introduction of the theory of relativity. But if Einstein's theories proved wrong, then it signaled a model crisis where the model breaks down.

In this case, there was a false paradigm shift. Big Science of the 20th century thought they took a turn into what they considered to be a paradigm shift but in reality, was a dead end.

And what fueled this wrong turn in science was a new "arrogance" where 20th century scientists began to play "god" by imposing their own mathematics and universal assumptions upon the universe, taunting the universe to try and "disobey" the genius of man.

This was the start of a very long and costly diversion from science and the scientific method. And in reality, it was the start of model crisis where the paradigm that physicists chose to shift to, was wrong. Abandonment of the Scientific Method

In 1905, Albert Einstein came along and changed the way we did science. Instead of observing the world around us, finding something new or different, and then trying to explain it, Einstein decided he would create laws of the universe that must be obeyed. This was an extreme shift in the scientific method which until then, required observing phenomena first, then coming up with theories or laws in response. Einstein set a fatal precedence that launched physics into a hundred-year crisis where inventing theories became the norm.

According to the science woke community, Albert Einstein was neither the start of end of a paradigm shift, it was the start of Kuhn's "Model Crisis"

Here are the laws of Physics which Einstein created for his special theory of relativity:

- The laws of physics are the same in the space of all moving systems or objects
- The speed is always measured to be the same no matter your relationship to the light source - moving or not

These "assumptions" causes big big problems in that it required time, mass, and length to change depending on your relative speed and there was no way to tell who was moving compared to whom. Einstein never measured mass increasing, time slowing down, or length contracting. He simply put forth with laws of the universe, and the mainstream world scrambled to find "proof" or data that would agree with Einstein. This continues to this day with science headlines regularly declaring experiments or analysis of data to "show once again that Einstein was right."

In 1915, Einstein tried to fix some of these problems introduced by his special theory of relativity by inventing general relativity and it's infamous "space-time". Through thought experiments and mathematics, Einstein once again imposed upon the universe new rules which it had to follow and In 1919, Edington claimed to verify that gravity bends light and mainstream science doubled down on Einstein's inventions and the apparent ability for scientists to dictate their theories and models to the universe and not visa-versa.

Bit not all was lost. A band of science woke critical

thinkers who saw through the arrogance and invention began to chip away at what mainstream 20th century science was producing, documenting what went wrong, and then proposing new models.

And as those critical thinkers slowly moved science back on track, Big Science was fulfilling Thomas Kuhn's prediction of model crisis on a grand scale.

E. Model Crisis Worsens

Wolfgang Pauli applied special relativity to radioactivity initiating the first "invented" particle later called the neutrino.

After Einstein, invention became the norm with the introduction of the first of many invented particles - particles that were postulated but never observed. In the early 1930s, Wolfgang Pauli applied special relativity to radioactivity and exclaimed that if special relativity is correct, that there must be more energy measured from radioactivity then what was measured. Even though the energy measured exactly balanced out during the experiment, once again, imposing laws on the universe took over. Pauli postulated a new particle later called the "neutrino" which invisibly carried away the energy. The particle had no charge and no mass and was essentially a ghost.

Many invented particles followed including quarks, gluons, w & z particles, and the latest: the Higgs boson.

One simple question you may have about this "reinterpretation" of Kuhn's Cycle: if these particles are not real, what are today's physicists finding? They answer: we don't really know. Particle accelerators depend on "signals" found during collisions and this is anything but an exact, engineering problem (See the "Higgs Fake" by Dr. Alexander Unzicker[5]).

Figure 2. "The Higgs Fake"[5] by Dr. Alexander Unzicker

The Higgs Fake by science woke author and physicist Dr. Alexander Unzicker presents damning arguments as to the dubious methods used in modern particle colliders and their claim of new particle discoveries.

Unzicker points out seven major flaws in the methods particle physics uses that show their claims of "confirming" particle existence to be impossible for any critical thinker to accept as valid. Model Revolution

Since the time of Newton's, critical thinkers have tried to find "physical models" for light, gravity, magnetic fields and the like. Newton talked about corpuscles being the force of gravity and in the 1800s, most all scientists working in what we call physics, were trying to prove the existence of an "aether" or medium for light.

In the modern era, Dr. Ricardo Carezani in the 1940s came up with a mathematical and physical error in Einstein's special relativity that allowed him to throw away special relativity and the neutrino, and describe the subatomic world of atom smashers to be classical mechanics throwing away relativity and space time and replacing gravity with a particle.

Today, we have dozens of proposed new models from critical thinkers that model light, gravity, and atomic structure that are great improvements from the "standard" model. This coincides with Kuhn's next cycle he calls "Model Revolution". This is a point which he says that the new data being collected is ample enough to simultaneously support various models that compete to eventually become the next paradigm shift or "Normal Science".

F. Real Advances During the Last 450 Years

Even though the science woke community recognizes that we have taken a wrong turn and have actually been in model revolution for over 400 years, advances in science have occurred. Two important advances have been made during this time that have been exploited and become extremely useful: the atomic periodic table and electronics.

The periodic table along with atoms and molecules have resulted in major advances in materials and healthcare while electronics have produced computers and communication devices that have proved invaluable to our society as a whole.

But when it comes to explaining the physicality of light, gravity, magnetism, and electricity, physicists have little to offer. It is exactly in those areas that today's science woke community are offering answers.

F.1. Modern Aether Models

Modern aether theories are theories which state that light are waves through a medium that permeates all of space that is call "aether". This is actually a fairly old notion and although Big Science has relegated it to the dust bin, modern aether theories flourish and are by far the largest group of new models and theories being proposed today by critical thinkers.

F.2. Particle Models

Particle models model light, gravity, magnetism and the like as all moving particles. The best example of a particle model is de Hilster and de Hilster's "The Particle Model" where light, gravity, electricity, the electron, and magnetic fields are all treated as the same particle.

F.3. Lattice Models

Lattice models are less common but they fill space with a lattice structure - something like a scaffold. Everything in the universe is described through this lattice including light waves to matter itself.

F.4. Structure Models

One example of a structure model is that of Dr. Bill

Lucas and his universal force equations. This is not for those squeamish with math. Dr. Lucas has come up with a universal force equation[6] (for the 3 or 4 forces of the universe) that match with current data from the subatomic level to the cosmological level. No Paradigm Shift Yet

So far, no one model has come to the forefront although the science woke world has more aether theories than other types. But why has no one theory come to the forefront? There are several reasons:

- No one current model alternative has captured the imagination of the dissident community
- The advancement of new models took a very long detour starting with Einstein in 1905 because of ego, power, and position
- Universities do not allow their students to challenge the foundations of today's "Standard Model" and propose new ones
- Those working outside the mainstream and universities get little or no support to advance their models and theories

Working outside the mainstream and universities get little or no support to advance their models and the better. We must be persistent in our pursuit of a better model we can all agree upon.

But we never, ever should reach the point that Big Science has reached today: where teaching "truth" has replaced the art and science of critical thinking.

Stay woke!

REFERENCES

1. PBS Space Time (YouTube), How the Quantum Eraser Rewrites the Past | Space Time | PBS Digital Studios, https://youtu.be/8ORLN_KwAgs
2. Moskowitz, Clara, String Theory May Create Far Fewer Universes Than Thought, Scientific American 2018
3. Lisi, A. Garrett, An Exceptionally Simple Theory of Everything, Cornel University, 2012
4. Kuhn, Thomas S., The Structure of Scientific Revolutions. Chicago :University of Chicago Press, 1970.
5. Unzicker, Dr. Alexander, The Higgs Fake. Createspace Independent Publishing Platform, 2013.
6. Lucas, Dr. William, The Universal Force - Volume 1, Common Sense Science, 2013.

Science Evangelists, YouTube, and the Woke Movement

David de Hilster

22936 Ironwedge Dr, Boca Raton FL, 33433 USA, david@dehilste.com

It used to be that journalism was based upon unbiased, investigative reporting that above all, would stick to the facts and present both sides of a story. But as we have become "woke" to the ways of modern journalism around the globe, we are now confronted not with journalists, but with "readers" or "mouthpieces" for news who read what they are told to read by their owners. Stories are carefully chosen to fit the narrative of the huge media companies and their sponsors and anything that goes against this narrative, will never make it to the airwaves and is often ridiculed.

Keywords: kuhn, paradigm shift, scientific revolution

A. Introduction

Reporting on Big Science in the mass media is no different. Big Science has their self-appointed ambassadors that are the mouthpieces for Big Physics and Big Cosmology who loudly toot their for horns for Einstein, Hawking, Dark Matter, the Big Bang and the latest particle found in their greatest temple: the "Large Hadron Collider". These mouthpieces or what I like to call "science evangelists" are promptly called to arms by Big Journalism and mass media to help "explain" big, complicated "science truths" to the public. And unlike politics, there are no dissident voices out there to present "both sides" of Big Science issues.

But YouTube and the "woke" revolution has changed all that.

B. YouTube Realized

When YouTube came out in 2005, the idea was apparent from it's name: YouTube. A place where you could make your own videos, your own movies, even your own channel. The prediction that with the explosion of the internet, that modern television as we knew it, would dissappear. But in the first years, even after Google purchased YouTube a year later, "YouTubers" as they commonly called, barely existed and YouTube was simply a place for humans to upload their videos.

Early adopters of YouTube had loyal followings but no one was watching their news on YouTube or making news channels. As YouTube collected the largest online repository of videos, it lingered for many years with some YouTubers having a cult-like following, but the masses were still not participating. Two things changed all this:

- Monetization for YouTube content creators
- The "Woke" revolution

C. Monetization

YouTube noticed that some "YouTubers" were accumulating the number of subscribers that would attract mainstream advertisers. Although at first it was foreign for big companies to advertise on YouTube thinking it would not be effective, that myth was quickly broken when advertisers started seeing return from their YouTube adverts grow substantially. What this meant was that original content providers could actually make a living at what they love to do. Today, monetization has created the first YouTuber millionaires and celebrities with some YouTubers reaching rock-star status among the younger generation. Woke

The second piece of the puzzle came with the fact that the Internet provided a place for real truths to be found in repressed areas of the globe. The "Arab Spring" where countries run by repressive governments were lead by the youth who saw the freedoms of other societies on the internet and took to the streets, often dying for the cause of free speech and free and open soceities. One google executive who was Egyptian even choose to stay in his country and fight against repression.

Then in 2015, Bernie Sanders, an independent Senator from the United States started shouting at the American people about how things were not as it seems. This message was being shouted by Sanders for decades but everyone was too busy surving to pay much attention. But when Sanders message that what we were seeing on mainstream media was a narrative that favored the rich and the corporations and the war machine and not the people, it finally happened: humans became "woke" to the fact that what they were seeing in mass media was a lie.

D. Journalism Changed

Once the population became woke, YouTube was ready and waiting. Since 2015, the journalist as seen on CNN, MSNBC, NPR, Fox, the BBC, and other mass media outlets were seen a mouthpieces, "readers" of the news, "personalities" - high paid celebrities without any journalistic integrity. Those who voiced truths on the air were fired and forced underground and many of them ended up on YouTube.

Speaking truth to power became the anthem from the masses and random voices who were neither trained journalists nor polished speakers became the voices of the people where live broadcasts, interviews, and real journalism took place. Real journalism found its home on YouTube on channels where YouTubers went from hundreds, thousands, to millions of viewers with shows and production costs becoming so cheap that anyone with a computer, a webcam, and a YouTube channel could become a truth teller, journalist, and new channel attracting enough followers or "subscribers" for some to quit their job and devote fulltime to telling the news, or creating a channel with content that interested many people. Science Evangelists

Before this golden age of "woke" and YouTube where journalists could not be found and mouthpieces thrived, science mouthpieces also started to appear. Self-appointed mouthpieces for Big Physics and Big Cosmology and Big Science began to popup on television with their skill of being able to explain complex science to the common man. These science evangelists like Bob Nye the Science Guy, Neil DeGrasse Tyson, and Michio Kiku became regular gotos when some big science story broke and someone needed to explain it to the masses.

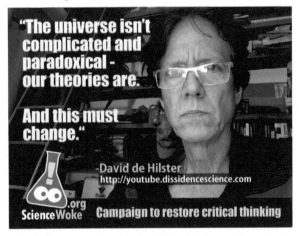

Figure 1. Complicated Theory according to David de Hilster

When the awakening of the masses happened during the past few years, physics and cosmology stood alone in that no dissident voices were heard. After all, who cares about "theoretical" science. It doesn't affect anyone negatively - doesn't make them go hungry, repress them politically, cause them to loose their jobs. With larger problems in the world like income inequality, the destruction of the earth, and unequal treatment of many parts of our society, particle physics and cosmology was just not on the radar.

E. Science Dissidents on YouTube

Ever since it started, there was dissident science on YouTube. Independent minds and critical thinkers were posting experiments, videos, and even making documentaries that were challenging mainstream physics and cosmology. YouTubes of explanations as to why Big Physics and Big Cosmology was wrong appeared including attacking the very foundations of physics and cosmology itself. Relativity, the big bang, particle physics, quantum mechanics and even plate tectonics were under attack and although from only a few voices in the beginning, now number in the thousands world-wide - and some of them on YouTube.

Eventually, the dissidents on YouTube and the science evangelists from main stream media would clash, none more that in this video where a YouTuber asks the most famous science evangelist, Neil deGrasse Tyson if Einstein could be wrong. Tyson's first answer: a laugh.

It then became painfully apparent that mainstream's science evangelists were not different from mainstream media journalist: they were simply mouthpieces for Big Science. Their job was not to present Big Science in an unbiased way. Their job was to impart the "narratives" of Big Science to the masses and crush any dissident voices out there.

F. Dissident Science YouTube

Inspired by YouTubers from the progressive political movement in the United States, I decided to start my own YouTube channel telling "truth to power" but this time, the power was Big Physics and Big Cosmology. I started simply recording my thoughts of Big Science from the dissident point of view, something that I had done for over 20 years. I noticed that people liked talking to me about physics because I had the perspective of a critical thinker, something I cultivated by hanging out with some of the greatest scientists of our time outside the mainstream.

Eventually, the channel grew from 50 to 100 to 300 and now to amost 1300 subscribers world wide. I took the time to learn what made channels grow on YouTube, how to make titles, graphics, even use a green screen. I now have a professional mic and lighting and am looking to create my YouTube studio when we move to a new house later this year.

I even made a video about the video of the answer from Neil deGrasse Tyson where he laughed accusing Tyson of being arrogant which is one of my most popular videos.

G. Parroting Big Science

Truth be told, the science evangelists themselves don't understand the theories they talk of. They claim they do, but most of the time they don't. They even tell us when confronted with "understanding" that they "trust" their colleagues and that they are just communicating the complexities of modern physics and cosmology to the masses.

So in the end, they are simply repeating what they have been told by Big Physics and Big Cosmology. They study the explanations and prepare themselves for questions from the public and the try to explain in "plain language" what Big Science is exposing.

In the process of explaining, more often than not, the explanations are above the public's ability to comprehend and the evangelists come off as "super brains" who are way smarter than everyone else. They then become reveered by the public whose minds are tickled by the magic of a complicated universe.

This is a win-win situation for the science evangelists and Big Physics and Big Cosmology who are looked upon in awe as if they were science gods and goddesses to be held up on the pedestals of the highest and smartest of the human race.

But this could not be further from the truth.

H. To Complicated - But What?

These self-appointed mouthpieces for Big Science create the illusion of being able to explain the inexplicable to the public. After all, the universe is very complicated and you need a very high IQ and a much larger brain to understand what seems impossible to understand.

But the truth is, the universe is not complicated, it is our theories that are complicated. And when the public or a news "reader" on a major network doesn't understand something, it is not because the theory or idea is paradoxical or wrong, it is because the public is too stupid to understand the concept. Crowning Themselves Kings and Queens

In the end, it is fame and fortune that the science evangelists seek. They are not seekers of scientific truths or teaching critical thinking to the masses. If there were truly critical thinkers, they wouldn't laugh at a question of whether Einstein is wrong and entertain that possibility. Instead, they pontificate about the universe, fill auditoriums, and make people marvel at their clever thought-provoking quips and carefully crafted stories - not to enlighten, but to sell T-Shirts with photos and sayings from them. Some of the T-Shirts even blatantly showing them as "saints".

Figure 2. Worshiping of Science Evangelists

I. Science Woke YouTubers

Even though we are in the infancy of the science woke movement, there are clear signs that it is working. We now have three other channels that regularly put out material including Jeff Yee, Robert de Hilster, and Nick Percival, Lori Gardi and videos from our CNPS including conference videos and weekly like Saturday Morning presentations for the science woke. There are other channels that have been around for sometime including Robert Distinti, Bill Gaede, and Jean de Climount and new ones that are doing quite well like the Sky Scholar.

There are large groups out there with world-wide followings like the Electric Universe which boasts over 150,000 subscribers. Our CNPS group which is more general in nature is starting to grow slowly but surely

We are just starting and have plans for growing even larger. This website is a big part of our "awaking" to the fact that Big Physics and Big Cosmology need truth spoken to their power to bring science back on track and advance once again.

J. Journalism is YouTube

To my teenage daughter, YouTube is television. She has no idea and never watches mainstream TV. She has no idea what CNN or MSNBC or FOX or NPR is. Her media world revolves around YouTube, SnapChat, and the like and her celebrities are from those arenas.

The science books she brings home reflect the narrative of Big Physics and Big Science and she knows that when I help her, that there is a different narrative out there. I know we still have work to do in getting the word out. But I now see it working. I see that there is an audience for being science woke and it is the silent majority.

The masses are not yet science woke. But between this new online science magazine, our YouTube channels, and decades of amazing work done by dissident voices in physics and cosmology, I am certain that those of us who speak truth to power in science, will be able to change the narrative and create the new voices who are true critical thinkers and not bias mouthpieces for a science that is wrong, stuck, and needs true unbiased critical thinkers to move it forward once again.

Ether to Matter to Ether

Francis Fernandes

The stages in the transformation of ether to matter to ether are as follows. Matter can collapse from visible mass back into the etheric sea at faster than light speed FTL, $3.481819 * 10^{12} m/s$ as "involution". In contrast, by "evolution", the etheric fabric changes into visible matter, as an act of creation at slowed speed VK,25812.8076 m/s. The creation of matter is thus understood in terms of a living changing texture with changing velocities. And, instead of change in time, we must talk in terms of time-period ... of pulsating gravitons and aitherons and protons. Thus, ether-to-matter, matter-to-ether is, on an etheric scale, a reversible process. Inverse of time period is frequency. The material fabric of space is ether. The field is ether and is expressed mathematically as $MR = 1.34 * 10^{27} kg/radial\ meter$. The field is comprised of myriads of 186-ether tori each of mass $1.859222909 * 10^{-9} kg$. At the heart of the Universe twin mass gravitons exist where one acts as a seed for proton formation and thus a proton particle is born. The other graviton becomes the ether toroid comprised of 186-ether tori. The diagram of a twin mass of two gravitons depicts one graviton emerging as 186-etheric mass which is measured as intrinsic elementary charge the source of electricity. The second graviton spins a fiber to form a toroid which is comprised of 186-etheric torii the source and measure of wavelength of light. A quantum of such ether torii now clustered together form what is known to science as tangible matter. Ether mass of the infinitesimal magnitude of 10^{-51} kg is herein called an aitheron from the Greek, $\alpha\iota\theta\eta\rho$, for ether, in order to distinguish it from other ether particles. A frequency of an aitheron of mass $7.3724936 * 10^{-51} kg$ is a fundamental building block of protons. The energy of this mass is equal in magnitude to Planck's constant under the condition of one second. This is the point mass of the material Universe. The aitheron material is created from 10^7 gravitons each of mass $7.3724936 * 10^{-58} kg$.

Keywords: kuhn, paradigm shift, scientific revolution

A. ETHER AND ITS MANIFESTATIONS

Ether Mass and Radial Length

$$G = \frac{B}{\wp}c^2 \ \ or \ \ G = \frac{1.380668031 * 10^{-36}}{1.859222909 * 10^{-9}}c^2 \quad (1)$$

Ether: Planck Mass and Planck Length

$$\pi B^2 (137.036) = \pi (Plancklength)^2 \quad (2)$$

I have discovered this correspondence in the dynamic living pulsation of ether.

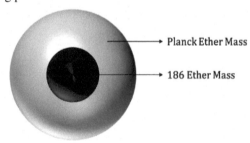

Figure 3. Ether Mass

$$m_{Pl} \equiv \sqrt{\frac{c}{G}} = PlanckMass = 2.176450474 * 10^{-8} kg \quad (3)$$

$$B = 1.380668031 * 10^{-36} \ m \ Torus \ radius \quad (4)$$

See Figure 2 on the next page

B. Ether Model

The yellow to blue to purple to green toroidal rings represent ether to matter. The black graviton sphere nested in a torus spun by another graviton at ten to the power 48 Hz depicted in yellow is ether.

Ether Mass: Yellow Ring - Twin Gravitons. One graviton point mass nested in a torus spun by another graviton point mass moving at faster than light speed.

Coulomb Mass: Blue Ring - The nested graviton now manifests as an aitheron; first step in the creation of tangible matter. The ether toroid is the reason for the Coulomb constant, k.

Proton Mass: Purple Ring - The frequency of the aitheron is the measure of proton mass. The frequency in Planck's energy equation is not of the proton rather an attribute of the aitheron. The ether toroid now has a property of angular momentum with faster than light speed change to a slowed velocity measured in SQUID.

Elementary Charge: Green Ring - The frequency of the proton yields the measure of elementary charge. The ether toroid is now the source of Compton wavelength of a proton.

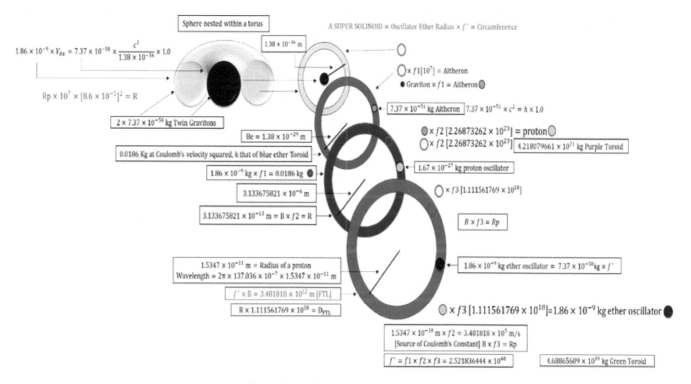

Figure 4.　Sphere Nested within a Torus

Particle	f (Hz)	Graviton (Matter)	
		Mass (kg)	Radial length (m)
Graviton		7.372496×10^{-58}	$5.474851611 \times 10^{-85}$
Aitheron	f1	$10^{-58} \times f1 = 7.37 \times 10^{-51}$	$5.474851611 \times 10^{-78}$
Proton	f2	$7.37 \times 10^{-51} \times f2 = 1.67 \times 10^{-27}$	$1.242097444 \times 10^{-54}$
Ether Oscillator	f3	$1.67 \times 10^{-27} \times f3 = 1.86 \times 10^{-9}$	$1.380668031 \times 10^{-36}$

Figure 5.　Chart A

Particle	f (Hz)	Graviton (Ether Toroid)	
		Mass (kg)	Toroid length (m)
Graviton	f'	$7.37 \times 10^{-58} \times f' = 1.86 \times 10^{-9}$	$1.380668031 \times 10^{-36}$
Aitheron	f1	$1.86 \times 10^{-9} \times f1 = 0.0186$	$1.380668031 \times 10^{-29}$
Proton	f2	$0.0186 \times f2 = 4.218079661 \times 10^{21}$	$3.133675821 \times 10^{-6}$
Ether Oscillator	f3	$4.218079661 \times 10^{21} \times f3 = 4.68865609 \times 10^{39}$	3.481818×10^{12}

Figure 6.　Chart B

C. Atomic Frequency

The ether model mathematically apportions a distribution of ether tori within a time-period of one second. A graviton pulsates at a frequency, f. There is a curious relationship between frequency, f, and "f-number" of aitheron particles. In other words, factor f, if multiplied by a single aitheron mass would yield the proton. The wave frequency of rippled ether, f, finds its origins in this aitheron quantum, f. The aitheron is comprised of 10 million gravitons.

$$f^* = f1 * f2 * f3 = 2.521836444 * 10^{48} \ Hz \quad (5)$$

$$f1 = 10^7 \ Hz \quad (6)$$

$$f2 = 2.26873262 * 10^{23} \ Hz \quad (7)$$

$$E = h * f2 \ for \ a \ proton \quad (8)$$

$$f3 = 1.111561769 * 10^{18} \ Hz \quad (9)$$

See Chart A in Figure 3 on page 2.

The (radial length) $*1.346611109 * 10^{27}$ kg/m = the particle mass

See Chart B in Figure 4 on page 2.

Example:
$1.242097444 * 10^{-54}m * 1.346611109 * 10^{27}$ Kg/m = $1.672622216 * 10^{-27}$ kg proton mass

Speed of Light Squared

$$c^2 = 3.481819 * 10^{12} m/s * 25812.8076 m/s \quad (10)$$

*Mass * Velocity * Distance = h*

A] $1.86 * 10^{-9} * 3.4818 * 10^{12} * [1.38 * 10^{-29}] * [2\pi * 10^{-7} * 137.036] * [2\pi * 10^{-7} 137.036] = h$

Boltzmann constant Q where:
$Q^2 = 1.86 * 10^{-9} * [1.38 * 10^{-29}] * [2\pi * 10^{-7} * 137.036] * [2\pi * 10^{-7} * 137.036]$

The two angles are postulated to be the reason for angular momentum and hence motion in the Universe.

B] $1.8610^{-9} * 25812.807 * 1.38 * 10^{-29} = h$

The product of the velocities in A and B is speed of light squared

SIGNIFICANCE

The reason for light speed is explained as emanating from the green ring and purple ring.

The source of faster than light speed squared is shown to be the result of one faster than light speed and another slow speed. A common error would be to think of light speed squared to be c x c. The speed of light squared is associated with Boltzmann's constant henceforth called Q. The Boltzmann constant has units of Coulombs.

I postulate that the reason for motion in the Universe is due to two toroidal precessions, $[2\pi * 10^{-7} * 137.036] * 2\pi * 10^{-7} * 137.036]$. The precessions of ether generate angular momentum. The momentum of one Coulomb of ether oscillators [in the green ring] is the measure of electric current as measured by an ammeter.

The evolution of ether to the material world can be depicted as follows - gravitons aggregate to form aitherons to form protons to form elementary charge. Cocooning these particles are ether toroids comprised of myriads of 186-ether tori. Creation is a snapshot of evolution. Proton matter and elementary charge are the building blocks of the periodic table. All of life emanates from here. The chicken and egg arrive at the same time. Some stem cells become the chicken and some the egg.

Intrinsic Redshift in Quasi-Stellar Objects (QSOs) - Mass Dependence and Quantization?

Raymond HV Gallucci, PhD, PE

8956 Amelung St., Frederick, MD 21704, email=gallucci@localnet.com

I tackle the topic of quantization of intrinsic QSO redshifts, especially based on the lifetime work of Halton Arp, examining first the potential relationship between intrinsic QSO redshift and QSO mass, then the phenomenon of quantization for both QSO mass and redshift. My approach is primarily a mathematical one, as developing a theory for intrinsic QSO redshift, let alone its quantization, is beyond my expertise. I postulate a geometric explanation of intrinsic redshift given a possible dependence on mass to the 2/3 power, related to possible attenuation of light energy (and therefore frequency) within the "emitting nucleus" of a QSO, compounded by a further "dilution," and therefore energy (and frequency) decrease due to spread over the surface area. To do the quantization aspect justice, I summarize three theories by other experts and examine the plausibility of the two within my realm of knowledge. Finally, I offer at least a mathematical representation of the quantization aspect as "food for thought."

Keywords: Cosmological Redshift, Quasi-Stellar Objects, Quantization, Halton Arp, Variable Mass

A. Introduction

"Viktor A. Ambartsumian suggested the idea that new galaxies are formed through ejection from older active galaxies (1958). This idea has had a certain continuity in the research carried out over the last 40 years based on the hypothesis that some extragalactic objects, and in particular high redshift [quasi-stellar objects] QSOs, might be associated with low redshift galaxies, thus providing a non-cosmological explanation for the redshift in QSOs (e.g., [1], [2], [3], [4], [5], [6], [7], [8], [9]); that is, a redshift produced by a mechanism different from the expansion of the Universe or the Doppler effect. Ambarsumian never accepted the idea of non-cosmological redshifts; however, the scenario of QSOs ejected by galaxies is a common theme of the Armenian astrophysicist and in proposals of discordant QSO-galaxy redshift associations." [10] More recently, this has been advocated by Tifft - "There appears to be little doubt that redshift is a quantized and variable quantity" - who has been pursuing this since his dissertation in 1963. [11]

Redshift (z) periodicity has been observed at z = 0.3, 0.6, 0.96, 1.41 and 1.96, with two others predicted at z = 2.63 and 3.46. [12] An additional preferred peak at z = 0.061 has been observed by several others as well. [13] Various explanation have been proposed for this phenomenon, including: (1) strictly Dopplerian redshifts; (2) partial Dopplerian and non-Dopplerian redshift; (3) "tired light" (non-Dopplerian) redshift; (4) periodic oscillation of physical constants (e.g., the gravitational constant); (5) interaction between radiation and cold Rydberg material in intergalactic space close to the observed parent galaxy of the QSOs; (6) three-dimensional quantized time; (7) oscillating atomic lines (due to temporal changes of the fine structure constant); (8) oscillating luminosity of galax-

ies; [12] (9) Quantum Temporal Cosmology (QTC), which assumes time is three-dimensional with matter flowing out radially from a near-singular time origin such that, as energy decays, doubling processes produce quantization [11]; (10) local ether theory with gravitational redshift [14]; and (11) variable particle mass that changes in discrete steps [15]. And, while I do not have a pet theory of my own as to why these QSO redshifts should be quantized, it occurred to me that perhaps a simple explanation might be based on gravitational effects, something that might be examined at least for plausibility given the measured redshift peaks and estimates of QSO masses.

Reference [16] provided a tabulated source of data for QSO masses that has already considered over 50,000 QSO observations. For redshift increments of z = 0.2 from z = 0.2 to z = 2.0, Table 1 lists the observed values, which includes combining those for the 3a and 3b increments into one for convenience. Increments 3a and 3b were combined into one (Increment 3) with 3665 + 4727 = 8392 data, weighting the log of the mass ratio as follows: $\frac{3665x8.69+4727x8.59}{8392} = 8.63$ Conveniently, the z range covers all but the lowest observed peak at z = 0.061.

B. Gravitational Redshift?

The fairly smooth trend shown in Figure 1 suggested a correlation between QSO mass and measured redshift, and our first thought was to examine the possibility of a gravitational effect. Gravity is postulated as being capable of redshifting light as the light travels outward from a gravitational mass (such as a star or QSO). The redshift follows this relationship: [17] $\lim_{r \to \infty} z(r) = \frac{1}{\sqrt{1 - \frac{2GM}{R^* c^2}}} - 1$

where: G = gravitational constant, 6.674E-11 $m^3/kg - s^2$, M = gravitational mass (kg), R^* = radial coordinate of emission point (analogous to classical distance from center

Table 1. QSO Data for z from 0.2 to 2.0 [14]

#	Z Range	Z Midpoint	Number of QSOs	Log of Mass Ratio (to Sun's Mass)		Mass Ratio (to Sun's Mass)
1	0.2-0.4	0.3	2690	8.27		1.86E+08
2	0.4-0.6	0.5	4250	8.44		2.75E+08
3a	0.6-0.8	0.7	3665	8.69	8.63	4.30E+08
3b			4727	8.59		
4	0.8-1.0	0.9	5197	8.76		5.75E+08
5	1.0-1.2	1.1	6054	8.89		7.76E+08
6	1.2-1.4	1.3	7005	8.96		9.12E+08
7	1.4-1.6	1.5	7513	9.07		1.17E+09
8	1.6-1.8	1,7	6639	9.18		1.51E+09
9	1.8-2.0	1.9	4900	9.29		1.95E+09

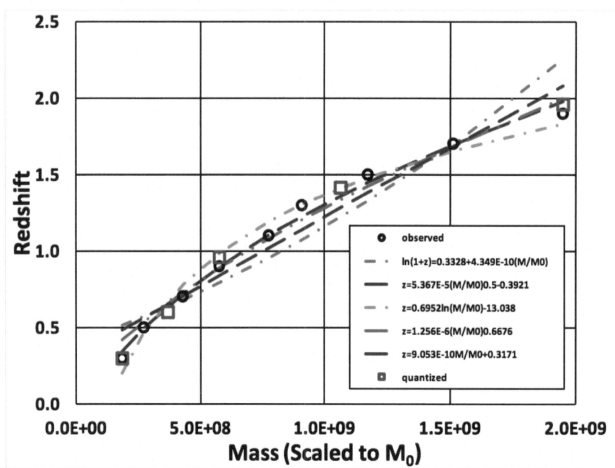

of gravitational mass) (m), r = radial distance to observer (effectively infinite, since this formula is for a limit) (m), c = speed of light, 3.00E+8 m/s.

Rearranging the equation as follows yields the unknown R^* as a function of z (replacing the limit designation since the observation distance is assumed to be "infinite"): $R^* = \frac{\frac{2GM}{c^2}}{1 - \frac{1}{[z+1]^2}}$. Using 1.99E+30 kg as the Sun's mass, M_0, we calculate $1.35E + 12m \leq R^* \leq 6.53E + 12m$ for the range of redshifts in Table 1, based on the incremental midpoints (i.e., $0.3 \leq z \leq 1.9$).

If QSOs are ejections from the nuclei of parent galaxies, we would expect their size to be significantly less than those of these parent nuclei. Reference [18] cites a radius for the nucleus of the Milky Way of 800 parsecs, or 2.47E+19 m, six to seven orders of magnitude greater than the estimated range for R^*. If this is typical of galaxies from which ejected QSOs have been observed, then their sizes must be quite small relative to the parent nucleus to generate the observed redshifts solely by gravitational effects. At least one theorist (C-C. Su) cites gravity as a potential cause for intrinsic redshift: [14]

... [T]he high redshift can be due to the gravitational redshift as an intrinsic redshift. Based on the proposed local-ether theory, this intrinsic redshift is determined solely by the gravitational potential associated specifically with the celestial object in which the emitting sources are placed. During the process with which quasars evolve into ordinary galaxies, the fragmentation of quasars and the formation of stars occur and hence the masses of quasars decrease. Thus their gravitational potentials and hence redshifts become smaller and smaller ... in accord with the aging of redshift during the evolution process. In some observations, the redshifts of quasars ... exhibit a series of preferred peaks in their distributions ... Based on the local-ether wave equation, it is shown that the quantum-state energies and transition frequencies of atoms or ions placed in a celestial object decrease under the influence of the associated gravitational potential ... [I]n the evolution process with quasar fragmentation and star formation, the masses of quasars decrease and their gravitational potentials become weaker. Thus their redshifts become lower and lower, while the starburst makes their luminosities stronger.

However, another has noted that "... the redshift was quantized and not continuous as required by gravitational dynamics." [11] Nonetheless, this does not rule out a gravitational dependence for QSO redshift over a continuous spectrum, although the calculation above suggests that QSOs must be extremely small at "birth" relative to the nuclei of their parent galaxies to exhibit the observed redshifts. I form no conclusion as to the plausibility of a gravitational cause for intrinsic redshift of QSOs, but merely suggest that such would require the QSOs to be relatively extremely small when ejected.

C. "Tired Light" Attenuation?

Another idea as to the dependence of redshift on QSO

mass is that, as the light travels outward from inside the QSO, it loses energy through interaction with the matter inside the QSO (presumably plasma) according to the typical formula for attenuation with distance: $E(r) = E_0 e^{-\mu r}$ where: E(r) = energy at distance r from the source, E_0 = energy when emitted at r = 0, μ = attenuation coefficient (m - 1 when r is measured in m). Since redshift at a distance r from the source is defined as $z(r) = \frac{v_0 - v(r)}{v_0}$ and $E(r) = h v(r)$, we can express the redshift in terms of the previous equation as follows: $z(r) = e^{\mu r} - 1$ then linearize it and perform a simple regression analysis using the values from Table 1 (using the z midpoints) if we assume: (1) The "emitting nucleus" of the QSO has a relatively constant size (assume spherical) that does not change but loses mass as material emanates outward, i.e., its density decreases with age; (2) Attenuation is a function of this density, decreasing with decreasing density, thereby reducing redshift by attenuation as the QSO ages.

Note that this does not suggest that the QSO ceases to "grow" in size with age, but only that the "emitting nucleus" remains relatively constant in size as its mass spreads outward and density decreases. Since density and mass are directly proportional for a constant volume, we can rewrite the preceding equation in the following linear form suitable for regression: $\ln(z[r] + 1) = a_0 + a_1 \frac{M}{M_0}$. Reference [19] is an online tool for various forms of regression analysis. For this equation, it yields the following result with an R^2 coefficient of 89.1 percent: $a_0 = 0.3328, a_1 = 4.349E - 10$. As might be expected from the less than ideal R^2 value, the fit to the observed data is not satisfactory, showing a different trend (see Figure 1). [1]

D. Other Explanations?

The next trial was to perform non-linear regression using Reference [19] to see what correlations might fall out and see if any might suggest a physical model for the dependence of QSO redshift on mass. The following three were the "simplest" that also exhibited a high value of R^2:

$z = 5.367E - 5\sqrt{\frac{M}{M_0}} + 0.3171, R^2 = 99.3 percent$;

$z = 0.6952 \ln \frac{M}{M_0} - 13.038, R^2 = 98.3 percent$;

$z = 1.256E - 6(\frac{M}{M_0})^{0.6676}, R^2 = 98.2 percent$.

A simple linear fit, $z = 9.053E - 10\frac{M}{M_0} + 0.3171$, yielded an R^2 of 94.9 percent. All these are plotted in Figure 1 along with the observed values from Table 1 (using the z midpoints). [2]

These three equations show the best fits vs. the observed data, although none passes through all of those points. The linear fit is better than the previous one for the attenuation assumption, but is noticeably weaker than the best three.

---

[1] While both redshift trends increase with mass, the observed redshift shows a slightly descending rate of increase while the regression equation shows a slightly ascending rate of increase.

[2] Also shown are the quantized redshifts, discussed in the following section.

Of the three, the last with its dependence on the scaled mass to essentially the 2/3 power suggests a possible physical phenomenon for the dependence of QSO redshift on mass, given the previous assumptions.

Light presumably is emitted at the "surface" of the QSO, taken as an approximate sphere such that its surface area is proportional to the square of its radius. We have assumed the radius of the "emitting nucleus" portion of the QSO remains relatively constant. Therefore, any decrease in mass is the result of a decrease in density as mass emanates outward with the growing QSO (but not the growing "emitting nucleus"). Since the radius is proportional to the cube root of the mass (given the relatively constant volume as well), the surface area is proportional to mass to the 2/3 power. While I do not know what physical phenomenon might cause redshift to be directly proportional to the area of the emitting surface (possibly some sort of "dilution" of the light energy, corresponding to both energy and frequency decrease?), IF this relationship is true, then the correlation with mass to the 2/3 power follows - for a relatively constant emitting volume and surface area, as the density decreases, so does the redshift. One possible mechanism again returns to the attenuation effect, albeit somehow directly proportional to the radius, i.e., the distance through which the light must pass to reach the emitting surface. With decreasing density and relatively constant radius, the attenuation decreases, allowing light to pass through more readily with less energy loss and, therefore, less decrease in frequency and less redshift.

If all this seems implausible, remember that the mainstream cosmological explanation requires a Big Bang with an ever expanding universe where QSOs observed to be relatively close to "parent galaxies" is purely coincidental. Halton Arp and others have estimated the probability of such a purely coincidental occurrence to be astronomically small ("less than one in ten million" [15]). Therefore, is my speculation any more implausible?

E. Redshift Quantization?

At the Kronia Group Conference in Portland, Oregon, on Sept. 23, 2000, Halton Arp presented his theory on "Intrinsic Redshift." [15] ... [I]n the early 1950s ... they saw these thin connections [between galaxies and radio lobes] going from the central galaxy out to the radio lobes on either side ... [T]his material is actually being ejected (that's about the only way you could get this configuration) ... [T]his large amount of material is coming from this very small active spot ... [I]f the galaxy is going to eject something, it's going to eject along the path of least resistance, which is out the poles ... [Y]ou have this nice relationship that as the quasars ... proceed out as time goes past, they age and drop in redshift ... [T]hey don'ât drop smoothly ... [but] in preferred quantized redshifts ... What I have interpreted this to mean is that these quasars move out, evolving to low redshift ...

Arp's theory is that QSOs are ejected at high redshift and, as they travel outward from the ejecting galaxy, expe-

rience a decrease in redshift but in discrete increments.

We can use the three non-linear regression equations to estimate the QSO mass at each of the redshift peaks 0.30, 0.60, 0.96, 1.41 and 1.96. The estimates and averages from the three are presented in Table 2.

Now, if there is some sort of quantization phenomenon as the QSO is ejected and travels outward, with redshift decreasing in specific increments, we expect some relationship between redshift, and therefore mass, of the QSO with time and/or distance, with time or distance increment 1 being associated with the newly ejected QSO (redshift = 1.96 and mass [scaled] = 2.05E+9) and increment 5 associated with the oldest QSO (redshift = 0.30 and mass [scaled] = 1.65E+8). As before, we exercise the online non-linear regression program [19] to generate the following five correlations between scaled mass and time or distance increment (i.e., t = 1, 2, 3, 4, 5):

$\frac{M}{M_0} = (3.775E+9)e^{-0.6106t}, R^2 = 100.0 percent$;

$\frac{M}{M_0} = (-1.189E+9)\ln t + 1.992E+9, R^2 = 99.1 percent$;

$\frac{M}{M_0} = (2.095E+9)t^{-1.163}, R^2 = 97.2 percent$;

$\frac{M}{M_0} = (-1.525E+9)\sqrt{t} + 3.410E+9, R^2 = 95.7 percent$;

$\frac{M}{M_0} = (-4.549E+8)t + 2.219E+9, R^2 = 89.9 percent$.

All these are plotted in Figure 2 along with the averaged values from Table 2.

The last two equations have the undesirable property that, at time or distance increment 5, the scaled mass drops below zero, an impossibility. Clearly the first equation fits the data best, passing through all the quantized values. The second equation is nearly as good, just missing at time or distance increment 5. The third one is slightly weaker, but still acceptable within the limits of accuracy assumed. The first and third equations are also the simplest, one being a decreasing exponential, the other a decreasing power. Does either suggest a quantization mechanism?

E.1. Variable Particle Mass? Halton Arp's Theory

At the Kronia Group Conference, Halton Arp also presented his theory for quantization of intrinsic redshift for QSOs. He first laid the groundwork for particle mass being variable with time: [15]

The conventional theory is the Einstein field equations of general relativity ... The solution made [in] 1922 made an approximation, which I think was wrong - ... the particle masses were constant everywhere in the universe ... They then solved this equation with this approximation and they got that the ... scale factor of space varied as the redshift, and so this is the expanding redshift solution; this is the Big Bang solution, and they predict expanding coordinates, singularities at time equals zero, and it demands that all the redshifts are velocities of recession ... This whole approach has to be abandoned ... Jack Narlikar, who's a student of Fred Hoyle, and Hoyle had investigated the general solution of this equation, which was not to assume that particle masses were constant in time ... [T]hey got a very simple solution that the masses varied with the

Table 2. QSO Mass (Scaled) vs. z Peak

Z Peak	$Z \propto \sqrt{M/M_0}$	$Z \propto \ln(M/M_0)$	$Z \propto (M/M_0)^{0.6676}$	Average
	M/M₀			
0.3	1.66E+08	2.15E+08	1.14E+08	1.65E+08
0.6	3.42E+08	3.31E+08	3.21E+08	3.31E+08
0.96	6.35E+08	5.55E+08	6.50E+08	6.13E+08
1.41	1.13E+09	1.06E+09	1.16E+09	1.11E+09
1.96	1.92E+09	2.34E+09	1.89E+09	2.05E+09

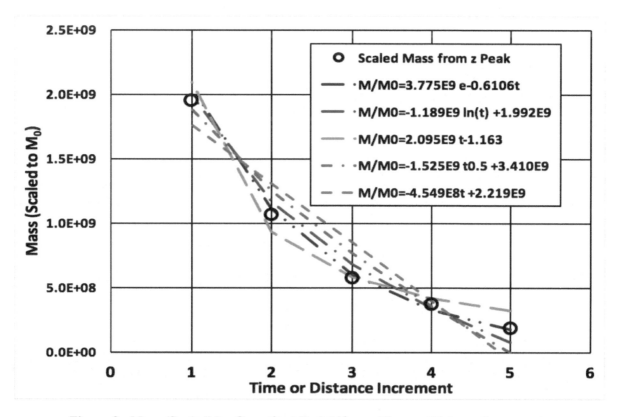

Figure 2. Mass (Scaled) by Quantized Redshifts vs. Time or Distance Increments

time squared, i.e., in the beginning, when they were first created, there are zero masses, and as time went on they communicated with more and more of the universe and their mass grew (this is a Machian theory), and so, if the electron mass, when it makes its transition in the atom and emits the photon, if the mass is small, the photon is weak and it's redshifted. As the electron grows in mass, the photon which is emitted is stronger and it drops in redshift. So this is a perfect explanation for what we've been seeing that younger objects are high redshift[ed] and ... the sacred Hubble constant is just the inverse age of our galaxy ... It makes a link between quantum and classical mechanics because the creation of the matter is in very small particles in the quantum regime; there's no more singularities ... The most important point is ... that this is in flat space-time, Euclidean space-time ... You don't need any of these complicated curved space-time coordinates ... [T]he conventional solution needed these to account for the incorrect treatment of the mass particles ...

He continued by linking his theory of variable particle mass to redshift quantization: [15]

... [W]e live in a hierarchical universe ... [I]f you start in the galaxy nucleus, you get a high density ... In the center of this active nucleus, this mysterious engine where the stuff is created, ... the new particles are in that environment, and they're gaining mass from their environment very rapidly. When they step out of the nucleus, they go into a different, much lower density, environment into the bulge of the galaxy; and, then, if they come out in the plane [of the galaxy], they go out of here; if they come out along the axis, they drop here [into the local group]. These are enormous drops in density ... And finally, when they drop out of the local group, they take another step down [into the local supercluster], and out the local supercluster, they take another drop down ... This means that these particle[s] ... will be gaining mass very rapidly, and the redshift will be dropping very rapidly on one of these steps; and then it levels off; and there goes another step in the drop; and there are just about ... six drops, and there are six major quantization levels [1.96, 1.41, 0.96, 0.6, 0.3 and 0.061] ... [M]aybe this redshift quantization that we're seeing in the quasars is a reflection of the density hierarchy in the whole universe.

While not the most easily viewed schematic, Figure 3 illustrates Arp's quantization scheme as presented at the conference. The discrete drops in density from galactic nucleus to galactic bulge to galactic plane to local group to local supercluster (Virgo in the case of the Milky Way) and finally into intergalactic space(?), corresponding to the discrete drops in QSO redshift, are clearly evident.

E.2. Gravity-Induced Quantization? C-C. Su's Theory

C-C. Su's theory that gravitational redshift explains intrinsic redshift was introduced above. Here we continue with his theory explaining the quantization effect (with a minimum of equations, for simplicity): [14]

... According to the ejection model, quasars are formed from [the] gas of atoms, plasma and dust ejected from

the parent active galaxy ... [S]uppose that the material of the gas cloud together forms a local ether associated with the quasar ... [T]he gravitational potential on the surface of the quasar ... is extraordinarily strong, [although] the gravity of acceleration on the surface of ... a massive quasar is less than one percent of that on the surface of the Earth ... [B]ased on the ejection model and the local-ether theory, the wide variation in redshift can be ascribed to a variation in density and size of the gas cloud, which in turn can be due to the strength of the initial ejection from the parent galaxy, the speed at which the cloud moves away from the galaxy, to the gas expansion, to the fragmentation of gas clouds, and to ... star formation. As the size and density tend to vary widely, it seems that the redshifts of quasars vary in a random way. However, from an analysis of about 600 quasars, it has been found that the redshifts have some preferred values and, thus, the distribution of the redshifts exhibits some preferred peaks ... Due to non-uniformity in particle velocity and density, or to some internal disturbance, a quasar may break into pieces of smaller sizes. By reason of symmetry, it seems to have a good chance to break into pieces of identical or similar sizes. Suppose the fragments are also spherical and the density remains unchanged. Thereby, their radius is shorter than the previous one by a factor of $2^{-1/3}$ and the gravitational potential on the surface of either fragment will decrease by a factor of $2^{-2/3}$ ... [A]fter the nth splitting in half, the gravitation-induced intrinsic redshift ... is given by

$$1 + z_n = \sqrt{1 + 2^{\frac{-2n}{3}}([1+z_0]^2 - 1)}$$

where the quantity $(1 + z_0)^2 - 1$ denotes two times the normalized gravitational potential corresponding to the zeroth redshift. For the cases of very high redshifts, the preceding formula can be approximated as $1 + z_n \approx 1.26^{-n}(1 + z_0)$.

By adopting the preferred value of 1.956 as the zeroth redshift again, [this] formula leads to the prediction that the preferred intrinsic redshifts are z = 6.08, 4.65, 3.53, 2.64, 1.96, 1.42, 1.02, 0.71, 0.49, 0.33, 0.22, 0.14, 0.09 and 0.06 with n = -4 to 9 ... A redshift distribution around 0.6 may actually be a merger of two close distributions around 0.71 and 0.49, respectively ... [L]ow redshift peaks are expected to be smeared, since other affecting factors of uneven splitting, gas expansion and star formation, will accumulate with time ...

Unlike Arp's theory, Su's does not postulate that the series of quantized redshifts represents QSO evolution with time and/or distance, although he does agree that QSOs are formed by ejection from a parent galaxy. His quantizations are static for each QSO and dependent upon various initial conditions and interactions until the QSO "stabilizes" and exhibits one of the characteristic, preferred redshift values.

E.3. Quantum Temporal Cosmology? William Tifft's Theory

William Tifft, as mentioned in the Introduction, has been

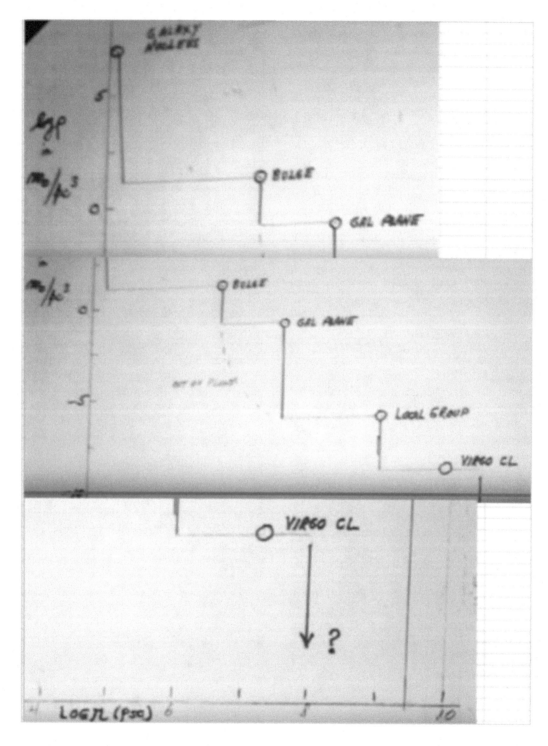

Figure 3. Arp's Redshift Quantization Scheme [15]

investigating this phenomenon for over 50 years. From his work over the past quarter of a century, he has developed the theory of Quantum Temporal Cosmology (QTC) which "has proven to be consistent with redshift quantization, particle properties and observational evidence." [11]

The theory is founded upon time being three dimensional (called tau-space) with matter (in spaces called sigma-spaces) flowing out radially from a near-singular origin in time ... As energy decays, doubling processes produce quantization, define properties of matter and generate observational effects ... The upper left diagram in Figure 11 [Figure 4 below] is a conceptual picture of tau-space expansion where sigma-spaces (galaxies) flow out radially on timelines. There are two expansions from the point of view of galaxies, which are effectively "particles" in tau-space. There is a temporal (radial) and spatial (lateral) expansion as timelines grow and separate sigma-spaces, which seems to resolve the dark energy problem. The diagram at lower left shows the dual redshift prediction in QTC appears to fit supernova data. The different structure further indicates that look-back geometry in 3-D time corresponds to a logarithmic spiral. The figure at right illustrates time-time look-back geometry with observed redshifts marked. Present maximum observed redshifts are far from the origin (since the dual expansion in QTC is absent in classical cosmology and ascribed to dark energy).

Commenting on Tifft's QTC is beyond my expertise, other than noting that he derives quantized redshifts at 1.9, 1.5, 1.1, 0.59 and 0.24 which correspond reasonably well with the accepted observed values of 1.96, 1.41, 0.96, 0.6 and 0.3, respectively.

E.4. Speculation on My Part

My efforts have been focused on mathematical representation of the potential relationship between QSO intrinsic redshift and QSO mass, with or without quantization, although the latter phenomenon is so obvious that it cannot be ignored. As Arp indicates, QSO quantized redshift varies with QSO distance from the parent galaxy, which could be either (or both) a time or distance phenomenon. In Arp's theory, QSOs are ejected with high redshift, which appears to correlate well with high mass (density) so long as the "emitting nucleus" of the QSO remains relatively constant in size. Redshift decreases as QSO mass (density) within the "emitting nucleus" decreases, both a time and distance phenomenon in Arp's theory. Arp offers a reason for the observed quantization based on variable particle mass, which increases with time, and correspondingly with distance, as the particles "evolve" and travel outward from higher to lower density regions in a piecewise, not continuous, manner. If you accept Arp's variable mass postulate, this certainly appears reasonable.

Su's theory does not require any time dependence, as he postulates that quantized QSO redshift (and mass) results from initial conditions and subsequent interactions. Presumably, the spatial distribution around the parent galaxy, whereby the higher redshifted QSOs are closest and the lower ones farthest, is the result of the initial energy of the QSO's ejection, its initial size and interactions with surrounding material. The more energetic ones travel outward farther and interact more with material, thereby losing more mass and showing lower redshift with distance. And while he derives a formula that predicts at least some of the quantized values, he does not appear to offer a definitive reason for the quantization. Thus, his theory appears less plausible than Arp's.

As I said previously, Tifft's QTC is beyond my expertise, so I do not comment. What I can offer is another possible mathematical observation for quantization that could have a yet to be identified physical basis. I previously cited two of my regression equations as the simplest ones that reproduce well the quantized, decreasing QSO redshifts as a function of uniformly increasing time or distance intervals. The first equation suggests an exponential "decay," while the second suggests roughly decay as a function of inverse time or distance.

Note: The $t^{-1.163}$ dependence in this equation can be viewed as a reasonably close representation of a t^{-1} dependence.

Exponential decay is a fairly common physical phenomenon (e.g., radioactive decay), but the discrete aspect appears unique to QSO redshift. An inverse distance dependence is characteristic of a magnetic or electric field around an infinitely long string of charges, or current-carrying wire, which suggests the possibility of some connection with Electric Universe Theory where intergalactic Birkeland currents are postulated to pervade the universe. Galaxies formed where these currents flow could exhibit surrounding magnetic or electric fields with the inverse distance dependence. What is more difficult to ascertain is the quantization aspect.

While I leave speculation as to the basis for quantization to experts, such as Arp, Su and Tifft, I make the following mathematical observation that the quantization of both QSO mass and redshift can be represented by the following sine curve with decreasing amplitude of the same decaying exponential form as my first equation, such as shown in Figure 5:

$$\frac{M}{M_0} = |(2.73E + 9)e^{-0.6106t}\sin(\pi[t - 0.55])|$$ where | | indicates absolute value, 2.73E+9 has been inserted as a scaling factor to correspond to the quantized masses from Table 2, and -0.55 as a shift factor to set the peaks at integer values.

The peaks in Figure 5 occur at scaled masses of 2.05E+9, 1.11E+9, 6.04E+8, 3.28E+8 and 1.78E+8 for increments 1 through 5. Comparison with the average values in Table 2 shows excellent agreement to within 10 percent at worst. What type of phenomenon might exhibit such a sinusoidal behavior with exponentially decaying amplitude is unknown (possibly some form of harmonic dependence?) and beyond my conjecture. I offer it as "food for thought."

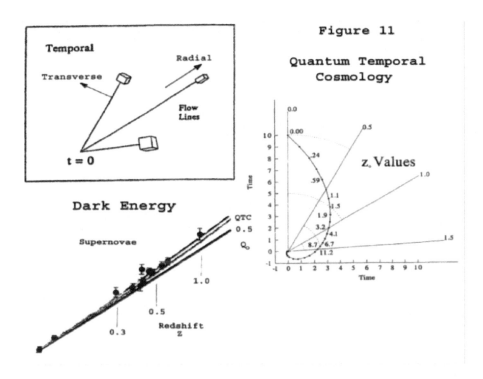

Figure 4. Tifft's Quantum Temporal Cosmology [11]

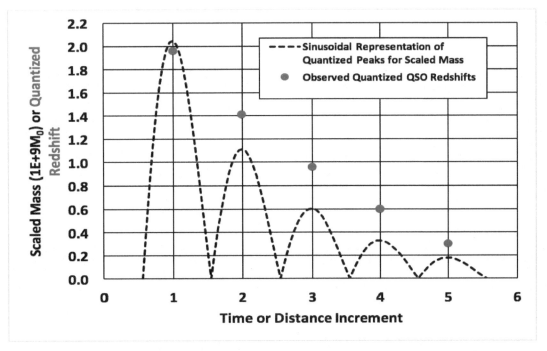

Figure 5. Quantized QSO Scaled Mass as a Sinusoidal Function (Shown with Quantized QSO Redshift)

F. Summary

I have attempted to tackle the topic of quantization of intrinsic QSO redshifts, especially based on the lifetime work of Halton Arp, examining first the potential relationship between intrinsic QSO redshift and QSO mass, then the phenomenon of quantization for both QSO mass and redshift. My approach has been primarily a mathematical one, as developing a theory for intrinsic QSO redshift, let alone its quantization, is beyond my expertise. Based on my mathematical analyses for QSO mass vs. redshift, I postulate a geometric explanation of intrinsic redshift given a possible dependence on mass to the 2/3 power, related to possible attenuation of light energy (and therefore frequency) within the "emitting nucleus" of a QSO, compounded by a further "dilution," and therefore energy (and frequency) decrease due to spread over the surface area. To do the quantization aspect justice, I have summarized three theories by other experts and examined the plausibility of the two within my realm of knowledge. Finally, I offer at least a mathematical representation of the quantization aspect as "food for thought."

REFERENCES

1. H. Arp, QSOs, Redshifts and Controversies, Interstellar Media, Berkeley (1987).
2. H. Arp, Catalogue of Discordant Redshift Associations, Aperion, Montreal (2003).
3. J. Narlikar, , Space Science Reviews, 50, 523 (1989).
4. G. Burbidge, , Publications of the Astronomical Society of the Pacific, 113, 899 (2001).
5. M. Bell, , The Astrophysical Journal, 506, 755 (2002).
6. M. Bell, , The Astrophysical Journal, 567, 801 (2002).
7. M. Bell, , astro-ph/0602242 (2006).
8. M. Bell, , The Astrophysical Journal, 667, L129 (2007).
9. M. Lopez-Corredoira and C. Gutierrez, First Crisis in Cosmology Conference, American Institute of Physics Conference Proceedings 822), Melville, NY, p. 75 (2006).
10. M. Lopez-Corredoira, Apparent Discordant Redshift QSO-Galaxy Associations, arxiv:0901.4534v1, January 28, 2009.
11. W. Tifft, The Nature of the Redshift, https://williamtifft.wordpress.com/paper-1-the-nature-of-the-redshift/ (2013).
12. K Bajan and P. Flin, Redshift Periodicity, Concepts of Physics, Vol. IV, No. 2, pp. 159-201 (2007).
13. H. Ratcliffe, A Review of Anomalous Redshift Data, Second Crisis in Cosmology Conference, CCC-2, The Astronomical Society of the Pacific Conference Series, Vol. 413, pp. 109-115 (2009).
14. C-C. Su, A Proposed Mechanism for the Intrinsic Redshift and its Preferred Values Purportedly Found in Quasars Based on the Local-Ether Theory, arXiv:physics/0608164v1 (August 16, 2006).
15. H. Arp, Intrinsic Redshift, ronia Group Conference, Our Violent Solar System, Portland, Oregon, Sept. 23, 2000, https://www.youtube.com/watch?v=EckBfKPAGNM.
16. C. Steinhardt and M. Elvis, The Quasar Mass-Luminosity Plane - I.A Sub-Eddington Limit for Quasars, Monthly Notices of the Royal Astronomical Society, 402, pp. 2637-2648 (2010).
17. Wikipedia, Gravitational redshift, https://en.wikipedia.org/wiki/Gravitational-redshift.
18. R. Freitas, Jr., , Chapter 4.3 - The Milky Way Galaxy, 2008 (http://www.xenology.info/Zeno/4.3htm).
19. www.Xuru.org, Regression Tools, http://www.xuru.org/rt/TOC.asp.

Plausibility of Earth Once Having a Thick Atmosphere - Examining the Rate of Impact Cratering

Raymond HV Gallucci, PhD, PE

8956 Amelung St., Frederick, MD 21704, email=gallucci@localnet.com

Theories abound as to how dinosaurs and other prehistoric creatures could have grown to such immense sizes, inconsistent with the spectrum of sizes for today's creatures and Earth's living conditions. Some focus directly on changes in the governing physics of the universe, such as a different gravitational constant. Some postulate that, rather than this difference, the earlier Earth experienced lower gravity due to differences in its size and mass. The majority focus on biological and aerodynamical anomalies that may have prevailed to explain these gargantuan sizes. This paper focuses on the latter group, offering an independent means by which to test the hypothesis that a (much) thicker atmosphere provided the buoyancy needed by these creatures to exist on land. This means is astronomical, an examination of possible differences in the rate of impact cratering on Earth due to atmospheric differences. With the Earth's atmosphere allegedly experiencing eras of much greater thickness than current, and alternating between these "thick" and "thin" atmospheric eras, it is postulated that, in addition to the biological and aerodynamical anomalies, a difference in the cratering rate from meteor impacts on Earth should be evident. Thicker atmosphere would "burn up" more meteors, reducing the cratering rate when compared to that during thinner atmospheric eras. This paper explores this, using the cratering rate from meteor impacts on the Moon as a "control" since it has no atmosphere to attenuate meteors but also is in Earth's orbital vicinity and should have experienced a nearly equivalent rate of meteor influx per unit surface area.

Keywords: Earth, Moon, Atmosphere, Volcanism, Carbon Dioxide, Dinosaurs, Meteors, Impact Cratering

A. Introduction

Some dinosaurs (and other prehistoric "leviathans") were inexplicably large, especially in light of today's spectrum of creature sizes. Various theories to "explain" how they could have functioned given such sizes have been postulated. Some focus on postulates that the gravitational constant was lower, such that Earth's gravity would have been lower, or a varying size of the Earth may explain the paradox. Others pursue biological arguments, with connections to aerodynamics, for an explanation. We will not consider the first set, but rather focus on the second as being the more plausible. After reviewing the arguments for the biological/aerodynamical postulates, we examine an independent means of ascertaining the plausibility of these, both of which contend that Earth had a much thicker atmosphere in the past. For that independent means, we select an astronomical approach, namely examination of possible differences in the cratering rates due to meteor impacts on the Earth during "thicker" and "thinner" atmosphere eras, representing eras of greater and lesser attenuation ("burn up") of incoming meteors, thereby affecting the cratering rate per unit surface area on Earth relative to what has been experienced on the geologically and climatologically dead Moon. Since the Moon is in the same orbital neighborhood as the Earth, it should have experienced the same meteor influx per unit surface area over the same eras.

Much of the material in Section 2, especially regarding dinosaur physiology, is provided only as background to the thick atmosphere theories, i.e., this material is not necessarily used in the analysis for cratering rates due to meteor impacts. The reader interested only in the latter may skip to the last paragraph in Section 2.

B. Two Prominent Theories for Thick Earth Atmosphere

Two prominent theories supporting the proposition that Earth has previously experienced (much) thicker atmospheric conditions are examined. Both focus on biological and aerodynamic arguments regarding dinosaur and other prehistoric creatures having sizes incongruously large when viewed in terms of how they could possibly exist today.

B.1. Levenspiel, Fitzgerald and Pettit

In "Earth's Atmosphere before the Age of Dinosaurs," Levenspiel, Fitzgerald and Pettit state: [1]

... [T]he giant flying creatures of the dinosaur age could only fly if the atmospheric pressure was much higher than it is now: at least 3.7-5.0 bar. If this is so, it raises several interesting questions. For example, how did the atmosphere get to that pressure 100-65 million years ago (Mya)? What was the pressure before that? And how did it drop down to today's 1 bar? Although we have no definite answers to these questions, let us put forth reasonable possible explanations.

What was the air pressure for the 97 percent of Earth's life before the age of dinosaurs? We have three possible

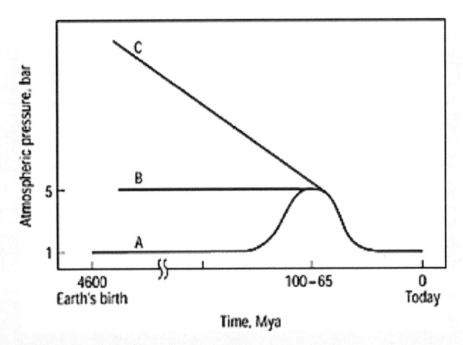

Figure 1. Three possible alternatives for the atmospheric pressure early in Earth's lifetime, *given that it was at ~5 bar, ~100 Mya.*

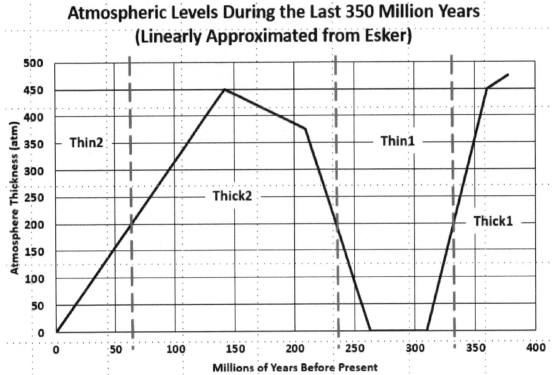

Figure 2. Atmospheric Levels during the Last 350 Million Years with Assumed Transition Times

alternatives, as shown in Figure 1: [3] *(1) The pressure could have been at 1 bar throughout Earth's earlier life, risen to 4-5 bar approximately 100 Mya (just at the time when the giant fliers needed it), and then returned to 1 bar (curve A). (2) The pressure could have been approximately 4-5 bar from Earth's beginning, 4600 Mya; and approximately 65 Mya, it could have begun to come down to today's 1 bar (curve B). (3) The atmosphere could have started at higher pressure and then decreased continuously through Earth's life to approximately 4-5 bar approximately 100 Mya and down to 1 bar today (curve C). The third alternative seems to be the most reasonable ... Geologists believe that most of the carbon on the young, hot Earth, >4000 Mya, was in the form of gaseous carbon dioxide, carbon monoxide, and methane. With time, the CO and CH_4 reacted with oxide minerals and were transformed into CO_2. These reactions did not change the total amount of carbon in the atmosphere.*

Our sister planet and nearest neighbor, Venus, has an atmosphere of 90 bar pressure, consisting of 96 percent CO_2. Why should Earth be so different? ... [W]hy did Venus's atmosphere remain at 90 bar while Earth's decreased to a few bar during the age of dinosaurs and then declined to the 1 bar it is today? What happened to Earth's CO_2 and by what mechanism did it virtually disappear? ... Being thinner, Earth's crust was fragile and broke up under the action of the mantle's convective forces. In contrast, Venus's thicker crust remained rigid and did not permit the mechanisms that removed the CO_2 from its bound state. In addition, because Venus is closer to the Sun and hotter than Earth, free liquid water cannot exist on it, whereas Earth has giant oceans that cover two-thirds of the planet. The oceans played an important secondary role in removing CO_2 from the atmosphere ...

Today, vast deposits of sedimentary carbonate rocks are found on land and on ocean bottoms, >1,000,000 km^3 throughout Earth's crust. Above the continents, the CO_2 was taken up by rainwater and by groundwater. This CO_2-rich water reacted with rocks to form bicarbonates, followed by transport to the ocean and precipitation as calcium and magnesium carbonates. In the ocean, dissolved CO_2 combined with the calcium hydroxide to form deposits of chalk, or it was taken up by coral, mollusks, and other living creatures to form giant reefs. A study of the distribution through time of these deposits gives us clues to the history of CO_2 in the atmosphere ...

With time, the concentration of CO_2 steadily decreased, primarily because of the formation and deposition of limestone and other carbonaceous materials. CO_2 was also lost by photosynthesis followed by the deposition of carbonaceous substances such as coal, petroleum, peat, oil

shale, and tar sands; however, this loss was quite minor. Calculations show that the deposit of what are now considered fuel reserves lowered the atmospheric CO_2 by «1 bar. At the same time, the concentration of oxygen slowly rose. These two changes, the decrease in CO_2 and the rise in oxygen, thinned the forests and the dead material began to be oxidized more rapidly, so that dense layers of dead organics were no longer deposited. Evidence of this change in atmospheric conditions is that we cannot find any massive coal deposits younger than 65 million years. Animal life found this changed atmosphere to its liking, so mammals and dinosaurs flourished, first as very small creatures but then increasing in size as a result of evolutionary competition. This led to the giant flying creatures close to the end of the dinosaur age. It could be that these creatures died out as the total pressure of the atmosphere dropped below their sustainable level ...

If we assume that Earth's early atmosphere was very different, both in composition (mainly CO_2) and total pressure, that would answer some puzzling questions from a variety of disciplines. (1) How did the flying creatures from the age of dinosaurs have enough energy to fly when physiology, biology, and aeronautics say that this was impossible? (2) How could life have developed on Earth when astronomy says that Earth was too cold to sustain life? (3) If Earth's atmosphere had stayed at approximately 1 bar throughout its history, where did the equivalent of 50-70 bar of CO_2 in limestone and other carbonates on Earth's surface come from? This picture of high CO_2 concentration and high pressure in the past also explains why most massive coal seams are older than 65 million years and why most limestone caves are younger than 100 million years. Although we do not know the values for the atmospheric pressure in those early times, and although each of the arguments in this paper only leads to suggestions, when taken together, the evidence from these various sources leads to the same conclusion: The atmospheric pressure was higher in the past than it is today and consisted primarily of CO_2. This hypothesis presents a picture of our evolving planet that should be examined and that could have interesting consequences.

B.2. Esker

In a subsequent, more comprehensive look at this topic, "Scientific Theory Solving the Dinosaur Paradox and Numerous Other Paradoxes Regarding Earth's Evolution," Esker states: [2]

... [T]he large dinosaurs and pterosaurs of the Mesozoic era present a scientific paradox. Four areas of scientific incongruities regarding these animals' large size are identified: (1) insufficient muscle strength, (2) insufficient bone strength, (3) unacceptably high blood pressure within the tallest dinosaurs, and (4) the paradox of pterosaurs having grossly insufficient power to fly in atmospheric conditions similar to the present ... [T]he development of airplanes has always been more of an art than a science. The absence of a theoretical understanding of flight becomes most apparent when the paleontologists make their foolish

---

[3] Figure 1, and the review of the thicker atmosphere theory of Levenspiel, Fitzgerald and Pettit, are presented only to show that there are multiple analysts presenting theories of prehistorically thicker atmospheres. It is not used in the subsequent analysis, which focuses solely on Esker's thicker atmosphere theory.

attempts trying to explain how the giant pterosaurs flew. Common sense tells everyone that a reptile the size of a horse should not be capable of flight, but until now there has not been a theoretical understanding of flight enabling us to scientifically clarify what is wrong with the paleontologists' claim that there is nothing odd about gigantic flying reptiles ... The Thick Atmosphere Solution's ability to solve the dinosaur paradox qualifies it as being a strong hypothesis, but with additional evidence it can be shown that the Thick Atmosphere Solution is actually a new scientific theory ... [T]he Thick Atmosphere Theory solves the long-standing paleoclimatologist puzzle of how the Mesozoic era Earth had the same pleasant climate over its entire surface ...

Just as the largest animals have the lowest relative bone strength, it is also true that the largest animals have the lowest relative muscle strength. Absolute strength can be defined as how much weight an animal can lift regardless of the animal's own weight, and clearly the larger animals have greater absolute strength than the smaller animals. But when we look at relative strength, the lifting ability of an animal relative to its own weight, it is the smallest animals that have the greatest relative strength ... For most physically fit human beings we have more than enough relative strength so that getting out of bed in the morning is not outside our physical capacity. But the larger animals that have lower relative strength lifting their body off the ground can be a serious issue. Large farm animals such as cattle or horses exert all the strength that they have when they pick themselves up off the ground. Likewise the large wild animals such as elephants and giraffes need all their strength to perform this task that is not challenging for the smaller animals. As a consequence of these difficulties, it is not surprising that many of these larger animals evolved the behavior of sleeping while standing up. Yet numerous dinosaurs were much larger than these animals. Their greater size would mean that their relative strength would be substantially less than that of the large animals of today. It is not realistic to imagine that the large dinosaurs never fell or otherwise found themselves on the ground throughout their entire lives. If a Jurassic Park was actually created, any sauropod or other large dinosaur would be stuck lying on the ground much like a helpless whale stranded on a beach ...

The buoyancy force is best described by Archimedes' principle that states that when an object is partially or fully submerged in a fluid, an upward buoyancy force lifts up on the submerged object that exactly equals the weight of the fluid displaced. ... [B]uoyancy ... is what gives a lifting force to hot air balloons. The main difference in the buoyancy effect provided by these two fluids [air vs. water] is the amount of fluid volume that needs to be displaced to achieve flotation. For terrestrial vertebrates, it is the net force produced by their weight that often limits their size. But this is not true for species that exist in the water. For the latter species it is not their weight but rather other factors, such as the availability of food that might limit the size of these species. Without the weight limitation some of these aquatic species grow to display gigantism. It is the buoyancy of water that allows the whales, the largest animals of today, to grow so large ... Without this buoyancy to counteract gravity, the poor whale that finds itself stuck on a beach is soon having its bones broken from its own weight. To produce an effective buoyancy force on dinosaurs the Earth's atmosphere would have to be thick enough to have a density comparable to the density of water. By summing the forces acting on a typical dinosaur such as a Brachiosaurus the density of the necessary atmosphere is calculated ... to be $670 \ kg/m^3$. This says that to produce the necessary buoyancy so that the dinosaurs could grow to their exceptional size,[4] the density of the Earth's air near the Earth's surface would need to be 2/3 of the density of water ...

It may be hard to imagine that the Earth's air could be so thick that its density would be comparable to water. Nevertheless, there is no reason why a gas cannot be compressed so much that it has properties similar to that of a liquid, and in fact compressing a gas into a liquid is a common industrial process ... 150 million years ago the Earth's atmospheric pressure near the surface was about 370 atmospheres ... 370 times thicker than what it is today ... [C]onsider the pressure that currently exist at the deepest depths of the oceans. The average ocean depth is 3790 m and at this depth the pressure is 380 atmospheres. So for all practical purposes, the present day pressure at the average depth of the ocean is the same as the pressure at the bottom of the Mesozoic atmosphere. Yet there are numerous species that live at this depth and many more that live much deeper. Extremely high absolute pressure has no ill effect on our present creatures of the deep that have evolved in these environments; likewise, the extremely high pressure of the Mesozoic era had no ill effect on the terrestrial species of the Mesozoic era ... If both the inside and outside of an enclosed container are at the same absolute pressure, no matter what the absolute pressure might be, there will be no net force on the sides of the container ...

Within the Phanerozoic eon [current geologic eon ... during which abundant animal and plant life has existed - 541 million years to the present] we can identify two thick atmosphere eras and two thin atmosphere eras ... Twice during the Carboniferous and the Cretaceous/Paleogene periods, the atmosphere transitioned from being extremely thick to being relatively thin ... With a massive amount of CO_2 being removed from the atmosphere we would expect to see large carbon deposits during these times and indeed that is the case ... [T]he only time that the atmosphere transitioned from being relatively thin to being extremely thick was when the earth was void of most life ... around

---

[4] Esker's discussion makes it clear that the buoyancy provided by a thicker atmosphere benefitted not only flying dinosaurs (pterosaurs) but also those that walked on land.

the time of the P-T [Permian-Triassic] mass extinctions and continuing into the Triassic period ...

Figure 2 is a linearized approximation of Esker's graph of "Atmospheric Levels during the Last 350 Million Years," on which I have arbitrarily drawn transition times between the two Thick and Thin Atmosphere Eras using an arbitrary transition atmosphere of 200 atm. Starting around 350 million years ago with an atmospheric thickness of nearly 500 atm, he presents alternating periods of decreasing and increasing atmospheric pressure up to today's present "Thin" atmosphere, which I have assumed to be "Thick" and "Thin" as shown in my approximation of Esker's figure. This results in two Thin and Thick Eras, as shown. They transition at approximately 340, 230 and 53 million years ago, with the Thick1 Era assumed to begin 2.4 billion years ago, since this is the reported age of the oldest recorded Earth crater, the 16-km Suavjarvi crater in Asia (see Table I at the end).

C. Thick Atmosphere Theory and Earth Cratering Rates

The previous discussions by Levenspiel, et al., and Esker supporting a Thick Atmosphere Theory focus on mainly biological and aerodynamic arguments. After reading these discussions, I seek an independent means by which to examine this theory at least for plausibility, as anything definitive is currently beyond achieving. Reasoning that a thicker atmosphere should "burn up" more incoming meteors than a thinner one, I examine the cratering rate for impacting meteors on the Earth, based on the Earth Impact Database (see Table I at the end).[5] From the Earth Impact Database I compile a list of all Earth craters from meteoric impacts that have been recorded (including some still cited as "unconfirmed" [red italics]). For reasons that will become evident, only craters at least 4 km in size are counted. To the present 163 such craters have been identified, which reduces to 111 if only those at least 10,000 years old are counted (roughly up to the end of the last Ice Age). Note that this affects only the last Esker Era, labelled as Thin2. This somewhat arbitrary truncation results from the preponderance of North American craters of most recent age relative to similar craters worldwide. The intent is to remove possible bias from more extensive crater identification having been performed on our continent.

Before proceeding, it is important to ascertain the time history of what the cratering rate would have been for the Earth in the absence of an atmosphere, its geologic activity, etc. This may be possible by assuming the time history of the Moon's cratering rate would be closely representative, on a per unit area, given its proximity to the Earth. Figure 3 presents an estimate of the lunar cratering rate over the assumed roughly five-billion-year lifespan of the Moon. [3] Corresponding to the four Esker Atmospheric Eras is this figure showing the estimated rate of cratering on the Moon since its alleged birth in terms of the rate per unit surface area (km^2) for craters > 4 km in size. Table II shows the starting and finishing times for each of the Esker Eras, with the corresponding cratering rates at the start and finish of each based on the "constant production rate" curve (dashed). For each Era, the geometric mean (given the logarithmic plot) between the starting and finishing rates is assumed to be characteristic for that Era. For example, for Thick1, the geometric mean is just the square root of the cratering rates at the start and finish, i.e., $\sqrt{(8.5E-5km^{-2})(1.1E-5km^{-2})} = 3.06E-5km^{-2}$. Consistent with the curve, this decreases with time, from approximately $3E-5/km^2$ during the earlier Thick1 Era down to approximately $2E-6/km^2$ for the present Thin2 Era, slightly over a factor of 10. When the time-weighted rates for both Thick and Thin Eras are calculated, we see that the weighted cratering rate for the Thin Eras is about one-quarter of that for the Thick ones.[6] This is expected given the Thick Eras always precede the Thin ones, such that their cratering rates are relatively higher, and the cumulative time periods for the Thick Eras (approximately 2.2 billion years) is over 10 times longer than for the Thin ones (approximately 160 million years).

For each of the Esker Eras, I estimate the cratering rate on Earth (for craters at least 4 km in size, to place on an equivalent basis for comparison with the Moon) as the number of craters identified for that Era divided by the length of the Era and the approximately 29 percent of the surface area of the Earth that is land ($[0.29][4\pi][6371km]^2 = 1.5E+8km^2$). This is evaluated on an annual basis, e.g., for Thick1 to the end of the Ice Age: $\frac{43}{(1.5E+8km^2)(2.4E+9y-3.4E+8y)} = 1.41E-16y^{-1}km^{-2}$.

Then I weight over the two Thick and Thin Eras, as shown.[7] Table III presents two sets of estimates, one where I truncate the counting of Earth craters at the end of the last Ice Age (10,000 years ago) and one without truncation (i.e., counting all craters to present time). This has no effect on the cratering rate for the Thick Eras (4.87E-7 km^{-2}), which is a factor of 59 lower than the corresponding lunar cratering rate (2.85E-5 What is of particular interest is the ratio of the weighted cratering rates (red italics in Table III). When truncated at the end of the Ice Age, the cratering rate during the Thin Eras is reduced by nearly a factor of two relative to that for the Thick Era, somewhat to be expected given the lunar result which showed roughly

---

[5] "List of Impact Craters on Earth," Earth Impact Database (available at https://en.wikipedia.org/wiki/List-of-impact-craters-on-earth).

[6] Weighting over the two Thick and two Thin Atmospheric Eras is accomplished as follows (shown for the Thick Eras - it is analogous for the Thin Eras):
$\frac{(3.06E-5km^{-2})(2.4E+9y-3.4E+8y)+(5.05E-6km^{-2})(2.3E+8y-5.3E+7y)}{2.4E+9y-3.4E+8y+2.3E+8y-5.3E+7y} =$
$2.85E-5km^{-2}$

[7] This weighting is slightly different from that used for the lunar rates, as follows, e.g., for the two Thick Eras: $(1.41E-16y^{-1}km^{-2})(2.4E+9y-3.4E+8y) + (1.10E-15y^{-1}km^{-2})(2.3E+8y-5.3E+7y) = 4.87E-7km^{-2}$. Note that this is the same as combining the two Thick Eras initially: $\frac{43+29}{1.5E+8km^2} = 4.87E-7km^{-2}$.

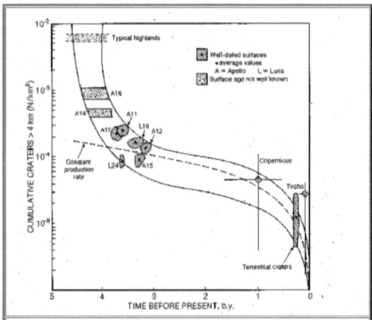

Figure 1. Lunar crater production rates through geologic time as reconstructed from the measurement of crater densities on the lunar surface and from absolute age dating of returned lunar rocks. Firm correlations can only be reconstructed for (1) the well-characterized basalt surfaces (3.8-3.2 Gyr) and (2) the contemporary meteorite flux based on current astronomical observations (t = 0). The ages of Tycho and Copernicus are inferred from indirect evidence. From F. Horz et al. p.84.

Figure 3. Lunar Crater Production Rates through Geologic Time

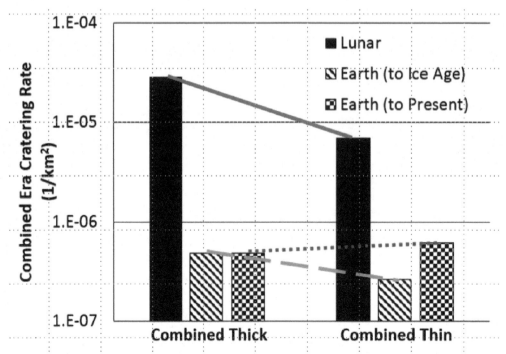

Figure 4. Comparing Trends in Cratering Rates for the Earth and Moon over the Combined Thick and Thin Atmosphere Eras

a factor of four reduction. The fact that the Earth cratering rate during the Thin Eras is reduced by less compared to the Moon rate may be indicative of the effect of atmospheric thickness. That is, the thinner Earth atmosphere allowed more cratering during the Thin Eras than would be expected relative to the cratering rate during the Thick Eras when compared to the ratio for the Moon which is climatically and geologically dead (compare ratios of 0.542 to 0.245 [red italics in Table II]). If the Earth crater counting is not truncated, i.e., counted to present time, this difference is much more pronounced. In fact, the cratering rate during the Thin Eras now is slightly higher than during the Thick Eras, by about one quarter (ratio = 1.26, in red italics). Figure 4 shows this graphically by the three different trend lines (solid red for the Moon; dashed green for the Earth to the Ice Age; and dotted blue for the Earth to Present). The lunar trend line is the steepest downward. That for the Earth to the Ice Age is also downward, but not as steep, while the trend line for the Earth to Present is slightly upward.

The Earth to Present trend is completely different from the lunar, which saw a reduction by about a factor of four rather than this increase by one quarter. This may be indicative even more so of the atmospheric thickness effect, although the caveat previously mentioned about the preponderance of the most recent craters having been identified in North America somewhat tempers it. Nonetheless, even the comparison for truncation at the end of the Ice Age shows a noticeable difference relative to what would be expected for a body without an atmosphere subjected to the same meteor influx, represented by the Moon. Another factor, though likely not as dominant as the potential atmospheric effect, could be a decreasing geologic activity on Earth with time, since the Thick Eras each preceded the Thin Eras. However, given Earth is still quite geologically active, likely not much less so than around two billion years ago, this effect is expected to be dwarfed by the atmospheric thickness difference.

D. Summary

Given all the assumptions and approximations employed, and the fidelity of cratering data for both the Earth and Moon, no definitive conclusion can be drawn. However, at least this cratering rate analysis does not contradict the postulate that Earth's atmosphere has varied substantially in thickness as per Esker and offers an independent means to test the hypothesis to supplement the more biological and aerodynamic ones that both he and Levenspiel, et al., provide. During the Thick Atmosphere Era, meteor impact on the Earth would be decreased by a relatively greater degree vs. the Thin Atmosphere Era when compared to what would be expected on a per unit surface area for the geologically and climatologically dead Moon. Given two meteors of comparable size, speed and entry angle, the one hitting the thick atmosphere would be less likely to survive to impact than the one hitting the thin atmosphere on Earth.

This has been demonstrated by the analysis presented here, which considers two scenarios, varying with the truncation time for the cratering rates. The first truncates at the end of the Ice Age; the second does not truncate, but extends to the present.

For the first scenario, the ratio of lunar cratering rate between the Thin and Thick Eras (as defined for Earth) is 0.245, indicating that the Moon, without an atmosphere, experienced roughly four times the cratering rate during the Thick Eras vs. the Thin Eras ($1/0.245 \approx 4$). For truncation at the end of the Ice Age, the corresponding ratio for the Earth during these same Eras is 0.542, slightly more than twice as high ($1/0.542 \approx 2$). This indicates that, on Earth, the cratering rate during the Thick Eras was slightly less than twice that during the Thin Eras. Therefore, the effect of Earth's Thicker vs. Thinner Atmosphere Eras was to reduce the cratering rate more during the Thick Eras than the Thin Eras relative to what the reduction would have been without an atmosphere, as evidenced by the Earth's higher Thin vs. Thick ratio relative to that for the Moon (0.542 vs. 0.245). That is, instead of exhibiting a Thick Era cratering rate four times as high as that for the Thin Era, as per the Moon without an atmosphere, the Earth exhibited a rate only twice as high during the Thick vs. Thin Era. This ratio difference supports the conjecture that thicker atmosphere reduces cratering rate.

For the second scenario, this tendency is even more pronounced when the cratering rate is not truncated at the end of the Ice Age but extended to the present. Now the ratio between the Thin and Thick Eras on Earth is 1.26, indicating a Thin Era cratering rate 26 percent higher than during the Thick Era. Contrasting against the Moon's ratio of 0.245, one sees a pronounced decrease during the Thick Era relative to the Thin Era on Earth vs. what would have been experienced without an atmosphere, as evidenced by the Moon. Again, this ratio difference supports the conjecture that a thicker atmosphere reduces cratering rate, aligning with Esker's conjecture, which is based on biological/aerodynamical arguments.

REFERENCES

1. O. Levenspiel, T. Fitzgerald and D. Pettit, Earth's Atmosphere Before the Age of Dinosaurs, Chemical Innovation, Vol. 30, No. 12, pp. 50-55, December 2000 (available at http://pubs.acs.org/subscribe/archive/ci/30/i12/html/12learn.html).
2. D. Esker, Scientific Theory Solving the Dinosaur Paradox and Numerous Other Paradoxes Regarding Earth's Evolution, http://www.dinosaurtheory.com/index.html.
3. Muller, Space Lunar Crater Production Rates through Geologic Time, http://muller.lbl.gov/pages/crateringrates.htm.

Table I. Complete List of Identified Earth Craters

#	Name/Location	Continent	Size (km)	Age (yr)
1	Suavjärvi	Asia	16	2.4E+09
2	Vredefort	Africa	300	2.0E+09
3	Yarrabubba	Australia	30	2.0E+09
4	Dhala	Asia	11	1.9E+09
5	Keurusselkä	Europe	30	1.8E+09
6	Paasselkä	Europe	10	1.8E+09
7	Shoemaker (was Teague)	Australia	30	1.5E+09
8	Matt Wilson	Australia	7.5	1.4E+09
9	Ullapool	Europe	50	1.2E+09
10	Amelia Creek	Australia	20	1.1E+09
11	Lumparn	Europe	9	1.0E+09
12	Suvasvesi North	Europe	4	1.0E+09
13	Jänisjärvi	Asia	14	7.0E+08
14	Strangways	Australia	25	6.5E+08
15	Söderfjärden	Europe	6.6	6.0E+08
16	Acraman	Australia	90	5.9E+08
17	Luizi	Africa	17	5.8E+08
18	Spider	Australia	13	5.7E+08
19	Sääksjärvi	Europe	6	5.6E+08
20	Kelly West	Australia	10	5.5E+08
21	Massive Australian Precambrian/ Cambrian Impact Structure, MAPCIS	Australia	1250	5.5E+08
22	Foelsche	Australia	6	5.5E+08
23	Lawn Hill	Australia	18	5.2E+08
24	Glikson	Australia	19	5.1E+08
25	Wilkes Land	Antarctica	485	5.0E+08
26	Gardnos	Europe	5	5.0E+08
27	Mizarai	Europe	5	5.0E+08
28	Neugrund	Europe	8	4.7E+08
29	Decorah crater	North America	5.6	4.7E+08
30	Lockne	Europe	7.5	4.6E+08
31	Kärdla	Europe	4	4.6E+08
32	Ishim	Asia	350	4.5E+08
33	Tokrauskaya	Asia	220	4.5E+08
34	Agatha Knob	North America	43	4.3E+08
35	Kaluga	Asia	15	3.8E+08
36	Ilyinets	Europe	8.5	3.8E+08
37	Siljan	Europe	52	3.8E+08
38	Panther Mountain	North America	10	3.8E+08
39	Alamo bolide impact	North America	assumed > 4 km given age	3.7E+08
40	Woodleigh	Australia	90	3.6E+08
41	Piccaninny	Australia	?	3.6E+08
42	Gweni-Fada	Africa	14	3.5E+08
43	Aorounga	Africa	12.6	3.5E+08
44	East Warburton Basin	Australia	200	3.3E+08
45	West Warburton Basin	Australia	200	3.3E+08
46	Wanbleazu-Osceola	North America	17.5	3.3E+08
47	Unnamed impact	Australia	130	3.0E+08
48	Unnamed impact	Australia	120	3.0E+08
49	Serra da Cangalha	South America	12	3.0E+08
50	Dobele	Europe	4.5	2.9E+08
51	Ternovka	Europe	11	2.8E+08
52	Kursk	Asia	6	2.5E+08
53	Bedout	Australia	200	2.5E+08
54	Araguainha	South America	40	2.4E+08
55	Saqqar	Asia	34	2.4E+08
56	Saqqar*	Asia	34	2.4E+08
57	Rochechouart	Europe	23	2.1E+08
58	Gusev	Europe	30	2.0E+08
59	Riachão Ring	South America	4.5	2.0E+08
60	Obolon	Europe	20	1.7E+08
61	Puchezh-Katunki	Asia	80	1.7E+08
62	Vepriai	Europe	8	1.6E+08
63	Morokweng	Africa	70	1.5E+08
64	Gosses Bluff	Australia	22	1.4E+08
65	Mjølnir	Europe	40	1.4E+08
66	Tookoonooka	Australia	55	1.3E+08
67	Mien	Europe	9	1.2E+08
68	Oasis	Africa	18	1.2E+08
69	Mount Toondina	Australia	4	1.1E+08
70	Kebira	Africa	31	1.0E+08
71	Dellen	Europe	19	8.9E+07
72	Praia Grande	South America	20	8.4E+07
73	Lappajärvi	Europe	23	7.3E+07
74	Kara	Asia	65	7.0E+07
75	Tin Bider	Africa	6	7.0E+07
76	Chukcha	Asia	6	7.0E+07
77	Bow City	North America	8	7.0E+07
78	Vargeão Dome	South America	12	7.0E+07
79	Boltysh	Europe	24	6.5E+07
80	Shiva	Asia	600	6.5E+07
81	Vista Alegre	South America	9.5	6.5E+07
82	Chicxulub	North America	170	6.5E+07
83	Wembo-Nyama ring structure	Africa	41	6.0E+07
84	Connolly Basin	Australia	9	6.0E+07
85	Silverpit	Europe	20	6.0E+07
86	Goat Paddock	Australia	5	5.0E+07
87	Kamensk	Asia	25	4.9E+07
88	Jabal Waqf es Suwwan	Asia	5.5	4.7E+07
89	Ragozinka	Asia	9	4.6E+07
90	Chiyli	Asia	5.5	4.6E+07
91	Victoria Island structure	North America	5.5	4.3E+07
92	Logoisk	Europe	15	4.2E+07
93	Logancha	Asia	20	4.0E+07
94	Beyenchime-Salaatin	Asia	8	4.0E+07
95	Popigai	Asia	100	3.6E+07
96	Flaxman	Australia	10	3.5E+07
97	Crawford	Australia	8.5	3.5E+07
98	Tons Canyon	North America	22	3.5E+07
99	Vichada Structure	South America	50	3.0E+07
100	Ross	Antarctica	550	2.8E+07
101	Nördlinger Ries	Europe	25	1.5E+07
102	Karakul	Asia	52	5.0E+06
103	Karla	Asia	10	5.0E+06
104	Bigach	Asia	8	5.0E+06
105	El'gygytgyn	Asia	18	3.5E+06
106	Corossol	North America	4	2.6E+06
107	Bosumtwi	Africa	10.5	1.1E+06
108	Pantasma	North America	10	1.0E+06
109	Zhamanshin	Asia	14	9.0E+05
110	Rio Cuarto	South America	4.5	1.0E+05
111	Iturralde	South America	8	2.1E-04
112	Zeralia West	Europe	250	7.0E-03
113	Zeralia East	Europe	150	7.0E-03
114	Sudbury	North America	250	1.9E+03
115	Steinheim	Europe	127.5	1.7E+06
116	Santa Fe	North America	9.5	1.2E+03
117	Beaverhead	North America	60	6.0E+02
118	Rock Elm	North America	6	5.1E+02
119	Presquile	North America	24	5.0E+02

#	Name/Location	Continent	Size (km)	Age (yr)
120	Glover Bluff	North America	8	5.0E+02
121	Ames	North America	16	4.7E+02
122	Slate Islands	North America	30	4.5E+02
123	Calvin	North America	8.5	4.5E+02
124	Pilot	North America	6	4.5E+02
125	Couture	North America	8	4.3E+02
126	Glasford	North America	4	4.3E+02
127	Nicholson	North America	12.5	4.0E+02
128	La Moinerie	North America	8	4.0E+02
129	Elbow	North America	8	4.0E+02
130	Charlevoix	North America	54	3.4E+02
131	Serpent Mound	North America	8	3.2E+02
132	Crooked Creek	North America	7	3.2E+02
133	Decaturville	North America	6	3.0E+02
134	Middlesboro	North America	6	3.0E+02
135	Île Rouleau	North America	4	3.0E+02
136	Lac à l'Eau Claire Ouest	North America	36	2.9E+02
137	Lac à l'Eau Claire Est	North America	26	2.9E+02
138	Des Plaines	North America	8	2.8E+02
139	Gow	North America	4	2.5E+02
140	Tunnunik	North America	25	2.4E+02
141	Saint Martin	North America	40	2.2E+02
142	Manicouagan	North America	100	2.1E+02
143	Wells Creek	North America	12	2.0E+02
144	Red Wing	North America	9	2.0E+02
145	Cloud Creek	North America	7	1.9E+02
146	Upheaval Dome	North America	10	1.7E+02
147	Carswell	North America	39	1.2E+02
148	Sierra Madera	North America	13	1.0E+02
149	Deep Bay	North America	13	9.9E+01
150	Kentland	North America	13	9.7E+01
151	Avak	North America	12	9.5E+01
152	Steen River	North America	25	9.1E+01
153	Wetumpka	North America	7.6	8.3E+01
154	Santa Marta	South America	10	8.3E+01
155	Maple Creek	North America	6	7.5E+01
156	Manson	North America	35	7.4E+01
157	Eagle Butte	North America	10	6.5E+01

#	Name/Location	Continent	Size (km)	Age (yr)
158	Marquez	North America	12.7	5.8E+01
159	Montagnais	North America	45	5.1E+01
160	Haughton	North America	23	3.9E+01
161	Wanapitei	North America	7.5	3.7E+01
162	Mistastin	North America	28	3.6E+01
163	Chesapeake Bay	North America	90	3.6E+01
164	*Bowers*	*Antarctica*	*100*	*Unknown*
165	*Snows Island*	*North America*	*11*	*Unknown*
166	*Cerro Jarau*	*South America*	*10*	*Unknown*
167	Brent	North America	3.8	3.1E+08
168	Suvasvesi South	Europe	3.8	2.5E+08
169	Steinheim	Europe	3.8	1.5E+07
170	Flynn Creek	North America	3.8	3.6E+02
171	Colônia	South America	3.6	2.1E+01
172	Kgagodi	Africa	3.5	1.8E+08
173	Zeleny Gai	Europe	3.5	8.0E+07
174	Ouarkziz	Africa	3.5	7.0E+07
175	Pingualuit	North America	3.44	1.4E+00
176	Zapadnaya	Europe	3.2	1.7E+08
177	Newporte	North America	3.2	5.0E+02
178	Goyder	Australia	3	1.4E+09
179	Iso-Naakkima	Europe	3	1.0E+09
180	Granby	Europe	3	4.7E+08
181	Gusev	Asia	3	4.9E+07
182	Agoudal	Africa	3	1.1E+05

#	Name/Location	Continent	Size (km)	Age (yr)
183	*Ramgarh*	*Asia*	*3*	*Unknown*
184	*Gatun structure*	*North America*	*2.85*	*2.0E+07*
185	*Mahas*	*Africa*	*2.85*	*Unknown*
186	Shunak	Asia	2.8	4.5E+07
187	Rotmistrovka	Europe	2.7	1.2E+08
188	Ritland crater	Europe	2.7	5.2E+02
189	Mishina Gora	Asia	2.5	3.0E+08
190	Roter Kamm	Africa	2.5	3.7E+06
191	Viewfield	North America	2.5	1.9E+02
192	West Hawk	North America	2.44	3.5E+02
193	Holleford	North America	2.35	5.5E+02
194	Tvären	Europe	2	4.6E+08
195	BP Structure	Africa	2	1.2E+08
196	*Brushy Creek Feature*	*North America*	*2*	*2.1E+04*
197	Tenoumer	Africa	1.9	2.1E+04
198	Lonar	Asia	1.83	5.2E+04
199	Xiuyan crater	Asia	1.8	5.0E+04
200	Talemzane	Africa	1.75	3.0E+06
201	Liverpool	Australia	1.6	7.7E+08
202	Saarijärvi	Europe	1.5	6.0E+08
203	Karikkoselkä	Europe	1.4	2.3E+08
204	Tabun-Khara-Obo	Asia	1.3	1.5E+08
205	Hummeln structure	Europe	1.2	4.6E+08
206	*Darwin Crater*	*Australia*	*1.2*	*8.0E+05*
207	Barringer	North America	1.19	4.9E-02
208	Tswaing (was Pretoria Saltpan)	Africa	1.13	2.2E+05
209	Malingen	Europe	1	4.6E+08
210	Wolfe Creek	Australia	0.87	3.0E+05
211	*Temimichat*	*Africa*	*0.75*	*Unknown*
212	Kalkkop	Africa	0.64	2.5E+05
213	*Chelo*	*Asia*	*0.5*	*1.0E+02*
214	Monturaqui	South America	0.46	1.0E+06
215	Amguid	Africa	0.45	1.0E+05
216	Aouelloul	Africa	0.39	3.0E+06
217	Macha	Asia	0.3	7.0E+03
218	*Hickman Crater*	*Australia*	*0.27*	*3.2E+04*

#	Name/Location	Continent	Size (km)	Age (yr)
219	Boxhole	Australia	0.17	5.4E+03
220	Odessa	North America	0.168	5.0E-02
221	Henbury	Australia	0.16	4.2E+03
222	*Patomskiy*	*Asia*	*0.16*	*3.0E+02*
223	Wabar	Asia	0.116	1.5E+02
224	Kaali	Europe	0.11	4.0E+03
225	Morasko	Europe	0.1	1.0E+04
226	Veevers	Australia	0.08	2.0E+04
227	Ilumetsa	Europe	0.08	6.6E+03
228	Sobolev	Asia	0.053	1.0E+03
229	Campo del Cielo	South America	0.05	4.0E+03
230	Kamil	Africa	0.045	2.0E+03
231	Whitecourt	North America	0.04	1.1E-03
232	Sikhote-Alin	Asia	0.026	7.0E+01
233	Dalgaranga	Australia	0.02	3.0E+04
234	Haviland	North America	0.015	1.0E+03
235	Carancas	South America	0.0135	7.0E-06

Italicized entries *(red)* indicate "unconfirmed" craters. For size and age, if listing indicates finite range, midpoint value is assumed (geometric if range is order of magnitude or more); if open-ended range (i.e., > x or < x), minimum or maximum cited value (x) is assumed. Unknown entries excluded except for Alamo Bolide Impact which, given age, is assumed originally > 4km in size to be detectable today.

Plausibility of Shaw's "Aether Concept of Gravity"

Raymond HV Gallucci, PhD, PE

8956 Amelung St., Frederick, MD 21704, email=gallucci@localnet.com

Shaw has proposed an aether explanation for gravity, publishing several papers over the current decade (see http://www.duncanshaw.ca/). These have evolved into his "Aether Concept of Gravity," by which inflowing aether into cosmic bodies produces an accelerating "ram force" that manifests as the "attractive" gravitational force without the need to postulate "action at a distance." While examination of the full theory is beyond the scope of this paper, it is feasible to examine three of the key aspects which lend themselves to modeling in the form of mathematical constructs. While no attempt is made to explain the physics behind Shaw's theory, an investigation into its plausibility, at least from a mathematical perspective, is undertaken and appears to support at least this level of plausibility.

Keywords: Aether, Gravity, "Ram Pressure," Bernoulli, Solar System

A. Introduction

In "Aether Concept of Gravity," Shaw has proposed a model where gravity is a pushing, not pulling (attractive) force. He chooses the simple analogy of a vacuum cleaner which, by creating lower air pressure inside, causes air from the outside, at higher pressure, to push itself "inward" toward the artificially lowered pressure region. Rather than "sucking in air," a vacuum cleaner allows air to "push itself inward." Shaw's gravity concept postulates "that the inflow is caused by the pressure of 'aether' in cosmic bodies being lower that the pressure of aether in space. Pressure in cosmic bodies is lowered by the emission of aether from cosmic bodies. The resulting pressure differential causes aether in space to flow toward the partial vacuum - much like the emission of air from a household vacuum cleaner creates a partial vacuum into which surrounding air flows. Pressure in cosmic bodies is also lowered by the acceleration of inflowing aether from space to the relatively narrow targets of cosmic bodies. This is an application of Bernoulli's principle pursuant to which the pressure of a fluid that is flowing in a narrowing channel reduces as the speed of fluid accelerates." [1]

With all this aether flowing into a cosmic body, Shaw must address whether there is an outflow to maintain equilibrium and prevent runaway heating of the body. "Outflow is essential because: (1) it replenishes the supply of aether in space required for continuous inflow; and (2) it provides a mechanism to dissipate into space the heat that is transferred to cosmic bodies by the ram force of inflowing aether ... [H]eat generated by the ram force of inflow causes inflowing condensed aether to vaporize or evaporate into its gaseous state and flow back into space by way of diffusion and convection. When gaseous aether is back in space, it condenses into droplets of liquid aether ... [T]hey gradually come into contact with other aether cells and with droplets of condensed aether ... [T]he supply of condensed aether in space is replenished." [1]

There are three concepts that lend themselves to constructing mathematical models within Shaw's theory: (1) Accelerating rate of radial inflow of aether as it approaches a cosmic body (assumed spherical for convenience); (2) Creation of a pressure differential between inflowing and outflowing aether at the surface of the cosmic body, such that the inflow pressure is greater and represents "attractive" gravity; and (3) Dependence of inflow vs. outflow pressure differential on mass of the cosmic body, such that two bodies of equal size and shape experience different "gravities" depending upon their masses (densities). The following proposes a mathematical construct for each of these. These are purely mathematical exercises, not intending to address the physics that may be involved in the phenomena, in an attempt to at least gauge whether the concepts are plausible.

B. Radially Accelerating Aether Inflow

Shaw envisions this inward flow of aether to be dominated by the most massive member of our solar system, namely the Sun, as illustrated in Figure 1, overwhelming that of any planet except in the immediate vicinity of the planet. Envisioning this in three dimensions, where the Sun and planets are essentially spheres, the rate of aether "inflowing" from an infinitesimal shell of radius "d," where d = distance from planet center to Sun center, and thickness "Δd" over a time increment "Δt" is $4\pi d^2 \frac{\Delta d}{\Delta t}$, i.e., $4\pi d^2 v$, where $v = \frac{\Delta d}{\Delta t}$ can be viewed as the radially inward velocity of the aether at planetary distance d. If we define the rate of aether inflow (velocity) at the Sun's surface to be 1 and the inflow rates at the planet and Sun, since aether is not building up anywhere in the Solar System, we obtain $4\pi R^2(1) = 4\pi d^2 v(1) \rightarrow v = (\frac{R}{d})^2$ where "R" = radius of the Sun. Since R « d, the velocity of inflowing aether at the planet will be much less than that at the Sun, decreasing as one proceeds outward from the Sun.

The force of gravity generated by this inflowing aether results from the momentum imparted on the planet by the dominant inflowing aether due to the Sun, which is proportional to the amount of aether "mass" impinging on the cross-sectional area perpendicular to the radially inward flow toward the Sun. If the planet has radius "r," the mass is proportional to πr^2. Thus, the gravitational push inward due to the inflowing aether on the planet of radius "r" at distance "d" from the Sun is proportional to $vr^2 = (\frac{rR}{d})^2$, dropping the constant terms since we will be dealing with ratios among the planets.

The "impact" effect of the aether particles likely will differ significantly when impinging on a "solid" surface, such as Earth's, vs. a "gaseous" one, such as Jupiter's. Therefore, one might consider comparing the effects between the "solid" (denser) four inner planets and the four "gas giants" (less dense) to be somewhat of an "apples" to "oranges" comparison. To try to compensate somewhat for this possibility, consider treating the four gas giants as "solid" planets with a density equal to the average of those for the four inner planets ($\rho_{av} = 5.030E + 12kg/km^3$) and equivalent radii ($r_{eq}$) based on their respective masses (m), i.e., , where "ρ" and "r" are the planet's actual density and radius. This results in the equivalent radii and densities shown in Table 1 for the four gas giants.

When scaled to the Sun's gravitational force on Earth equal to unity, the ratios for each planet of the aether vs. Newton gravitational forces calculated in Table 1 are shown in Figure 2. As can be seen, except for, at most, roughly an order of magnitude difference for the gas giants and Pluto, the agreement is quite good, especially with respect to the trend.

C. Aether Pressure Differential

Shaw's inflowing, condensed aether can be viewed as an aether "capsule," shown as a tetrahedral package of four aether particles, each a sphere of unit radius, inflowing into a sphere in Figure 3. The tetrahedron represents the simplest three-dimensionally symmetric array of equal-sized spheres. As the aether capsule flows "into" a large spherical body, it displaces four individual aether particles in a "straight" line. This is analogous to Shaw''s concept of the ram force of inflow causing the inflowing capsule to vaporize or evaporate into its constituent particles. The inflowing aether tetrahedron has an equivalent spherical volume of $4\frac{4\pi}{3}(1)^3 = 16.76$, which corresponds to a sphere of equivalent radius = $(\frac{16.76}{\frac{4\pi}{3}})^{1/3} = 1.587$ (relative to unit particle radius), shown in dashed red in Figure 3. The volume of the four "expelled" aether particles is assumed to correspond to a cylinder of equivalent length = $\frac{16.76}{\pi(1)^2} = 5.333$ that proceeds outward in a straight line, the average distance being half the length, or 2.667.

Because the inflowing aether is in the form of a tetrahedral capsule, with equivalent spherical radius = 1.587, its "depth" of penetration is less than the equivalent average distance traveled by the expelled individual aether particles, 2.667. Radially, this corresponds to the expelled particles traveling at $\frac{2.667}{1.587} = 1.680$ times the speed of the inflowing capsule. By Bernoulli's equation (ignoring

gravity), a positive pressure differential results between the inflowing and expelling aether, derived as follows:
$$P_{in} + \frac{\rho v_{in}^2}{2} = P_{out} + \frac{\rho v_{out}^2}{2} \rightarrow P_{in} - P_{out} = \frac{\rho}{2}(v_{out}^2 - v_{in}^2) > 0,$$
since $v_{out} > v_{in}$.

Given neither the density of aether nor the inflow or outflow radial speed is known, one can only make some very crude estimates of what this pressure differential might be. To accomplish this, the following very subjective assumptions are made.

(1) As per Reference [5], "[i]n all phases, the interstellar medium [ISM] is extremely tenuous by terrestrial standards. In cool, dense regions of the ISM, matter is primarily in molecular form, and reaches number densities of 10^6 molecules per cm^3 ... In hot, diffuse regions of the ISM, matter is primarily ionized, and the density may be as low as 10^4 ions per cm^3." The geometric mean of this range of about 10 orders of magnitude would be approximately $10/cm^3$. Assuming this to consist of individual hydrogen atoms (separated protons [1.67E-27 kg mass] and electrons [9.11E-31 kg mass] in equal numbers if ionized), the ISM density would be approximately $\frac{(10)(1.67E-27kg+9.11E-31kg)}{(1cm^3)(0.01m/cm)^3} = 1.67E - 20kg/m^3$.

(2) Shaw assumes "... that the spacecraft [returning from the moon] are being carried by aether that is flowing toward the Earth ... [I]t follows that the speeds of the spacecraft en route to the Earth should be essentially the same as the velocities of the inflowing aether. Thus, for example, the velocity of the aether at the point where the vehicles reach the Earth's atmosphere must be about 11 km/s [... where they start to encounter the braking effect of the Earth's atmosphere ...]. One may conclude that the speeds of aether flowing toward and into the Earth are no more than tiny fractions of the speed of light ... One can speculate, however, that inflow speeds at or near a black hole might be at or beyond the speed of light." [6] Shaw's estimate exceeds by more than an order of magnitude the maximum terminal velocity quoted for skydiving, 1342 km/h, or 0.373 km/s, "... held by Felix Baumgartner who jumped from a height of 128,100 feet (39,000 m) ..., though he achieved this velocity at high altitude, where extremely thin air presents less drag force." [7] Let us use Shaw's estimate of 11 km/s as the speed of aether flowing into the Earth at it approaches its surface.

Returning to Bernoulli's equation with these very crudely assumed values, the pressure differential between inflowing and outflowing aether (at least for the Earth) becomes (assuming that $v_{in} = 11000$ m/s and $v_{out} = 1.68v_{in}$):
$$P_{in} - P_{out} = \frac{1.67E-20kg/m^3}{2}(1.68^2 - 1)(11000m/s)^2 = 1.68E - 16nt/m^2 = 1.68E - 21bar.$$

With respect to Table 2, this is roughly one-millionth the atmospheric pressure on the Moon. If we use light speed (3.00E+8 m/s) as the radial speed of aether, the pressure differential rises to 4.57E-17 bar, still below the Moon's atmospheric pressure. However, if we use the maximum estimate for ISM density (approximately $10^6/cm^3$), the estimates for pressure differential rise to 1.68E-16 bar (for

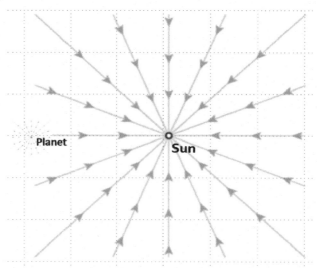

Figure 1. Approximate Reproduction of Shaw's Figure for Inflowing Aether [2]

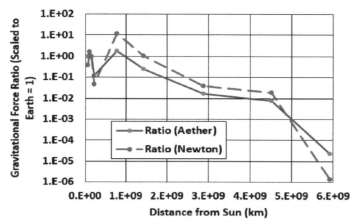

Figure 2. Ratios of Aether vs. Newton Gravitational Forces on the Planets (Scaled to Earth = 1) vs. Orbital Distance

Table 1. Gravitational Forces on Planets due to Aether vs. Newton (with Equivalent Radii for Gas Giants)

ORB	EQ. RADIUS (km)	MASS (kg)	DENSITY (kg/km^3)	DISTANCE (km)	VELOCITY	AETHER		NEWTON	
						Force	Ratio	Force (nt)	Ratio
SUN	6.957E+05	1.989E+30	1.408E+12	6.957E+05	1.000E+00				
MERCURY	2.440E+03	3.301E+23	5.427E+12	5.791E+07	1.443E-04	8.592E+02	9.789E-01	1.307E+19	3.689E-01
VENUS	6.052E+03	4.868E+24	5.243E+12	1.082E+08	4.134E-05	1.514E+03	1.725E+00	5.520E+19	1.558E+00
EARTH	6.371E+03	5.972E+24	5.514E+12	1.496E+08	2.163E-05	8.778E+02	1.000E+00	3.542E+19	1.000E+00
MARS	3.390E+03	6.417E+23	3.934E+12	2.280E+08	9.311E-06	1.070E+02	1.219E-01	1.639E+18	4.626E-02
JUPITER	4.483E+04	1.899E+27	5.030E+12	7.784E+08	7.989E-07	1.605E+03	1.829E+00	4.161E+20	1.175E+01
SATURN	2.999E+04	5.684E+26		1.429E+09	2.369E-07	2.130E+02	2.427E-01	3.693E+19	1.042E+00
URANUS	1.603E+04	8.681E+25		2.875E+09	5.854E-08	1.504E+01	1.714E-02	1.394E+18	3.935E-02
NEPTUNE	1.694E+04	1.024E+26		4.504E+09	2.385E-08	6.844E+00	7.797E-03	6.699E+17	1.891E-02
PLUTO	1.187E+03	1.303E+22	1.860E+12	5.915E+09	1.383E-08	1.949E-02	2.220E-05	4.943E+13	1.396E-06

Shaw's "aether speed" of 11 km/s) and 4.57E-12 bar (for "light-speed" aether), now at least comparable to the lowest atmospheric pressures within our solar system. Still, it is apparent that the differential pressure between inflowing and outflowing aether is miniscule, but apparently positive enough to produce the "attractive" gravitational force.

D. Effect of Mass

So far, mathematical constructs have been created to address (1) the increase in aether's radial inflow speed with the inverse of distance squared and (2) the pressure differential between inflowing and outflowing aether at a "planet's" surface to account for "attractive" gravity. What remains is to consider two equally-sized "planets" with different masses (densities), such that the more massive experiences the greater surface gravity. How does the inflowing aether "know" that, given the exact same geometry and distance, it must inflow faster for the more massive planet, thereby generating a greater pressure differential and, as a result, greater gravity? While I cannot answer "how," I propose yet another mathematical construct for visualization (Figure 4).

Assume that, as a result of the greater mass, a "larger" aether "capsule" (shown now as a cubic package of eight aether particles, each a sphere of unit radius) flows "into" the planet, now displacing eight individual aether particles in a "straight" line. The inflowing aether cube has a volume of $8\frac{4\pi}{3}(1)^3 = 33.51$, which corresponds to a sphere of equivalent radius $= (\frac{33.51}{\frac{4\pi}{3}})^{1/3} = 2.000$ (relative to unit particle radius), shown in dashed red. The volume of eight "expelled" aether particles is assumed to correspond to a cylinder of equivalent length $= \frac{33.51}{\pi(1)^2} = 10.667$ that proceeds outward in a straight line, the average distance being half the length, or 5.333. Radially, this corresponds to the expelled particles traveling at $\frac{5.333}{2.000} = 2.667$ times the speed of the inflowing capsule, 1.587 times higher than previously.

Returning to Bernoulli's equation with the previously assumed values, the pressure differential between inflowing and outflowing aether (at least for the Earth) now becomes (assuming that $v_{in} = 11000$ m/s and now $v_{out} = 2.67v_{in}$): $P_{in} - P_{out} = \frac{1.67E-20kg/m^3}{2}(2.67^2 - 1)(11000m/s)^2 = 5.63E-16nt/m^2 = 5.63E-21bar$.

If we use light speed (3.00E+8 m/s) as the radial speed of aether, and the maximum estimate for ISM density (approximately $10^6/cm^3$), the estimate for pressure differential rises to 1.53E-6 bar, comparable to Pluto's atmospheric pressure (see Table 2).

The numerical results really do not matter. What is key is that, via another mathematical construct, Shaw's Aether Concept of Gravity remains plausible, now accounting for the third effect, the dependence of aether inflow speed and pressure differential between inflow and outflow, and therefore gravity, on mass.

E. Conclusion

While no definitive conclusion regarding Shaw's Aether Concept of Gravity can be drawn from this examination, it is evident that at least mathematical constructs can be developed for three key aspects, such that Shaw's theory is plausible. That has been the only goal here, and further investigation into the physics involved hopefully will lead to greater insight into the potential validity of this theory.

F. Acknowledgment

The author wishes to acknowledge personal communications with Duncan Shaw throughout the development of this paper and expresses his gratitude for his support of this effort. This does not imply his agreement with any of my speculations, which are offered only as one out of what may be many possible and different mathematical models for Shaw's theory.

REFERENCES

1. D.Shaw, Aether Concept of Gravity, 2017 Proceedings of the Third Annual John Chappell Natural Philosophy Society, Vancouver, BC, July 19-22, 2017, pp. 180-185.
2. Mathews, Source-Sink Model, http://mathfaculty.fullerton.edu/mathews/c2003/SourceSinkMod.html.
3. Wikimedia, Monochrome Sphere, https://upload.wikimedia.org/wikipedia/commons/thumb/7/7e/Sphere-monochrome-simple.svg/2000px-Sphere-monochrome-simple.svg.png.
4. Blogspot, , https://1.bp.blogspot.com/-ywrqAz74Dsw/WIxr8AQhvwI/AAAAAAAAGxo/-YDhp-G9WnIUGe3QH-KjwlL5zg-VOUTjACLcB/s1600/Buckminster-2BFuller-2B7.jpg.
5. Wikipedia, Interstellar Medium, https://en.wikipedia.org/wiki/Interstellar- medium.
6. D. Shaw, Flowing Aether: A Concept, Physics Essays 26(4):523-530 (2013).
7. Wikipedia, Terminal Velocity, https://en.wikipedia.org/wiki/Terminal-velocity.
8. Smart Conversion, Surface Pressure of Planets and Sun, http://www.smartconversion.com/otherInfo/Surface-pressure-of-planets-and-the-sun.aspx.
9. FSU Chemical Lab, Simple Cubic, https://www.chem.fsu.edu/chemlab/chm1046course/simple-20cubic.JPG.

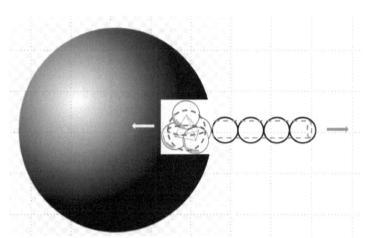

Figure 3. Mathematical Construct for Shaw's Inflowing and Outflowing Aether [3, 4]

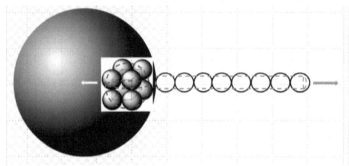

Figure 4. Mathematical Construct for Effect of Greater Mass [3, 9]

Table 2. Surface Pressures of the Planets and the Sun [8]

Surface Pressure of the Planets and the Sun

Name	Surface Pressure (bar)
Saturn	>>1000
Uranus	>>1000
Neptune	>>1000
Venus	92
Earth	1.014
Jupiter	0.2 - 2
Mars	$4 - 8.7 \times 10^{-3}$
Sun	8.68×10^{-4}
Pluto	3×10^{-6}
Mercury	10×10^{-15}
Moon	3×10^{-15}

Source: NASA

Gravity - When Push Comes to Shove?

Raymond HV Gallucci, PhD, PE

8956 Amelung St., Frederick, MD 21704, email=gallucci@localnet.com

Since first proposed by Fatio in 1690 and allegedly enhanced by LeSage in 1748, one possible explanation for gravity is that it is a pushing force theory that involves "shadowing" of omnidirectional gravity particles that impinge on all matter so as to make gravity appear as an attractive phenomenon. At least for a special case (large distance between spheres), a mathematical model that assumes gravity to be a pushing force, with shadowing and including the possibility of acting throughout the shadowed corridor of the sphere with attenuation effects, suggests a possible alignment with one of the known effects of gravity, namely that it is inversely proportional to the square of the distance between the spheres' centers. This hopefully lends some credence to the theories first proposed by Fatio and LeSage, and since supported by many dissident physicists, including Schroeder, et al., and members of the Gravity Group of the John Chappell Natural Philosophy Society. It is offered as one small contribution to furthering examination of this possible explanation.

Keywords: Gravity, LeSage, Particles, Shadowing, Attenuation

A. Introduction

Since first proposed by Fatio in 1690 before the Royal Society in London, and submitted poetically in 1731 to the Paris Academy of Science, the concept of gravity as a pushing force has existed (and been roundly discredited by mainstream physicists). Popularized and allegedly enhanced by LeSage in 1748 (and equally dismissed as Fatio's), this theory involves "shadowing" of omnidirectional gravity particles that impinge on all matter so as to make gravity appear as an attractive phenomenon (Figure 1). [1] Despite its repeated rejection, this theory has survived and even been revived by dissident physicists as mainstream physicists continue to struggle with an explanation for gravity and search for the elusive "gravity waves" or "gravitons" implied by their theories. Of especial note is the work of Schroeder, et al., and members of the Gravity Group of the John Chappell Natural Philosophy Society. [2] This paper builds on some of these efforts and others to offer one possible mechanism by which gravity can be viewed as "pushing" rather than "pulling."

B. Shadowing

Although proposed in connection with gravity as a four-dimensional wave phenomenon, the concept of shadowing is inherent to explanations of gravity as a pushing force. Simply said, as shown in Figure 2, "[i]f a force is transmitted to a body from 'something' pushing on it from all directions, the body would remain stationary as all the forces would cancel out [Figure 2.a]. However, if a second body is brought close to the first one, part of the impinging force on body 1 would be blocked out and cause a net push towards body 2 [Figure 2.b]. Similarly, body 1 would case a push on body 2 towards body 1, resulting in what would appear to an observer to be an attraction between the two bodies." [3]

With this concept, I examine a potential mathematical model that at least appears to align with one of the known effects of gravity, namely that it is inversely proportional to the square of the distance between the spheres' centers.

C. A Mathematical Model?

Figure 3 is a more detailed extension of Figure 2 where the shadowing from two bodies on one another is shown as the area between them enclosed by the dashed lines. The spheres are separated by a distance "d" between their centers and have respective radii and masses of "R" (larger), "r" (smaller), $4\pi R^3/3$ (larger) and $4\pi r^3/3$ (smaller), assuming densities of "P" (capital rho) and "ρ," respectively, for the larger and smaller spheres. The grey arrows represent the omnidirectional pushing forces (be they particles, waves or some combination) that remain "unshadowed" and exhibit "shadowing" angles of 2ϕ and 2θ on the smaller and larger sphere, respectively, due to the larger and smaller sphere, respectively.

The net pushing force on each sphere results from the area over which the pushing forces are not offset by equal and opposite pushing forces diametrically opposed, i.e., the cones of radii R and r with solid angles ϕ and θ, respectively. Considering the case where the spheres are far apart, i.e., d » R (and since $R \geq r, d >> r$), the geometry simplifies as shown in Figure 4 (relative lengths of r and R vs. d greatly exaggerated for clarity). Effectively, both triangles become right, such that $\sqrt{r^2 + d^2}$ and $\sqrt{R^2 + d^2} \to d; sin\theta \to R/d; sin\phi \to r/d$; and both $cos\theta$ and $cos\phi \to d/d = 1$.

The net pushing force on each sphere will be proportional to the cross-sectional area subtended by the cones of radii R and r, i.e., $\pi(Rsin\phi)^2$ and $\pi(rsin\theta)^2$, respectively for the larger and smaller sphere. Effectively the pushing force acts along a vector parallel to that between the centers of the two spheres. With d » R (and r), these each simplify to $\pi(\frac{Rr}{d})^2$. Each sphere also has inertia proportional to its mass, such that each pushing force will be resisted. Accelerating each sphere will be proportional to the exerted force divided by the mass, such that the accelerations become $\frac{\pi(\frac{Rr}{d})^2}{\frac{4\pi PR^3}{3}} = \frac{3r^2}{4RPd^2}$ for the larger sphere and $\frac{\pi(\frac{Rr}{d})^2}{\frac{4\pi\rho r^3}{3}} = \frac{3R^2}{4r\rho d^2}$ for the smaller sphere. Both are inversely proportional to the square of the distance between their centers ($\frac{1}{d^2}$).

Strictly, these accelerations must be multiplied by the change in momentum per unit area from the impinging particles, denoted here as "Δ" in units of $\frac{kg-m}{s^2}\frac{1}{m^2} = \frac{kg}{m-s^2}$. The first term represents the change in momentum ($\frac{kg-m}{s}/s$) from the impinging particles; the second the inverse of the impingement area. Therefore, the accelerations are more accurately written as $\frac{3r^2\Delta}{4RPd^2}$ for the larger sphere and $\frac{3R^2\Delta}{4r\rho d^2}$ for the smaller sphere. Each acceleration now appears in expected units of m/s^2.

C.1. Interaction throughout the Spheres

So far, we have only considered the spheres as solids, i.e., the pushing force acts only at the surface. However, Fatio, Le Sage, Schroeder, et al., and others who espouse gravity as a pushing force usually assume that it works throughout the target, i.e., throughout the sphere. If so, then we should consider the pushing force acting not only just at the cross-sectional area of impingement but throughout a cylinder extending through the sphere whose axis parallels the vector that connects the centers of the two spheres. Therefore, if we include the linear distance through each sphere, effectively multiplying the previous results by the diameter, we obtain the following for the accelerations: $\frac{3r^2\Delta}{4RPd^2}(2R) = \frac{3r^2\Delta}{2Pd^2}$ for the larger sphere and $\frac{3R^2\Delta}{4r\rho d^2}(2r) = \frac{3R^2\Delta}{2\rho d^2}$ for the smaller sphere. Again, the dependence on the inverse square of the separation distance is evident, but now without the inverse dependence on the radius of the sphere itself (the dependence on the square of the radius of the other sphere, that is the one that "shadows," remains).

Proponents of gravity as a pushing force sometimes assume that, in addition to the shadowing effect, the force itself may be somewhat attenuated as it passes through the sphere. Attenuation over a linear distance "x," such as passing along the axis of the interaction cylinder, is usually modeled as an exponential decrease, such as $\frac{1}{e^{\mu x}}$, where "μ" is some form of attenuation coefficient. For our example, it seems reasonable to assume that any attenuation coefficient should be some function of the density, i.e., $F(P)$ for the larger sphere and $f(\rho)$ for the smaller. Including this additional factor in the acceleration as another multiplier yields the following: $\frac{3r^2\Delta}{2Pd^2 e^{2RF(P)}}$ for the larger sphere and $\frac{3R^2\Delta}{2\rho d^2 e^{2Rf(\rho)}}$ for the smaller. Again, the dependence on the inverse square of the separation distance is evident, but now with some reduction due to attenuation.

C.2. Comparison

A ratio of the accelerations (larger to smaller) on the two spheres yields the following: $\frac{3r^2\Delta}{2Pd^2 e^{2RF(P)}} / \frac{3R^2\Delta}{2\rho d^2 e^{2rf(\rho)}} = (\frac{r^2}{R^2})(\frac{\rho}{P})e^{2(rf[\rho]-RF[P])}$. Since $R \geq r$, the squared first term likely dominates, unless $P >> \rho$ (e.g., comparing a neutron star to a typical star) or $F(P) >> f(\rho)$. Therefore, the acceleration on the larger sphere should most often be less than that on the smaller, implying less movement toward their mutual barycenter on the part of the larger sphere when compared to the smaller. This is consistent with what is observed.

D. Summary

At least for a special case (large distance between spheres), a mathematical model that assumes gravity to be a pushing force, with shadowing and including the possibility of acting throughout the shadowed corridor of the sphere with attenuation effects, suggests a possible alignment with one of the known effects of gravity, namely that it is inversely proportional to the square of the distance between the spheres' centers. This hopefully lends some credence to the theories first proposed by Fatio and Le Sage, and since supported by many dissident physicists, including Schroeder, et al., and members of the Gravity Group of the John Chappell Natural Philosophy Society. It is offered as one small contribution to furthering examination of this possible explanation.[8]

REFERENCES

1. Wikipedia, LeSage's Theory of Gravitation, https://en.wikipedia.org/wiki/Le-Sage-27s-theory-of-gravitation
2. Schroeder, Ramthun and de Hilster, Gravity is a Pushing Force, Proceedings of the First Annual Chappell Natural Philosophy Society Conference, August 6-8, 2015, Florida Atlantic University, pp. 47-51.
3. Esoteric Science, Gravity, http://www.esotericscience.com/Gravity.aspx.

---

[8] Subsequent to composing this article, I discovered a sophisticated derivation of Newton's gravitational equation from LeSage's attenuation concept which addresses not only the inverse proportionality to the distance between two objects but also the direct proportionality to the product of their masses (Mingst and Stowe, "Derivation of Newtonian Gravitation from LeSage's Attenuation Concept," *http://www.mountainman.com.au/le-sage.htm*).

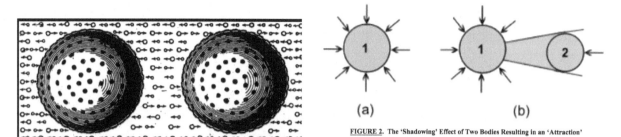

FIGURE 1. Le Sage's Original Illustration

FIGURE 2. The 'Shadowing' Effect of Two Bodies Resulting in an 'Attraction'

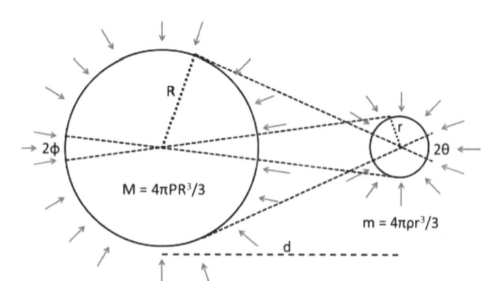

FIGURE 3. Schematic for Interaction of Two Spheres with 'Shadowing'

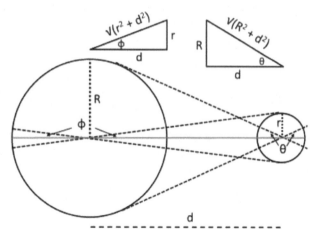

FIGURE 4. Schematic for Interaction of Two Spheres with 'Shadowing' when Far Apart

The Mirror Model - A Rosetta Stone for Fractal Biology

Sandro Guerra

Address, sandro_guerragarcia@hotmail.com

The mirror model is, in essence, a very simple idea; it is a model that synthesizes the incredible complexity of life into an elemental equivalence principle, or, as the name indicates, a mirror effect. This principle could be explained as a phenomenon similar to an equation. An equation is a statement with 2 parts divided by an equals sign. These 2 parts may look completely different at first glance, but they are indeed equivalent statements; they are 2 expressions of the same principle. The mirror model proposes that something very similar happens in complex life forms. It states that the body, like an equation, consist of 2 fundamental parts: the head and the body, and all the structures in the head are iterated onto the body.

At first, this idea may not make sense because the head does not look at all like the rest of the body. Furthermore, the brain is made out of nerve tissue, and the organs inside the abdomen and the thorax consist of a completely different set of tissues that have nothing to do with the brain; in fact, they do not even have the same origin. This idea also seems to contradict the Ed Lewis model of development by mosaics, which is the leading model of development today. How, therefore, can we resolve this tissue discrepancy, and how can we reconcile these two seemingly incongruent models? These questions are indeed highly relevant, and they will be addressed as the model is described.

Keywords: Gravity, LeSage, Particles, Shadowing, Attenuation

A. Introduction

Biology today is usually concerned with very tiny things. This approach has been very successful so far, and thanks to the detail-oriented work of many eminent scientists, we are able to grasp concepts such as DNA, Hox genes, epigenetics, and many others. But even though we know so much about many details, we still lack a complete, comprehensive picture of how the body takes shape. We do not understand how a duet of cells is able to transform coherently into the immense orchestra that is the human body. The strategy of the mirror model to tackle this problem is to take a step back, look at the big picture, and try to identify meaningful patterns hiding in plane sight.

To better understand how the mirror model may work we have to look at the pre-embryonic process. Humans develop from a "sandwich" of 3 germinal tissues; the ectoderm, mesoderm, and endoderm. The ectoderm divides into 2 parts; one part forms the skin and the other forms the nervous system. The mesoderm is responsible for the formation of the skeletal, muscular, and circulatory systems. The endoderm creates the lungs, liver, and digestive tract. If this model is correct, then the endoderm would follow the same principles to create the guts as the ectoderm follows to create the brain, producing what I call a mirror effect. I am not implying this happens simultaneously. I am aware these alleged mirror structures do not develop at the same rate, but I believe they do follow a similar morphogenic principle. On the other hand, the structures that develop from the mesoderm should also follow this mirror effect, but in this case the mesoderm mirrors itself instead of other germinal tissue. Therefore, the structures of mesodermal origin in the head would have counterparts

that also have a mesodermal origin in the body. Organs of mesodermal origin, such as the heart, kidneys, reproductive organs, and their respective counterparts, can be key to understanding the dynamics of this model. For this reason, I will devote special attention to these alleged mirror structures and explain why I believe these associations reinforce the coherence of this hypothesis.

To better explain the mirror model, I have created 3 catalogs of parallel structures. The first deals mostly with the skeletal system and its alleged analogous structures. The second one deals with the structures in the head and their alleged counterparts in the body, and the third one deals with heart and its alleged analogous structures in the head. I have gathered a body of evidence that support many of these parallels in the form of syndromes, symptoms, functional connections, mutations, and the surprising results of an experiment on the sexual behavior of rodents performed at Harvard University. I am aware that it is unconventional to include elements of the methods, and conclusion sections as part of the introduction. But, we live in an era where time is of the essence, and readers need substantial reasons to remain engaged. For the readers convenience I have summarized the catalogs and the evidence on this section including links with references and further information on the phenomena used as support. All this information will be reintroduced in the Discussion section as the catalogs are further explained.

Because no experiment has yet been done to test this hypothesis the Discussion section will be introduced first followed by the Methods section, which will contain general guidelines to future experiments, along with the initial observations that lead me to create this model.

Table 1: Alleged counterparts within the skeletal system:

Skull	Rest of the Skeleton
Orbits of the skull	Obturator foramina
Frontal bone	Rectus sheet/bone marrow on the ribs and crest of the ilium
Occipital bone	Sternum and manubrium
Sphenoid bone and cervical vertebrae	Sacrum bone and part vertebral column
Maxilla	Superior extremities
Mandible	Part of inferior extremities
Teeth	Nails
Temporal bone	Ilium
Pterygoid plates	Scapula

Table 2: Alleged counterparts in the head and the torso:

Head	Torso
Cerebellum	Lungs
Eye pineal complex	Heart thymus complex
Pituitary gland	Liver
Optic chiasma	Gallbladder
Putamen	Stomach (under consideration)
Hypothalamus	Pancreas (under consideration)
Hippocampus	Small intestine (under consideration)
Cerebrum	Colon
Auditory system	Kidneys
Lips	Anus
Nasal cavity	Vagina
Nasal meautus	Penis/clitoris
Palatine tonsils	Testicle and ovaries (under consideration)

Table 3: alleged counterparts in the Ocular-Pineal Complex and the Heart-Thymus Complex

Ocular-Pineal Complex	Cardio-Thymus Complex
Right and left eyes	Heart ventricles
Ciliari muscle	Papillary muscle
Zonular fibers	Cordeae tendineae
Muscles that control the movement of the eye and eyelids	Exterior layers of cardiac muscles
Pineal gland	Thymus gland

Go to next page!

A.1. Evidence Summary and References Material:

Tooth and nail syndrome (TNS) supports the parallel established between the teeth and the nails by the model:

[https://www.medicinenet.com/script/main/art.asp?articlekey=17699]

The antennapedia mutation in Drosophila supports the parallel established between the maxillary and the extremities by the model:

[http://www.ncbi.nlm.nih.gov/pubmed/2850265]

The reflection of congenital heart disease symptoms on the eyes supports the parallel established between the heart and the eyes by the model:

[https://www.rebuildyourvision.com/blog/vision-conditions/cardiovascular-diseases-eyes/]

[https://www.nature.com/articles/6701408]

The reflection of pituitary malfunction on the liver supports the parallel established between these structures by the model:

[http://www.ncbi.nlm.nih.gov/pubmed/15057893]

The correlation between spinal cord injury and cognitive impairment supports the relation stablished by this model between the brain and the digestive tract:

[https://www.researchgate.net/publication/308961103_Cognitive_impairment_and_mood_states_following_spinal_cord_injury]

The correlation found between Autism and bowel malfunction also supports the relation stablished by this model between the digestive tract ad the brain.

[https://www.spectrumnews.org/news/large-study-ties-gut-issues-autism-inflammation/]

The correlation found between dementia and irritable bowel syndrome (IBS) supports the parallel established between the cerebrum and the colon by the model:

[https://www.ncbi.nlm.nih.gov/pmc/articles/PMC4701489/]

The correlation found between colorectal cancer and the decline in cognitive function supports the parallel established between the cerebrum and the colon by the model:

[https://www.ncbi.nlm.nih.gov/pmc/articles/PMC5683012/]

The correlation shown between the kidneys and the auditory system by branchiootorenal syndrome supports the parallel established between these structures by the model:

[https://ghr.nlm.nih.gov/condition/branchiootorenal-branchiootic-syndrome]

The correlation shown between the reproductive organs and the olfactory system by Kallmann syndrome supports the parallel established between these structures by the model:

[https://ghr.nlm.nih.gov/condition/kallmann-syndrome]

The correlation shown between the reproductive organs and the olfactory system by the abundant presence of erectile tissue on the nose supports the parallel established between these structures by the model:

[https://en.wikipedia.org/wiki/Erectile_tissue]

The parallel established between the reproductive organs and the olfactory system is also supported by the results of an experiment on the sexual behavior of rodents performed at Harvard University by Dr. Catherine Dulac, Dr. Jennings Xu, and Dr. Tali Kimchi.

Short comprehensive article on the experiment:

[http://www.abc.net.au/news/2007-08-06/sex-not-on-the-brain-but-in-the-nose-study/2522574]

Original scholarly paper by Dr. Catherine Dulac, Dr. Jennings Xu, and Dr. Tali Kimchi:

[https://www.researchgate.net/publication/6163439_A_functional_circuit_underlying_male_sexual_behaviour_in_the_female_mouse_brain]

B. Discussion

B.1. Catalog 1 - The Skeletal System

When we look at the skeletal system, it is difficult to see the resemblance between the skull and the rest of the skeleton. However, there is a hint that gives everything away, and that is, as previously mentioned, the remarkable similarity between the obturator foramina and the orbits of the skull. After identifying these 2 structures, everything starts to fall into place. But there is a problem: if the obturator foramina are counterparts to the orbits of the skull, there should be an analogous frontal bone covering the abdomen, which is not the case. This apparent incongruence helps make an important point. I do not believe everything is expressed in a 1-to-1 relationship; otherwise, animals like snakes or fish would not fit into this model. Some organs and bones could be latent or expressed to a lesser degree. Fortunately, this seems to be the case with the inferior frontal bone because it would be very uncomfortable to walk with a bone over the abdomen. In this case, instead of a solid counterpart to the frontal bone, there are 2 analogous structures. One is the rectus sheet, which is the white tissue covering the abdominal muscles, and the other is the abundant bone marrow found in the crest of the ilium. So far, no one has been able to explain the reason for the significant presence of marrow in this area. However, if the mirror model is correct, this abundance of marrow would be justified by the absence of the counterpart of the frontal bone, and the marrow would be the expression of this latent structure.

On top of the abdomen, we find the ribcage, and if the counterpart of the frontal bone occupies the abdominal area, then the obvious counterpart for the ribs would be the parietal bones. But the parietal bones are 2 solid plates, and the ribs are a collection of individual bones. However, the ribs, like the ilium, also exhibit an abundant presence of bone marrow that has eluded the comprehension of experts. The presence of marrow in this area suggests that the ribs have the potential to be 2 solid plates, similar in shape to their alleged counterpart. This association explains the mysterious marrow that has puzzled scientists for many years.

Following this order, the sternum and the manubrium are counterparts to the occipital bone. The ilium is a counterpart to the temporal bones. The arms and legs are mirror structures to the maxilla and mandible, respectively. The scapula is parallel to the pterygoid plates. The sphenoid and possibly the cervical vertebrae are a counterpart to the sacrum bone and the rest of the vertebral column, and the clavicles are probably a counterpart of the hyoid bone.

The teeth are structures of ectodermal origin, but since they are always depicted as part of the skeletal system, I have decided to include them in this catalog, and the most obvious counterparts for the teeth are the nails.

The first piece of evidence related to the relationships established by this model is a genetic disorder called tooth and nail syndrome TNS. People with this condition exhibit poor formation of both the teeth and nails. The affliction generated by this condition on these alleged mirror structures supports the association established by the model between these structures. You can learn more about TSN in the following article:

[https://www.medicinenet.com/script/main/ art.asp?articlekey=17699]

Perhaps one of the most important pieces of evidence for this model is hiding in plain sight. The antennapedia mutation was the key to one of the most significant breakthroughs in the history of science. It was instrumental to proving Ed Lewis's theory of development by mosaics. Antennapedia is a gene first discovered in Drosophila, which controls the formation of the legs during development. The mutation of this gene can trigger the formation of legs in place of antennae. Contrary to popular belief, the antennapedia mutation is not really a mutation of the antennae; it is a mutation of the fly's maxillary, of which the antennae are substructures. This fact is highly significant because it is consistent with the relationship established by this model between the maxillary and superior extremities, and it can lead to further evidence on the validity of this hypothesis. You can learn more about the antennapedia mutation and confirm the claim about the fly's maxillary in the following article.

[http://www.ncbi.nlm.nih.gov/pubmed/2850265]

B.2. Catalog 2 - Parallels of Structures on the Head and the Alleged Counterparts in the Torso

The first organ we find looking at the body in descending order are the lungs. The lungs are one of the organs that best resemble their alleged counterpart: the cerebellum. If we look at a cross-section of these organs, we observe a fractal pattern in both cases: a tree-like structure on the cerebellum called the arbor vitae very much resembles the similar fractal shape created by the bronchi as they branch out to create the lungs. The lungs are responsible for the process of respiration. On the other hand, the cerebellum does not control respiration; the breathing process is an involuntary reflex controlled by the hypothalamus. However, it has been found that deep nuclei within the cerebellum are responsible for respiratory modulation [http://www.ncbi.nlm.nih.gov/pubmed/12879972]. The cerebellum is mainly responsible for coordinating movements. However, respiration is an important factor in

establishing coherent movement. Movements usually fall into a rhythm synced with the breathing process. This may not be obvious to many scientists, but it is something that athletes, musicians, and dancers know very well. A study conducted in the department of physiology at the University of Zurich in Switzerland by P. Bernasconi and J. Kohl showed that: "The degree of co-ordination during running increased slightly but not significantly with increasing work load and could be increased significantly by paced breathing."[1]

[https://www.ncbi.nlm.nih.gov/pmc/articles/ PMC1143984/]

According to this study respiration seems to be a significant factor in establishing coordination in movement, and this reinforces my suspicion of the lungs been a mirror counterpart to the cerebellum.

Right between the lungs is the heart. The counterpart of the heart is not easy to identify, since there are no structures in the head that seem to resemble this organ. But the first thing to take notice of in this case is the cytological origin of this structure. Unlike most of the organs in the torso, the heart does not develop from the endoderm; it develops instead from the mesoderm. For this reason, it is logical to infer that the heart's counterpart should also have a mesodermal origin. This dramatically reduces the prospects for an alleged mirror structure.

After careful examination of several structures of mesodermal origin within the head, I have concluded that the best candidates for the counterparts of the heart, as well as the thymus gland, are the eyes and pineal gland. Like the heart, the eyes are mainly formed by mesodermal tissue. Furthermore, the eyes are basically 2 hollow spheres, which resemble the structure of the heart's ventricles. This comparison is not too convincing at first glance, but a cross-section of the heart compared with cross-sections of the eyes shows remarkable similarities. Inside the eyes, there is a set of muscles called the ciliary body. These muscles connect to a set of fibers called the zonular fibers that are also connected to the lenses. The function of these structures is to pull the lens to focus the eye. Similarly, inside the heart, there are a number of muscles called papillary muscles. These muscles connect to a set of tendons called the chordae tendineae, which also connect to the heart valves. The function of these structures is to pull open the heart's valves. Looking at both sets of structures reveals a remarkable resemblance between the ciliary body and the zonular fibers on one hand and the papillary muscles and chordae tendineae on the other.

An important piece of evidence to support the analogy between the eyes and the heart or the ocular-pineal complex and the heart is the reflection of symptoms of cardiovascular diseases on the eyes. It has been found very recently that serious heart conditions can be accurately diagnosed just by looking at the patient's eyes. In a study published by Springer Nature, by A M Mansour, F F Bitar, E I Traboulsi, K M Kassak, M Y Obeid, A Megarbane, and H I Salti concluded that "patients with congenital heart disease (CHD) are at a high risk for ocular pathology and need screening for various ocular abnormalities."[2] You can learn more about this phenomenon in these articles:

[http://www.rebuildyourvision.com/blog/vision-conditions/cardiovascular-diseases-eyes/] Also see:

[http://www.nature.com/eye/journal/v19/n1/full/6701408a.html]

As previously mentioned, I not only associate the eyes with the heart, but also believe the eyes and the pineal gland are intrinsically related, and together they form a structure I call the oculo-pineal complex. I believe this complex is the mirror counterpart to both the heart and the thymus gland. I relate the pineal gland to the eyes because it has been found that most lizards, frogs, salamanders, certain bony fish, sharks, and lampreys possess an undeveloped third eye, also called the parietal or pineal eye. This pineal eye possesses a lens, and even a retina, that in many cases developed as an evagination of the pineal gland. More information on the parietal, or pineal, eye can be found in the following article:

[https://en.wikipedia.org/wiki/Parietal_eye]

I relate the thymus gland to the heart because of the connection found between the pineal gland and the eyes, the proximity of the thymus gland to the heart, and the resemblance I can observe between the pineal and thymus glands. The pineal gland is known for the production of melatonin, which is associated with the circadian rhythm. The circadian rhythm is regulated by the perception of light and by the hypothalamus, which also regulates the cardiac rhythm, along with many other involuntary functions of the body. The role of the hypothalamus in this relationship is still unclear to me, but I focus on the pineal gland because it seems to be the structure that induces sleep, which is relevant for answering a very important question: Is there a functional connection between the ocular-pineal and the cardio–thymus complexes? The main function of the heart is to pump blood, which is obviously not a function that can be attributed to the eyes. However, there is another significant connection between these structures. The heart produces the biggest electric field in the body, the intensity of which is modulated during each heartbeat. The brain also produces a potent electric field, but the peaks and valleys of this field are modulated by the circadian rhythm, which, as previously mentioned, seems to be associated with the pineal gland. This electric parallelism has led me to believe that the circadian rhythm is nothing more than a superior version of the heartbeat, or the heartbeat the lower version of the circadian rhythm. The association between these electric cycles can be central to understanding the mechanisms of this model. I believe the circadian rhythm and the heart beat are not only parallel phenomena, they are also the engine of this model and the process of development.

It has been found that the process of mitosis involves charge; this is not very well understood yet, but it has been observed that microtubules are charged when they assemble to connect to kinetochores. You can learn more about this observation on the following article: [https://europepmc.org/abstract/pmc/pmc2726302]. The knowledge of this electric phenomenon has led to the development of cancer therapies known as tumor-treating fields, or TTFields [https://www.youtube.com/watch?v=TpyWgNPrvGA].

This therapy inhibits cell division by the use of external electric fields that interfere with the formation of microtubules. This relationship between mitosis and electromagnetism allows us to speculate that the presence of a major electromagnetic cycle could be an excellent mechanism to regulate cell division during development. With both the heartbeat and circadian rhythm, major fluctuations of the electric fields around the heart and the brain can be observed. But what if these 2 fluctuating cycles exist not as a consequence of the organs but the organs as consequence of these cycles? What if these electromagnetic cycles exist even before the process of organogenesis, and what if these cycles are the organizing force behind development? If this hypothesis is correct, this phenomenon should be observable. More information on a possible of an experiment to test this hypothesis can be found on the Methods section.

Right below the lungs are the liver and gallbladder. I believe the analogous structures to the liver and the gallbladder are the pituitary gland and optic chiasma, respectively. I have reached this conclusion mainly because of the remarkable physical resemblance between these structures. It is also important to highlight that both the liver and the pituitary gland have important endocrine functions. Furthermore, liver problems like nonalcoholic fatty liver disease (NAFLD) have been associated with hypopituitarism. You can learn more about this association in the following article:

[http://www.ncbi.nlm.nih.gov/pubmed/15057893]

Next to the liver and the gallbladder is the stomach. From this point forward, there is a discrepancy I have not been able to resolve yet. The brain has 2 hemispheres, and we only seem to have 1 digestive tract. For this reason, the structures in the digestive tract seem to have 2 counterparts in the head instead of just 1. I do not claim to understand the reason for this discrepancy. I have speculated that the yolk sac could be the missing counterpart, but I am still uncertain on this issue. I am also unsure about assigning counterparts to organs such as the stomach, pancreas, small intestine, and spleen. I have speculated that the stomach could be a counterpart to the putamen because of their resemblance in shape. I have associated the hippocampus with the small intestine because of its proximity to the putamen and have also associated the pancreas with the hypothalamus because they are both part of the endocrine system. However, in all these cases, I have a lower degree of confidence in the validity of these associations because of the lack of significant evidence to support these alleged parallels.

Unlike other organs in the digestive tract, the colon seems to have a clearer functional connection to its alleged counterpart. Diseases like colon cancer, and irritable bowel syndrome have an impact on higher cognitive functions associated with the cerebrum. Irritable bowel syndrome has been linked with dementia, and patients with colorectal cancer show a decline in cognitive abilities. You can learn more about these relationships between Irritable bowel syndrome has and dementia on the following article:

[https://www.ncbi.nlm.nih.gov/pmc/articles/ PMC4701489/]

You can learn more about the decline in cognitive function in patients with colorectal cancer on the following article: [https://www.ncbi.nlm.nih.gov/pmc/articles/ PMC5683012/]

Autism, a syndromes associated with costive disfunction is also associated with bowels malfunction

[[https://www.spectrumnews.org/news/ large-study-ties-gut-issues-autism-inflammation/]

All these coincidences have led me to a strong suspicion that the cerebrum and the colon may indeed be mirror counterparts.

One of the greatest questions in science is the question of cognition. What is it, how does it work, and how does it come about? To answer these questions, scientists for many years have concentrated on conducting all kinds of studies on the brain. However, from the perspective of the mirror model, this is like trying to understand a soccer game by looking at only half of the arena. The position of the model on this issue is very different. The digestive tract has more than 100 million neurons intrinsically connected with the brain. Why do we have so many neurons in what seems to be a long tube for processing food? If this model is correct, all these connections suddenly make a lot more sense, but the perspective of the model on the cognition question goes further. I believe the body is something like a violin or a guitar. To operate one of these instruments, the musician does not just manipulate one side of the instrument. To make music with a guitar, a musician forms chords at the neck of the guitar with one hand while strumming the strings between the sound hole and bridge with the other hand. The coordination of these 2 actions produces what we perceive as music. I believe something very similar could be happening with the nervous system. Specifically, to produce the "music" we call cognition, we operate not only the brain but the entire nervous system. However, like the guitar, the most significant parts of this operation consist of the coordination between the neurons in the guts and the neurons in the brain. This hypothesis may be refuted bay arguing that there is not enough time for nerve impulses in the gut to travel all the way to the brain to simultaneously produce a thought. Therefore, let us go back to the guitar metaphor. To play a guitar, one does not do the same thing with both hands at the same time. The hands do complementary actions; one hand forms a chord by pressing certain strings at the neck, and the other hand strums the strings to play the notes. The important part here is that one hand makes it possible for the correct notes to be played by the other hand. I think some-

thing similar happens on the body. In this analogy, the neck of the guitar would be the gut, and the bridge would probably be the brain. I believe the process of thinking consists of opening channels or "pressing strings" at the gut level, so the brain is then able to play the "chords" we call thoughts. This would explain why we so often see emotional distress reflected in the gut and diseases of the gut affecting the brain. It has been broad to my attention hat sections of the colon can be removed without provoking a noticeable impact in cognitive function. I have to point that although this not always true, the same can be said about the brain, I presume the nervous system automatically compensates for the missing parts. The following article shows a clear correlation between spinal core injury and cognitive impairment:

[https://www.researchgate.net/publication/ 308961103_Cognitive_impairment_and_mood _states_following_spinal_cord_injury]

The kidneys, along with the heart, are among the special organs in the body that develop from the mesoderm. The heart was previously associated with the eyes, which are known as sensory organs. Therefore, it would make sense if the alleged counterparts to the kidneys were not only of mesodermal origin but sensory organs as well. There is a syndrome called branchiootorenal syndrome (BOR), which is an autosomal dominant condition that disrupts the development of tissues in the neck and causes malformations of the ears and kidneys, caused by loss of function of the SIX1 and EYA1 genes. You can find more information on BOR on the following article:

[https://ghr.nlm.nih.gov/condition/ branchiootorenal-branchiootic-syndrome]

This serendipitous coincidence has reinforced my suspicion that the ears are the mirror counterpart to the kidneys. If we look at a cross-section of the kidney and a cross-section of the cochlea, (see Fig. 13) some significant resemblances are noticeable. But this is not all, according to Oxford Medicine Online: "Malformations of the external ear may signal renal disease, but it is actually the disorders of the inner ear which reflect molecular pathways that are also crucial for kidney development. In a number of monogenic renal diseases, renal dysplasia is associated with deafness. Disorders of the kidney and inner ear are also linked in complex syndromes such as the human ciliopathies. In some cases, the loss of specific genes affects shared transport physiology, basement membrane assembly, or energy metabolism. The kidney and cochlea have a common susceptibility to toxins that are selectively concentrated by comparable uptake mechanisms in the two tissues."[3]

[http://oxfordmedicine.com/view/10.1093/med/ 9780199592548.001.0001/med-9780199592548- chapter-170]

Following the sequence of organs of mesodermal origin are the reproductive organs. If the alleged counterparts of the kidneys and the heart are sensory organs, it is logical to infer that the counterparts to the reproductive organs also follow this pattern. Thus, if the counterpart to the heart is the eyes and the counterpart to the kidneys is the ears, the choice for a counterpart to the reproductive organs is between the tactile and olfactory systems. The tactile system is distributed throughout the body and includes the reproductive organs, so it does not make too much sense as a viable counterpart. On the other hand, the olfactory system seems to share many parallels with the reproductive organs. The nose, like the vagina, is a humectated cavity, and in many animals, sense of smell plays a major role in sexual arousal and partner selection. However, perhaps one of the most remarkable coincidences between these structures is that the reproductive organs and nose are the 2 places in the body where most of the erectile tissue is found, a coincidence that is not at all trivial. More information on the presence of erectile tissue in the nose can be found in this article:

[https://en.wikipedia.org/wiki/Erectile_tissue.]

It is also important to point out that the reproductive organs are located on the pubic arch, which is the place where the nose would be if it is assumed that the obturator foramina is the counterpart of the eye sockets. Another significant association between these organs is made evident by Kallmann syndrome. Kallmann syndrome is a condition characterized by delayed or absent puberty and impaired sense of smell. Even more interesting is the fact that, occasionally, Kallmann syndrome occasionally affects the auditory system, along with the kidneys, structures that are also homologous in the model. More information on Kallmann syndrome can be found in this article:

[https://ghr.nlm.nih.gov/condition/kallmann-syndrome.]

Furthermore, a study conducted at Harvard University by Dr. Catherine Dulac, Dr. Jennings Xu, and Dr. Tali Kimchi showed that engineered mutation of a structure in the noses of mice, called the vomeronasal organ, triggers unusual sexual behavior in the subjects. This study is particularly significant not only because it supports the parallel established by the model, but also because it suggests that the validity of these alleged mirror structures can be tested in a lab using genetic engineering. More information on Dr. Catherine Dulac, Dr. Jennings Xu, and Dr. Tali Kimchi's experiment can be found in these articles: Short comprehensive article on the experiment:

[http://www.abc.net.au/news/2007-08-06/sex-not-on-the-brain-but-in-the-nose-study/2522574] Original scholarly paper by Dr. Catherine Dulac, Dr. Jennings Xu, and Dr. Tali Kimchi:

C. Methods

If we can learn something from Ed Lewis and many other outstanding scientists, it is that good science is usually based on simple comprehensive principles that are often counterintuitive. Sometimes to really understand things, it is not enough to look hard at all the details. Sometimes it is necessary to take a step back and see the broader picture. This is precisely how this model started to take

shape. One day I came across an image of the pelvic bone with the intestines exposed right on top. I thought it looked just like a skull with the frontal bone removed. At first, I only thought it was funny, but I could not stop thinking about this picture. The holes in the pelvic bone looked too much like the eye sockets, and the intestines like the cerebrum. These resemblances were hard to dismiss. (Now I consider the colon the counterpart to the cerebrum, but it took me a while to get to this conclusion.) I started to take this coincidence more seriously, and I asked myself: What if the obturator foramina (the holes on the pelvic bone) are indeed eye sockets? What if it is not just an amusing resemblance? I began to look further into this idea, and I started to put together many other strange coincidences that related structures in the body to structures in the head. Today, I have concluded that not only is the obturator foramina indeed an iteration of the eye sockets and the colon an iteration of the cerebrum, I now believe the whole body is in fact an iteration of the head. I am sure that it can be difficult for a serious scientist to entertain the possibility of an idea as bizarre as this. But, I hope that given the number and significance of the evidence listed, along with the experiments that will be proposed in this section, I will be able to convey an argument worthy of consideration. I am not a geneticist or a neuroscientist, so the observations that will be proposed will be general outlines. One of the purposes of this article is to find the funding and technical support to complete the design of these experiments, and test validity of these ideas.

C.1. Genetic experiments

It is logical to wonder how can this model help us understand life and its organizing principles when it seems to contradict the accepted theory of development? I do not think the Ed Lewis model is wrong; I think it is incomplete. I believe this idea I call the mirror model is a superstructure that encompasses development by mosaics and the Hox genes Dr. Lewis so accurately predicted. The mirror model proposes a symmetry principle consistent with a series of mutations gathered here as evidence. These mutations involve anomalies in specific genes that can be used as templates to engineer similar alterations in other parts on the genome. If the hypothesis proposed here is correct, these modifications should trigger mutations that will be consistent with the predicted mirror structures, unveiling an aspect of Lewis model not yet observed. Perhaps the most obvious subject to perform these experiments is the drosophila, since the antennapedia mutation is one of the most significant phenomena supporting this model. However, other mutations like Tooth and Nail Syndrome TNS, Branchiootorenal Syndrome BOR, and Kallmann, syndrome should also be consider for this extrapolation as well as the participation of other subjects. The experiment performed by Dr. Katherine Dulac on the behavior of rodents at Harvard University did not show a variation of the phenotype of the subjects but it did show a clear correlation between the nose and the sexual behavior of the rodents, supporting the relation stablished by this model between the genitals and the nose. I believe Dulac's experiment should also be taken in consideration, and should be extrapolated onto other parts of the genome in order to test this hypotheis.

C.2. Observation on the Circadian Rhythm and the Heartbeat as Leading Morphogenic Cycles.

I previously proposed that the cardiac and circadian rhythms exist not as a consequence of the organs that allegedly produce them, but that instead the organs are a consequence of these cycles. I believe that the cardiac and circadian rhythms could be leading electro-morphogenic cycles responsible for the coordination of the development process and could be found at the pre-embryonic stage. I believe these 2 electromagnetic centers could guide the development of the embryo by controlling the mitotic process through the peaks and valleys of their cycles. I believe that if the electric distribution of a fertilized egg is continuously monitored during the entire process of development, the presence of these electromagnetic centers will be detected. I have also speculated that these electromagnetic centers could begin as 1 pole, and periodically divide into many other sub-poles to guide the formation of different organs as the embryo complexifies. However, I also believe the cardiac and circadian rhythms will be the leading centers of this process and will always have a hire voltage than any other electromagnetic center that may be found.

C.3. Experiment on the Relation Between the Guts and the Brain.

On the previous section it was proposed that cognitive processes were the product not only of the brain, but of the interactions between the neurons on the digestive tract with the neurons on the brain. To illustrate this alleged phenomenon the body was compared to a guitar where 2 side of the instrument need to be operated in order to produce what we perceive as music. In the same way a guitar has different strings to produce different tones, the brain is divided into areas with specialized functions known as Brodmann areas. If this hypothesis is correct, reflections of specific functions of the brain should be observed in the neurons attached in the digestive tract. To test this idea, the head and the torso of a number of subjects should be monitored while performing tasks associated with specific Brodmann areas. The subjects for this observation should be divided in two groups, one group of people with normal cognitive, and neuronal functions, and another group of people with abnormal cognitive, and neuronal function. The second group should include people with conditions like: synesthesia, autism, Alzheimer, dyslexia, depression, bipolar disorder, schizophrenia, Parkinson, and others. If the hypothesis is correct the anomalies of these conditions should be expressed not only in the brain, but also along the digestive tract. The monitoring of this actions can be done with a combination of an EEG for the head and a dense distribution of electrodes throughout the torso. The same experiment can be repeated with an MRI scan of the whole body to observe different aspects of the reactions during the activities. One of the effects that is be expected is the reflection of Brodmann areas among the neurons distributed throughout the digestive tract.

Note to the reader

This has been a brief text considering the complexity and depth of the subject. Certainly, much more can be said about specific aspects of the model. I am aware that not all the organs in the body have been addressed and that this alleged mirror effect can have apparent variations among different species, and even different kingdoms. However, I hope the reader has been able to grasp the significance of the evidence that has been put forward, despite the unconventional nature of the hypothesis. The broad number of tangible connections that support this model cannot be regarded as trivial or random if observed from an impartial, honest, and objective perspective. So far, I have managed to put together this idea, despite many limitations in budget, time, and expertise, but the research necessary to test the validity of this model cannot be done singlehandedly. The purpose of this article is to capture the attention and the imagination of brave and adventurous scientists willing to sail into uncharted territory. I cannot offer grants or any benefits at the moment, but the implications of this idea could be far reaching, and the benefits that might unfold from it are in my opinion worthy of consideration.

REFERENCES

1. Analysis of co-ordination between breathing and exercise rhythms in man. By Bernasconiand J. Kohl:
   URL:
   https://www.ncbi.nlm.nih.gov/pmc/articles/PMC1143984/
2. Cardiovascular Diseases and the Eyes. By A M Mansour,F F Bitar, E I Traboulsi, K M Kassak, M Y Obeid, A Megarbane, and H I Salti:
   URLhttps://www.rebuildyourvision.com/blog/vision-conditions/cardiovascular-diseases-eyes/
3. Oxford Medicine online. Kidneys/ear syndromes:
   URL: http://oxfordmedicine.com/view/10.1093/med/9780199592548.001.0001/med-9780199592548-chapter-170

How the Electrostatic Field Works

Franklin T. Hu

19166 130th Ct. NE Bothell, WA, USA, franklinhu@yahoo.com

A fundamental question in physics is how do opposite charges attract and similar charges repel. What exactly is Charge and what exists between these charges that allows the transmission of these forces? This paper explains the electrostatic force as being the result of phased wave interactions between positive and negative charges. These waves are mediated by a special neutrally charged medium which transmits both normal electromagnetic waves and the special high frequency waves which make up the electrostatic force. This is a summary of a paper which can be found at: http://franklinhu.com/HowElectrostaticFieldWorks.pdf

Keywords: aether, ether, aether, charge, medium, electrostatic, field

A fundamental question is why do opposite charges attract and similar charges repel. We should try to understand the attraction of a positive and negative charge as somehow creating a region of low pressure between the charges which causes them to be sucked together and repulsion of similar charges as creating a region of high pressure between the identical charges.

In order to have regions of high or low pressure, we need some sort of medium like air which can fill all of space. It is proposed that this medium consists of positron/electron dipoles which are called 'poselectrons'. It is also proposed that positrons an electrons have a resonant frequency that they ring at when struck. The only difference between the positron and electron is that they ring 180 degrees out of phase.

So between a positron and electron, the waves are cancelled, which creates a region of low pressure between them. This causes the particles to appear to be attracted to one another. Similarly, between two electrons, the waves add up creating a region of high pressure between them which pushes the particles apart. So we have attraction of opposite charges and repulsion of similar charges This is the basic mechanism behind attraction and repulsion of charges. Charge itself is just a wave field emitted by a particle in only 1 of 2 phases.

This would mean that every electron would have to ring at exactly the same phase and rate as every other electron. This can be justified if time can be quantized. If there is a smallest unit of time, then everything has to change state at exactly the same time. If a particle like an electron is changing state from large to small at the fastest possible state, then it can only posses 2 binary states. This creates required lock-step for the entire universe just by saying that there is a smallest unit of time. If you find this hard to believe, then think of your digital computer which only has a binary 0 and 1 state and the computer changes in lock-step to the CPU clock. Certainly, there are systems which possess this quantization of time property. It has been speculated that the universe actually does run as a

simulation on digital hardware and that you will find this binary nature at the heart of physics.

If you still think it is unlikely that phased waves could generate the electrostatic force, it has actually been experimentally proven that such phased waves can generate forces similar to the electrostatic force. The experiment is described in the link:

http://historical.library.cornell.edu/cgibin/cul.math/ docviewer?did=02780002&view=50&frames=0&se q=11

This is an article written by Vihelm Bjerknes in 1905 called Fields of Force which demonstrated that pulses in water can generate the required forces.

If the poselectron sea exists, the question is, why hasn't it been found yet. There is experimental evidence already that such a sea exists. Some say that such a dipole cannot exist since they annihilate each other. However, the same experiments can also be explained as creating the neutral poselectron particle and emitting the kinetic energy of the collision as gamma rays. No particles are destroyed in this process. Also positrons and electrons can be kicked out of empty space in pair production. Energy is not converted to matter in these cases, energy is just just to break the bonding energy of the positron/electron dipole and kick out the separate components. There is also evidence accepted by the mainstream that the Lamb shift experiments shows that a sea of positrons and electrons must exist. If you are looking for the poselectron particle itself, it would be recognized as what we call neutrons. The only difference between an observed neutron and the surrounding sea, is that a neutron has kinetic energy and motion compared to the neutron sea that surrounds it. So in many ways, we have experimentally detected the particle that makes up aether space.

In conclusion, this paper has described what 'charge' is as a simple wave field emitted by positrons and electrons. These waves are propagated in a sea of poselectrons and the interaction of opposite phases cause attractive and repulsion effects.

How the Magnetic Field Works

Franklin T. Hu

19166 130th Ct. NE Bothell, WA, USA, franklinhu@yahoo.com

The existence of the magnetic field and the force it creates has been known for a long time, but just how this magnetic field works and what creates the forces that magnets exert has remained a complete mystery. This paper attempts to fully explain the origin and the physical mechanics behind the magnetic force as being mediated by an invisible positron/electron dipole sea which can be polarized as a magnetic field and can deflect electrons which are passing through it. This is a summary of a longer paper which can be found at: http://franklinhu.com/HowMagFieldWorks.pdf

Keywords: aether, ether, medium, electromagnetism, magnets, Lorentz, force, electrostatic, magnetism

What is the magnetic field? If we put a permanent magnet next to a nail, it can pick it up. At a minimum, a magnetic field needs to be able to specify a vector direction which determines the North/South directions and a magnitude of the field. A field of flags could represent a magnetic field with the wind blowing the flags to all point in a particular direction and the number of flags being blown representing a magnitude. However, a field of flags is not a magnetic field.

In order to have a 'field', it is proposed that there must be a material substance that fills all of space that can represent the vector direction and magnitude of the magnetic field - like a physical flag. If space consisted of nothing, then nothing cannot represent either of these values. It is proposed that the material substance that fills all of space is a positron/electron dipole particle which will be named the 'poselectron'. Since a dipole has 2 parts, you can draw an arrow from the negative side to the positive side and that can represent a directional vector that can point in any direction. The number of dipoles pointing in the same direction can represent the magnitude of the field. So a dipole is the simplest possible geometric structure that can represent a magnetic field.

The poselection is not 'hydrogen' which is a proton and an electron and it isn't positronium which is an electron orbiting a positron. The poselectron is the result of the bound state of a positron and electron. Mainstream science thinks these two particles annihilate each other, but the experiments can also be explained as producing the neutral poselectron particle and releases the collision energy as gamma rays. If we were to do experiments to find the resulting poselectron particle, we would find it.

If we start with a sea of poselectron particles, they would be randomly oriented. However, if you send a stream of electrons through this sea, it is proposed that this acts like a 'wind' and combs the poselectron particles to all point in the same direction like a field of flags. This is the fundamental reason why magnetic fields arises in the presence of moving electrical current.

Assuming we have a sea of poselectron dipoles which are all pointing the same direction, how does create the most basic effect of a magnetic field which is to deflect a moving electron. This is expressed as the Lorentz Force $F = qv \times B$. The force is proportional to the charge and the velocity of the charge and works at right angles to the magnetic field vector.

The basic mechanism is that if you line up dipoles, if you try to pass a negative electron charge between them, it will see a negative charge on the left and a positive charge on the right. As the electron passes, it will be repelled by the negative charge and attracted to the right. This causes a deflection to the right and this deflection is the fundamental origin of the magnetic force. This force depends upon the magnitude of the charge since it is fundamentally an electrostatic interaction of opposite charges. The number of dipoles a charge cuts through depends upon its velocity v, so we have a dependency upon velocity. Finally, the force will be perpendicular or at right angles to the charge direction. A charge attempting to move up through dipoles will be forced to the right. Thus, the Lorentz force law can be easily explained by a simple alignment of the dipoles of space.

While the Lorentz force law explains what happens to electrons through a magnetic field, what happens when a permanent magnet attracts an iron nail. It is proposed that the magnet and the nail are ferromagnetic because they host small superconducting current loops in the crystalline structure of magnet and nail. The conducting loops within the magnet work together to comb the poselectron field in one direction. When that field approaches the nail, it causes conduction loops to appear in the opposite direction. The electrons in both the magnet and nail are immersed in the field created by each other and causes their electrons to deflect towards each other. The electrons cannot escape the magnet or the nail, so they drag the bulk of the magnet and the nail with them by internally pushing them towards each other. This is fundamentally the force we feel as magnetic force and this is how the magnetic field works.

A Michelson-Morley Type Experiment Should be Performed in Low Earth Orbit and Interplanetary Space

James Marsen, MSME

63 Park St., Ridgefield Park, NJ 07660, james.marsen@caa.columbia.edu

This paper supports those who have proposed that a Michelson-Morley type experiment (MMX) be performed in outer space. It predicts results that will falsify the foundational postulates of Einstein's relativity. And it explains why these these unexpected results are predicted. The prediction is that a Michelson-Morley type experiment performed in low Earth orbit will show an unambiguous non-null result with a fringe or frequency variation proportional to the square of its orbital velocity ($7.6km/sec$ for a 500 km orbital altitude). If performed in interplanetary space, the result will be equivalent to the spacecraft's orbital velocity around the Sun ($\sim 30km/sec$). These predictions are based on an alternative ether concept proposed by the late Prof. Petr Beckmann in 1986 and independently developed by late Prof. Ching-Chuan Su in 2000. Prof. Su called it the local-ether model. It explains that the reason terrestrial MMX type experiments have reported null results is not because there is no "ether-wind" to detect; it is because the actual value of the "ether-wind" is due only to the velocity of Earth's rotation at the latitude of the laboratory ($464cos\theta$ meters/sec). And this is too small for even the most sensitive recent versions of the MMX to unambiguously detect. Finally we will discuss accomplishing the experiment with private funding.

Keywords: Michelson-Morley, Special Relativity, Ether, Sagnac Effect

A. Introduction

This paper presents a case for performing Michelson-Morley type experiments in low earth orbit (LEO) and (better) in interplanetary space. We predict that for low Earth orbit there would be a phase/frequency shift proportional to v^2/c^2 where v is the spacecraft's velocity with respect to the Earth Centered Inertial reference frame (the ECI) (essentially its orbital velocity). For a 500 km altitude v = 7.6 km/sec. If performed in interplanetary space, the phase/frequency shift is the spacecraft's velocity with respect to the Sun centered inertial reference frame ($\sim 30,000m/s$). This is the minimum velocity that all Michelson-Morley type experiments have expected to detect with terrestrial based interferometers.

This proposal is not new. Many have suggested it before. But the physics community is so certain of the validity of Einstein's Relativity that they believe it would produce the same null results that terrestrial implementations have reported. It would be a waste of time and money.

We will demonstrate that there are good reasons to expect a positive result:

1. Phenomena that involve the one-way point to point propagation of EM waves (including light) have shown that a the velocity of a terrestrial laboratory moves at the velocity of the Earth's rotation rate with respect to the ECI.

2. Recent MMX type experiments including the 1979 Brillet and Hall experiment probably have detected an "ether-wind" equal to the Earth's rotation rate. However, the experimenter are able dismiss the signal as "spurious" because of the low signal to noise ration and because it is unexpected.

B. A crucial experiment to falsify Einstein's Relativity and a viable alternative to replace it

The two postulates of Special Relativity imply that the speed of electromagnetic waves (including light) are independent of the motion of the receiver with respect to any reference frame. These postulates depend on the null results of MMX type experiments. are accepted as true physical reality, Special Relativity follows as an internally self-consistent representation of true physical reality (that many think is irrefutable). Since General Relativity is founded on Special Relativity, it follows as well. Therefore the most effective (and probably only) way to refute Special Relativity is to decisively demonstrate that its postulates are contradicted by experimental facts. It is also very important to provide an alternative physical model that is consistent with the physical facts. Hopefully this alternative model is simple and restores the classical concepts of absolute time and three dimensional space. Such an alternative model exists. And it suggests an experimental test that would convincingly contradict the postulates of Special Relativity.

The test is simple in concept: perform a Michelson-Morley type experiment with an interferometer on a spacecraft in low Earth orbit. Or better, launch the spacecraft into interplanetary space orbiting the Sun. It is predicted that there will be a positive result equivalent to the spacecraft's orbital velocity: $\sim 7.6km/sec$ for a 500 km altitude Earth orbit and $\sim 30km/sec$ for orbiting the Sun in interplanetary space. Special Relativity would (of course) predict null results for both. So positive results would directly contradict the reason Special Relativity was originally proposed. And since the null results of Michelson-Morley experiments done on Earth is so often cited as the fundamental proof of Special Relativity, a positive result should lead to a reevaluation of the concept of Special Relativity.

There are two arguments in favor of performing this experiment:

1. There is clear experimental evidence that the velocity rotation of the Earth is the actual velocity that terrestrial experiments should have been looking for.

2. This velocity indicates that the Earth's gravitational potential generated by the Earth's mass and is carried in it's orbit around the Sun is equivalent to a preferred reference frame. It has been detected by modern versions of the MMX but has been ignored by the experimenters as a systematic.

C. Why this experiment is worth performing

An alternative concept to Einstein's Relativity was proposed by the late Prof. Petr Beckmann in 1986 in his book, Einstein Plus Two [1] and independently by the late Prof. Ching-Chuan Su in 2000 [2]. They postulate that electromagnetic (EM) waves (including light) propagate classically via a material medium that is different than what is commonly imagined for the ether. It is not universally uniform and at rest with the Universe. They postulate that it has a variable density that is proportional to the gravitational potential/field generated by the mass of a celestial body. Like the gravitational potential, it is carried with the celestial body. It can be pictured as a "halo" surrounding the celestial body. A key difference with previous entrained ether concepts is that it doesn't rotate with the celestial body. Its direction is fixed with respect to the fixed stars and a celestial body rotates within its own halo. The halo extends out to where the gravitational field of another celestial body becomes dominant. For the Earth it is where the Sun's gravitational field becomes dominant ($\sim 10^6$ km). The outer boundary for the local-ether of the Sun and Solar System is ~ 2 light years from the Sun. An additional postulate is that the speed of light is a function of the magnitude of the local gravitational potential. Prof. Su calls this halo the local-ether.

A local-ether defines the unique preferred reference frame for the classical propagation of EM waves within its halo. "Classical" is meant in the Newtonian sense: Time is absolute (no time dilation) and space is Euclidean (no length contraction). For the Earth, this reference frame is called the Earth Centered Inertial frame (the ECI).

The Sun's local-ether is stationary with respect to the heliocentric inertial frame. There is a local-ether for the Milky Way Galaxy and one for the Local Group. A hierarchy of local-ethers of ever greater extent must exist. These local-ethers form preferred reference frames for the propagation of electromagnetic waves within their boundaries. Prof. Su further postulates that the speed of electromagnetic radiation is a function of the local gravitational potential. This is shown to account for the phenomena of General Relativity.

Based on the Local-Ether model, all experiments done on the Earth's surface are within the Earth's local-ether and are shielded from the Earth's orbital velocity around the Sun. The **only** motion of the laboratory with respect to the Earth's local-ether is due to the Earth's diurnal rotation within its local-ether halo ($464cos\theta$ meters/sec) where θ is the latitude. Also note that the direction of this velocity is always due west. This is too small to be detected by Michelson-Morley experiments that have been done before 1979. In low Earth orbit, the interferometer would also be within the Earth's local-ether and therefore also shielded from the Earth's orbital velocity around the Sun. However, the experiment would be moving within the Earth's local-ether with respect to the ECI as it orbits the Earth at $7600 meters/sec$ for a 500 km altitude orbit and it should be able to unambiguously detect that motion. It is 7600/360 = 22 times faster than the "ether-wind" for a terrestrial lab which would produce a $22^2 = 500$ times greater fringe shift/frequency variation.

Based on the local-ether model the "a function of the latitude of the laboratory (355 m/s) and that its direction is always due west. This velocity has been clearly detected by many experiments that involve the one-way propagation of EM waves. These phenomena include the pseudorange correction formula used to calculate the latitude and longitude of a GPS receiver [9] and the longer propagation times for intercontinental microwave signals sent transmitted east compared to when they transmitted west to east between the same locations [6][8]. This velocity is easier to detect than for MMX type experiments because the effect is proportional to v/c (i.e. first order).

Note that none of these phenomena show any influence from the Earth's motion with respect to the Sun, the Milky Way Galaxy, or the CMBR Dipole. Also note, one should be highly skeptical of any terrestrial experiment that reports an "ether wind" that is not equivalent to the Earth's rotation.

An MMX type experiment involves the two-way propagation (reflection) of a light source. This cancels out any effect proportional to v/c (first order). However a signal proportional to v^2/c^2 (i.e. second order) remains.

This explains why MMX type experiments have come up empty - at least until the Brillet and Hall experiment in 1979 [4]: they were not sensitive enough to detect the velocity of the Earth's rotation. The signal for a second order experiment at 40°latitude is $(355/30000)^2 = .00014$ times smaller then a signal due to the Earth's orbital velocity would be.

When MMX type experiments failed to detect a 30000 m/s "ether wind", 19th and early 20th century mainstream physics jumped to the conclusion that it meant there was no "ether wind" to be detected. This led inexorably to Einstein's Relativity.

But the physics of the propagation of electromagnetic waves and light **must** be the same whether the experiment is first order in v/c or second order in v^2/c^2.

The 1979 Brillet and Hall experiment detected a signal consistent with the Earth's rotation velocity that varied at twice the rotation rate of the base of the interferometer ($2\omega R$) but it was dismissed as "spurious" and was averaged out of the results. The goal of the experiment was to detect an anisotropy due to the Earth's motion relative to the CMBR dipole and this would only be detectable over a month or more.

More recent MMX type interferometers use cavity resonators for even greater sensitivity. Their goal has been to test for Lorentz invariance violations predicted by some recent theories. At least some of them also mention a $2\omega R$ signal (for ones that rotate the base of the device).

They also dismiss this signal as a systematic and average it out of their results. They are also expecting a signal that varies over the course of days or months. I assert that the $2\omega R$ signal is actually the long sought "ether wind". However the experimenters appear to be so certain of the correctness of Einstein's Relativity that they assume the $2\omega R$ signal must be spurious.

According to mainstream physics, all first order experiments involve rotation and are therefore examples of the Sagnac Effect. And since the mainstream claims that the Sagnac effect does not violate Einstein's Relativity they dismiss any first order experiment as not a disproof of Einstein's Relativity.

This is why an MMX type experiment in low earth orbit or interplanetary space experiment is necessary. It is necessary to show a positive result for the same experiment that led to Einstein's Relativity. If done in low earth orbit, the "ether wind" would be equal to the spacecraft's velocity with respect to the ECI: 7600 m/s. This would be much easier to unambiguously detect and therefore could not be dismissed. If done in interplanetary space, the spacecraft would be moving with respect to the Sun's local-ether so the full orbital velocity would be measured. According to Einstein's Relativity, the results would be null so this would be a falsification of the fundamental postulates of Special Relativity that could not be denied. If they expected non-null results, it would have been tried already. This makes it much more difficult to try to make an after-the-fact claim that positive results were consistent with Einstein's Relativity.

D. Analysis of Michelson-Morley type experiments based on the local-ether model

Prof. Su specifically discusses Michelson-Morley type experiments in §6.2 of "A local-ether model of propagation of EM wave" [2]:

"From physical reasoning, it is expected that the propagation mechanism in the Michelson-Morley experiment in no way can be different from that in GPS and earthbound microwave link experiments, from the standpoint of any plausible propagation model. The null effect of earth's orbital motion in the Michelson-Morley experiment reflects no Sagnac correction due to this motion in the GPS pseudorange. On the other hand, the Sagnac effect due to earth's rotation in the high-precision GPS and intercontinental microwave link should reflect a non-null effect of earth's rotation in the Michelson-Morley experiment. The difficulty in the Michelson-Morley experiment is that this effect becomes a term of the second order of the normalized speed, owing to the round-trip path and the lack of relative motion between transceiver and target."

And:

"According to the classical propagation model, the resonance frequency of a cylindrical cavity resonator is inversely proportional to the round-trip propagation time over the propagation path along the cylinder axis. Thus the motion of the cavity with respect to the unique propagation frame tends to affect the round-trip propagation time and hence the resonance frequency. The shift in propagation time can manifest itself as a corresponding variation in beat frequency between two waves from two perpendicular cylindrical cavities [28] or between a wave from a single cavity and a reference wave from a stable source [29,30].

Then, based on the local-ether model, the second-order round-trip Sagnac effect due to earth's rotation results in a quadrupole anisotropy in the resonance frequency of a cylindrical cavity, as the direction of cavity is changing.

That is, the resonance frequency is the lowest when the axis of the cavity points in the east-west direction; it is the highest when it is in the north-south direction. As the cavity is rotating slowly with respect to the ground in a horizontal plane, the beat frequency is expected to vary sinusoidally at twice the turntable rotation rate.

Moreover, the peak-to-peak amplitude Δf_{max} for the case of a single cavity can be found from the round-trip propagation time given in (13) as

$$\Delta f_{max}/f = v_E^2/2c^2 \simeq 1.2cos^2\theta_l \times 10^{-12}, \quad (14)$$

where $v_E = \omega_E R_E cos(\theta_l)$ is the linear speed due to earth's rotation with respect to an ECI frame, R_E is earth's radius, and θ_l is the latitude."

"Such a heterodyne system using a stable He-Ne laser at 3.39 μm (f = 0.88 $\times 10^{14}$ Hz) and a stable Fabry-Perot resonator has been developed [29]. According to the local-ether model, the amplitude Δf_{max} is expected to be 62 Hz, as the cavity heterodyne experiment is supposed to be conducted at a latitude of $40°$. In the measured data, a term varying at the expected rate has been reported. However, the peak-to-peak amplitude of this term is merely about $17 \times$ Hz and was attributed to a persistent spurious signal among other larger noises. It seems too early to make a decisive conclusion from this experiment. A more careful experiment is anticipated to test the second-order round-trip Sagnac effect supposed due to earth's rotation."

Reference [29] refers to the 1979 Brillet and Hall experiment [4]. This experiment was also analyzed by Prof. Howard Hayden [7][9]. He came to the same conclusion that the experiment most likely detected an "ether-wind" equal to the Earth's rotation rate but the signal to noise ration was low enough that it could be ignored as "spurious".

I again stress that a Michelson-Morley type experiment needs to be performed in low Earth orbit or (better) in interplanetary space to unambiguously resolve the discrepancy between first order and second order EM wave propagation experiments. The physics of EM wave propagation **must** be the same whether the propagation path is one-way point-to-point (first order in v/c) (e.g. GPS pseudo-range correction) or two-way round-trip second order in v^2/c^2 (e.g. MMX type interferometers).

E. The MMX "ether-drift" has been detected but dismissed

There have been several MMX type experiments done in the past 20 years with increasing sensitivity. They were looking for violations of Lorentz Invariance assuming the CMBR forms a universal inertial reference frame. They report null results with ever higher precision. However, they appear to detect (but dismiss) a signal consistent with the Earth's rotation with respect to the Earth Centered Inertial reference frame (the ECI). This is consistent with experiments that are sensitive to the first order of v/c that clearly detect this velocity. From one of the most recent experiments by Nagel et al. in 2015 using cavity resonators on a rotating platform [5]: "Taking error-weighted averages of relevant amplitudes from equation (1) we found a $2\omega R$ amplitude of 98±6 nHz. This value of interest, $2\omega R$, is only statistically significant, owing to the influence of systematic noise sources (see Fig. 3), the most dominant of which is the dependency of oscillator resonance frequency on external magnetic fields, arising from the presence of impurities in the sapphire crystal25 and ferrite-based microwave components. The frequency variations induced by moving the oscillators through the quasi-static magnetic field of the Earth in the laboratory **are indistinguishable from a Lorentz violating signal**." (my emphasis). I suggest that it could have been possible to shield the experiment from the Earth's magnetic field if they were not so confident that it must be only a systematic effect.

F. How to accomplish Low Earth Orbit MMX with private funding

So why haven't these experiments been done years ago? The probable answer is that the mainstream physics is so certain the Einstein's Relativity is correct that they believe the results would be the same null results as terrestrial based Michelson-Morley type experiments. It would be a waste of time and money. No committee would dare approve such a proposal.

Perhaps the best option would be to privately fund the experiment. The good news is that the cost of getting it done is much lower than in the past. There is now a commercial company that will launch a small satellite into a 500 km orbit for a relatively modest fee. The company is called Rocket Lab [12]. It has already had three successful launches. It supports the launch of small satellites called CubeSats [11] that use standardized off-the-shelf components that can share the ride with several other projects so the cost of the launch is only a fraction of what a dedi-

cated launch would cost. It's also developing a capability to design and implement small satellites using a standard base called "Photon" that provides common components for control and communications. I would think they would accept the project as long as it is paid for. At one point they were quoting $100K$ dollars for a single unit CubeSat.

It might be able to accomplish the project for around 500,000 dollars. It might be feasible to raise this amount by crowd sourcing.

Interplanetary MMX would be more expensive and there aren't any commercial launch services that support it yet. But if low Earth orbit MMX is successful, it would be a powerful argument for a NASA or other government space agency to sponsor the project.

G. Conclusion

We predict that a Michelson-Morley experiment performed in low earth orbit will produce an unambiguous positive result proportional to the square of the orbital velocity. If successful, Einstein's Relativity will be proven to be fatally flawed.

The first step is to perform the experiment in low earth orbit using private funds to be launched by a commercial company like Rocket Lab so approval by a mainstream committee would not be required.

After a successful result is achieved, then the more expensive version performed in interplanetary space would be more likely to be sponsored by NASA or the space agency of another country.

Please also see Prof. Su's full thesis from 2005 Quantum Electromagnetics [3] for further details on how he provides alternative qualitative and quantitative explanations for a wide array of physical phenomena based on his local-ether model. And he extends his model to unify electromagnetic, quantum, and gravitational phenomena.

I also recommend Questioning Einstein: Is Relativity Necessary? by Thomas Bethell. He describes Beckmann's theory for non-physicists and presents the case for MMX in outer space more clearly than I can.

REFERENCES

1. Beckmann, Petr Einstein Plus Two, 1987, Golem Press, New York, ISBN: 0-911762-39-61987.
2. Su, Ching-Chuan, "A local-ether model of propagation of electromagnetic wave", Eur. Phys. J. C 21, 701 (2001), https://preview.tinyurl.com/yyrkadvr.
3. Su, Ching-Chuan, Quantum electromagnetics: a local-ether wave equation unifying quantum mechanics : electromagnetics, and gravitation, https://preview.tinyurl.com/yyxonxb6. Note that the web page points to some brokein links. Prof. Su published his full thesis as an eBook that is available from: https://ebook.hyread.com.tw/bookDetail.jsp?id=19899 for about 17 dollars. (use Google to translate from Chinese).
4. Brillet, A., Hall,John L., Phys. Rev. Lett. 42, 549 (1979)
5. Nagel et al., "Direct terrestrial test of Lorentz symmetry in electrodynamics to 10(-18)", Nature Communications, volume 6, Article number: 8174 (2015)
6. Saburi, Y., Yamamoto M., Harada, K., "High-Precision Time Comparison via Satellite and Observed Discrepancy of Synchronization", IEEE Trans. Instrum.Meas. IM 25, 473

(1976)

7. Hayden, Howard C., "Is the Velocity of Light Isotropic in the Frame of the Rotating Earth?", Physics Essays Volume 4, Number 3 (1991)

8. Marmet, Paul., "The GPS and the Constant Velocity of Light", Acta Scientiarum, 22, 1269, 2000, https://preview.tinyurl.com/yxp5qrca.

9. Bethell, Thomas, Questioning Einstein: Is Relativity Necessary?, Vales Lake Publishing, Colorado, 2009.

10. Psimopoulos, M., Theocharis, Theo., "Testing Special Relativity", Nature 319 (1986) 269.

11. http://cubesat.org .

12. https://www.rocketlabusa.com .

Reason for a Cyclone to Spin
—Coriolis Force only Terminates It

Cameron Rebigsol

P.O. Box 872282, Vancouver, WA 98686. e-mail: crebigsol@gmail .com

Can Coriolis force accurately explain the spinning behavior of cyclones? One obvious observation about cyclones is that they all have converging movement while spinning about an eye, but Coriolis Effect is put up based on diverging movement. Convergence and divergence are two opposite concepts. More physics must have been involved in resulting in the converging movement patterns of cyclones.

Keywords: Cyclones, equator, air pressure, disk, walling effect

Clouds[1] in sky may contain various physical forms of water: vapor, mist, water droplets, rain drops, or even ice droplets. So averaged out, they have many occasions ending up with higher mass density than air. Suspending in high air with near zero restriction in horizontal movement, they may collect each other under the influence of mutual gravitational force among them. Whether they have come in contact or not, but when the distance is right, they may sooner or later organize the appearance of a prominent mass across a big area in the sky. We will call it a disk of cloud. It is natural that prominent mass has a prominent mass center. However, at where mass center is located, mass may not necessarily be found.

Our Earth keeps incessantly self-spinning. Its spinning drags the atmosphere to move over its surface and, the clouds, being "hijacked" by the atmosphere, must also move over the surface of the Earth. It is so natural that the spherical shape of the Earth would introduce speed difference between some clouds moving near the equator and other clouds that are more away from the equator but closer to Earth's pole, with those near the equator moving faster linear distance wise. If these two groups of clouds happen to belong to one big disk of cloud, the south part and the north part of the same disk must move out of pace with respect to the ground.

For clarity in explanation, let's focus on a cloud disk found in the north hemisphere. For this cloud disk, its south edge would have higher speed toward the east, while the north edge lower. If the higher speed is called V_1 and the lower speed is called V_3, we can easily figure out that the speed, called V_2, of the mass center of this disk should fit in this relationship: $V_1>V_2>V_3$. The speed difference between the south edge and north edge should have buried the seed of rotation with respect to the mass center of the disk of clouds, pending on the maturity of other physical conditions.

The centrifugal force produced by the Earth's spinning forces everything on it to have a tendency to be swung away toward the outer space (f_1 in Fig 1). This centrifugal force is parallel to the equatorial plane and be determined by $f_1 = m\omega^2 r$, where m is the mass under the influence of the centrifugal force, ω is the angular spinning speed of the Earth and r is the perpendicular distance between the mass in concern and the spinning axis of the Earth. According to this equation, the south edge of the disk of clouds, with a bigger distance from the Earth's axis, should have a higher elevation than the mass center with respect to the surface of the Earth (assuming a perfect sphere). Therefore, the south edge may produce certain fluid pressure due to gravity toward the mass center.

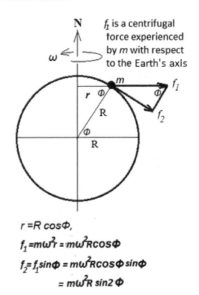

$$r = R\cos\Phi,$$
$$f_1 = m\omega^2 r = m\omega^2 R\cos\Phi$$
$$f_2 = f_1\sin\Phi = m\omega^2 R\cos\Phi\sin\Phi$$
$$= m\omega^2 R\sin 2\Phi$$

Anything m suspended in air tends to be pulled toward the Equator by force f_2

Figure 1. A pulling force toward the Equator

The pressure difference between the south edge and the mass center of the disk may be further escalated due to another force. Everything suspended in air tends to be herded toward the Equator by a force indicated as f_2 in Fig 1. Force f_2 has the maximum value at $\phi = 45^o$ and zero at $\phi = 0^o$ or $\phi = 90^o$. So, the mass center, located more northern than the south edge, would have a tendency ducking under the south edge. Meanwhile, being more northern than the mass center, the north edge would push itself toward the mass center, resulting in a wall towering over the mass center. The overall result is that the mass center has a tendency to sink itself lower than both the north edge and south edge and subsequently has the highest mass density among the three. We call this effect brought out by both edges but suffered by the mass center the walling effect.

While kneading the center part of the cloud disk being lower than the south and north edge, force f_2 further works out to turn the cloud disk into a spinning disk.

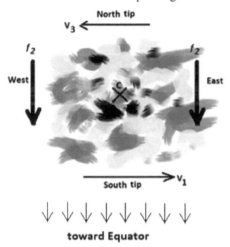

V₁, V₂ and both f_2 work together

motivating the cloud gathering into
a spinning disk

(Viewer is at rest with respect to
the mass center c)

Figure 2. A counterclockwise spinning disk is in the making

In Fig 2, both f_2 in the east and west should statistically have the same magnitude pointing toward the south, or the Equator. However, since the entire disk of clouds is a fluid body, f_2 in the west is beefed up by the momentum carried by the moving mass traveling at speed V_3 on the north edge. Meanwhile, f_2 in the east is crippled by the momentum carried by the moving mass in south traveling at V_1. Consequentially, due to $V_1 > V_3$, f_2 in the west ends up being stronger than the f_2 in the east. Then, with respect to the mass center of the disk, f_2 produces a stronger torque; torque usually ends up forcing a free body to rotate. The moving style so presented is applicable to any material forming a loop of any radius encircling the mass center of the cloud disk.

When a large cloud disk gets into a rotation state, what we call a cyclone[2] appears. With the information presented in Fig 2, a counterclockwise rotation is easily visualized out of it. This explains why cyclones in the north hemisphere normally appear spinning counterclockwise. Symmetrically, a clockwise rotating cyclone can also be visualized as shown in Fig 3 if the cyclone appears in the south hemisphere.

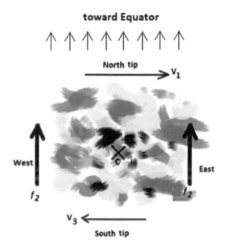

A clockwise spinnning cyclone in

the south hemisphere is
in the making

(Viewer is at rest with respect to
the mass center c)

Figure 3. A clockwise spinning disk is forming

In both Fig 2 and Fig 3, had speed V_1 and V_3 been nearly equal in magnitude, f_2 in the east and west would have always been nearly equal. Then this pair of force would most likely push the entire cloud disk coherently to move toward the Equator. Some local dimples may be made into spinning because of the friction agitated by V_1 and V_3, which are moving in opposite direction, but the entire disk would hardly get into spinning.

When the entire disk gets into a spinning state, at the beginning, the clouds at distance further away from the mass center have higher linear speed than those nearer the center. The air pressure below the outer edge of the disk therefore drops more than that is closer to the center. This is a common fluid phenomenon—at where an object travels at higher speed, the pressure of the ambient fluid drops more. To establish balance, the pressure below the center of the disk also correspondingly lowers itself, causing the central part of the disk, which has the highest mass density in the disk, further to sink lower.

The further sinking of the center creates chance for the neighboring clouds at bigger distance to roll in because of the pressure difference so created. As the distance shortened toward the center, the rolling in neighbors, due to momentum conservation, will circle about the center at higher speed, further reducing the air pressure below the cloud disk. It won't take long for the clouds closer to the center to travel at higher speed than those at the outer edge. This means that an area of the lowest air pressure below the entire disk begins to build up about the center, and the central clouds cannot help but only to keep sinking. If the cloud quantity of the disk is large enough, and if the original air pressure below the disk was already low enough at the start, the aforementioned neighboring-mass-rolling-in will continue with ever escalated intensity. This may lead to at some point that the clouds located in the central region center, being the densest portion, are totally sucked away toward the ground. A hole, or called the eye of the cyclone, is created.

When the eye is brought into shape, dramatic mechanical phenomena appear. Being the spot of the lowest pressure in the disk, the eye becomes a bottomless abyss keeping sucking materials from the adjacent area in the cloud disk. As materials rush to the eye, they must move at higher and higher speed, both linear and angular. With higher linear speed, the materials flying near the eye further cause the air pressure there to maximally drop. Higher angular speed, on the other hand, must produce stronger centrifugal force, forbidding the flying materials from truly approaching the dead center. Then, next to the eye, a circular wall of air current is formed. Within this wall, two forces fiercely compete and balance each other: (1) the centrifugal force, and (2) the sucking force of the eye. The higher the linear speed mentioned in (1), the lower the air pressure is in the eye.

The fierce turbulence of a cyclone must end itself because the disk must carry only a limited quantity of clouds, no matter how big it was at the beginning. After more clouds have been sucked toward the eye and dispersed at lower elevation, the disk gradually shrinks. Without continuous material carrying enough momentum to sustain the eye's sucking power, the cyclone must end up being self-extinct.

From formation to disappearance, the material movement within a cyclone is dominated by a converging movement; hardly any diverging movement is seen involved. However, it seems to this author that all contemporary popular explanations on the reason why cyclones appear are based on the so called Coriolis effect or Coriolis force [3]. Either Coriolis effect or Coriolis force is about diverging movement. As a matter of fact, some Coriolis effect we detect may have nothing to do with the supposed Coriolis force (Fig 4). Instead of having any force involved, the Coriolis effect may sometimes just be some visual effect, whose appearance is not a result of any dynamic consequence other than kinematic consequence. In Fig 4, the ball's actual traveling path has nothing to do with the turning table; therefore no Coriolis force or any kind of force appears during its movement, regardless.

If a physical influence is called force, it must have the quality of producing acceleration on some mass. Coriolis force should have no exception. In Fig 5, the ball has direct

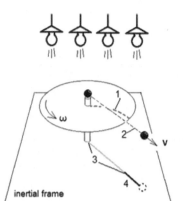

1. Loci of ball projected and recorded on turn table

2. Actual historical path of the ball

3. Path 2 projected and recorded directly below the turn table

4. Path 2 projected and recorded outside the turn table

Illusory Coriolis Effect

Figure 4.   Illusory Coriolis effect

contact with the turn table. When it is propelled leaving the center of the turn table, the turn table would inevitably exert influence on the ball's movement, no matter whether the movement is in the form of rolling or sliding over the table. It can be easily deduced that it is an accelerated movement, in which the ball must also move on a new radial line in every next instant of its movement. When it finally leaves the turn table, it would have obtained the maximum speed and would continue its movement at this speed and in a direction different from its initial velocity. The bigger the turn table is, the more this new direction would point at the center of the tern table with this final speed.

In comparison to the above analysis, we can regard the cloud collection portraying as a cyclone to be a collection of black balls in Fig 5 placed on a turn table (See Fig 6)

It is potentially possible that when a cloud gathering has become large enough and a spinning cyclone is on the way to flex its muscle, the Coriolis force loses no time to step up a process of tearing the cloud into pieces and throw them away from the edge of the gathering. For the tearing to be successful, the Coriolis force must overcome three forces: (1) the overall mutual gravitational force produced by the entire gathering, (2) the force caused by the walling effect on both the north and south edge of the cloud gathering, (3) the sucking power pointing toward the eye.

If the Coriolis force wins, the spinning cyclone mass would be disintegrated—the cloud gathering had been large enough to start a cyclone but not large enough to resist the destructive power of the Coriolis force and there-

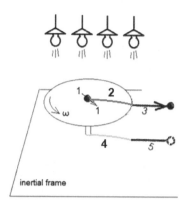

1-1 The ball's initial moving direction

2. The curved loci of the ball's movement printed on the turn table

3. Speed and direction the ball carries at the time it leaves the turn table

4. Loci 2 projected on the inertial frame

5. Loci 3 projected on the inertial frame

The movement of a ball under the influence of Coriolis Force

Figure 5.   Coriolis force in action

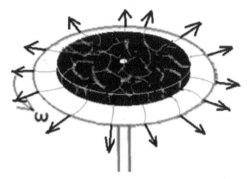

All arrows represent the velocity of all torn pieces from the cloud collection on the turn table when leavng the turn table.

The fine curved lines represent the loci they traced and left on the turn table

True Coriolis effect on a cloud collection as a candidate of a cyclone

Figure 6.   A cyclone disk is underway of dismantling due to action of Coriolis force

fore unable to sustain the cyclone to live on. It is not some rare events that from time to time certain expected cyclone said in the way to be spawned in meteorology report eventually vanishes itself.

Of course, if the Coriolis force fails, the three forces mentioned above would soon push up the appearance of a madly spinning cyclone. However, it does not mean the Coriolis force is willing to recede from the scene. When enough amounts of materials have been sucked by the eye and dispersed toward the ground, the cloud disk prominently reduces its diameter. Although the shrunk disk continues to spin about the eye with the high speed it has been "trained" to accomplish with, the angular momentum must reduce with its diminishing material stock. Eventually it must come to a point that all three forces working together cannot resist the Coriolis force, which keeps increasing in correspondence with the escalated spinning of the cloud disk. Being torn apart becomes an inescapable fate of the disk. Once adequately dispersed, the madly flying power of each cloud piece is braked by the adjacent air. The cyclone ceases.

Nevertheless, now we can see that the essential nature of Coriolis force is of a centrifugal force with two imperative characteristics: (1) its magnitude continues increasing, (2) with respect to a spinning reference frame that enables the Coriolis fore to grow in magnitude, this force must continuously change its radial line on this frame in every instant of its existence.

REFERENCES

1. Clouds, https://en.wikipedia.org/wiki/Cloud
2. Cyclones, https://en.wikipedia.org/wiki/Cyclone
3. Coriolis force, https://en.wikipedia.org/wiki/Coriolis_force

That the Universe Is Infinite Is Ironclad

Cameron Rebigsol

P.O. Box 872282, Vancouver, WA 98686. e-mail: crebigsol@gmail .com

This author do feel puzzled what has been found as evidence supporting the idea of a limited, or bounded universe. As far as this author can find, **none!**

(1) Arguments rejecting an infinite universe is self-refuted. (2) Arguments advocating or serving as frame work for a limited universe is self-refuted. (3) No fact preventing the existence of an unlimited universe has ever been found. (4) Facts tolerated and embraced only by an unlimited universe are gaining stronger and stronger credibility as our cosmological observation skill getting more and more advanced.

Overall, we have only two versions of argument regarding the size of the universe: infinite and limited. If the version of a limited universe must be rejected by evidence and logic, we have only the version of infinite universe left for choice.

Keywords: Olbers' paradox, stone wall, relativity, acceleration, light, CMB (cosmic microwave background), BBT (Big Bang Theory), pillars.

The most prevailing argument for a limited universe nowadays is the theory called the Big Bang theory (BBT). Generally, the BBT claims that everything we can detect as part of the universe came out from one single point called Singularity. The creation of this universe is a result of a onetime explosion of this Singularity and the explosion is completed in an extremely short duration of time. To defend their idea, people supporting the BBT naturally put up reasons to emphasize how an infinite universe being impossible. One of the arguments they feel most strongly serving their point of view is the Olbers' paradox [1].

Olbers' paradox holds that logic must lead to the appearance of infinite brightness in the sky if the universe is infinite and then has infinite stars in the sky. Unfortunately, due to history reason, Olbers' paradox is ignorant of two pieces of critical evidence: (1) stars all have different birth days, and (2) stars must have different life span from each other. These two phenomena tell us that at any instant, the sky is illuminated by limited stars that are taking turn to shine the sky. How can the limited stars give infinite brightness in the sky when the sky is infinite? Indeed, both of the above evidence are reinforced by a third piece of evidence in failing Olbers' paradox. It is the stars' red-shift.

The stars' red-shift reveals that the farther away from us, the younger the stars are found. The retrospective reasoning then naturally tells us that in space nearer and nearer to us, i.e. the observers on Earth, stars are more popularly getting older and dimmer or even having died. This would be a direct fact rejecting the possible existence of infinite (shining) stars in the sky. No infinite stars, no validity to Olbers' paradox, it is simple and direct.

Roughly, with respect to a certain distance in any direction of observation, stars have about the same age. Based on this isotropic observation, simple linear reasoning could easily encourage someone to conclude that all the materi-als that eventually evolved into stars must have initially started their journey from one single point, and further, so does the history of our universe. However, guided by this linear reasoning, the Big Bang believers would have to create many impassable stone walls for themselves in convincing other people to accept their cosmological model. These stone walls can only destine their model to a fate of self-refutation.

Stone wall one: Edge of the universe.

To the BBT believers, the isotropic movement and distribution of materials impeccably witness an expanding universe. Expansion imperatively needs the presence of some edge. Without being described by the movement of an edge, no volume can be said expanding. The problem of the edge now boils down to two issues: whether the edge only carries the sense of geometry or whether the edge is physically tangible.

If the edge has only geometrical sense, it means that this edge only serves to separate space with marks and it is not physically tangible. This equivalently advocates that only space on one side of the marked edge does exist what is called the universe by the BBT supporters. But then, what is the space on the other side? Obviously, the geometry edge cannot stop the BBT supporters' universe from being owned by one continuous space straddling across both sides of this edge. The concept of a limited universe must cease existing right at the geometrical edge.

If it is not a geometrical edge, the edge must be physically tangible. But then there would be two prominent difficulties challenging the BBT supporters for answer. (1) What is the material nature and material quantity of this edge? Remember, the BBT claims that everything of the universe is from a Singularity. Naturally, all materials, belonging to the edge or not, must be from the Singularity. (2) How this edge would interact with anything coming from the universe encircled by this edge, such as light, microwaves, or stars traveling at extraordinarily high speed toward it?

Regarding difficulty (1) above, no chemical element or compound known to human beings can satisfy this question—a material that can infinitely stretch to accommodate the expansion that has been going on for 13.5B years and the expansion is said still on the way continuing. Most critically, when was this material edge put in shape? ***Immediately*** at the instant the explosion occurred or *a while after*? If immediately, the thickness of this edge, or more properly termed, the shell, must have infinite thickness so that it still has enough material today tightly wrapping up the universe after 13.5B years of its expansion. Then, the existence of this infinitely thick shell contradicts and refutes the concept of a limited universe. How about *a while after* if not immediately? So far, ever since the BBT was debut, concerning the material evolution of the universe, all that this theory has put up is about the evolution of the material we know of through experience we learn in daily life on Earth, including the material we observe form the sky. Nothing about this edge material has been mentioned. So after 13.5B years, this "a while after" should be long enough to witness the BBT to have failed in having a physical boundary put up with material we know of to serve its concept of a limited universe.

If no physical boundary can be logically visualized, there can only be a geometry boundary, or edge, left as choice for the BBT.

Regarding difficulty (2), let's focus the interaction between the supposed edge and light. Given that the light sources are all the burning stars and "inside" the universe, a tangible edge can only have three types of interaction with light: (i) allowing light to penetrate and thus egress, (ii) no egress but reflection, (iii) absorption.

Obviously, type (i) is not allowed by the BBT. Allowing light to penetrate beyond the physical boundary is admitting the existence of an unlimited universe. Neither is Interaction type (ii) allowed by the BBT. If the edge is able to reflect light, it will turn Olbers' paradox into a weapon against the BBT itself because, logically, all lights collected from the stars will contribute a bright sky—a characteristic that the BBT considers only an infinite sky can have. How about type (iii), then?

Materials do absorb all kinds of electromagnetic energy, but not limitlessly. After reaching some saturation limit, it would radiate, although, frequency wise, what it radiates may be different from what it has absorbed. This radiation is in effect another type of reflection. If Olbers' paradox will end up introducing an infinitely bright sky in the argument of type (ii) interaction above, this paradox will introduce an infinitely hot sky in the universe, because, besides visible light, the absorption modifies type (ii) interaction to include every kind of electromagnetic waves: radio wave, microwaves, infrared, ultraviolet, X-rays, gamma rays.

Stone wall two: cosmic microwave background (CMB).

Here is a statement from some authoritative article regarding cosmic background noise: The CMB is electromagnetic radiation as a remnant from an early stage of the universe [2].

A remnant? A remnant must mean something left behind by a source that has no longer existed. According to the BBT, the source, the "early stage" of the universe producing the future remnant, is gone extremely near 13.5B years ago [3]. If expansion is an ever true concept for the universe, at the epoch that the electromagnetic radiation accompanying with the Big Bang explosion was not yet becoming a remnant, the universe must have occupied an extremely small volume. Now, the BBT must answer the following questions:

(1) Was the electromagnetic radiation as one form of energy fully occupying the entire universe in the entire processing of its expansion? Of course, the BBT can only have "yes" for answer. "No" is a suicidal answer for the BBT itself. "No" means the propagation speed of the radiation cannot catch up with the expansion speed of the universe and must continue to chase after the expanding edge before it can return back to us and show to us as background noise.

(2) But, if yes, how did the pace of propagation of the "remnant" happen to be the same as the pace of expansion of the universe? Remember, electromagnetic energy propagates at constant speed, but today we have a concept of accelerated expansion for the universe. Furthermore, all versions of the BBT claim that in the early phase of the Big Bang, the universe was very rapidly expanding. But how rapidly, at speed equaltl to the speed of light or even higher? Adding the accelerated expansion to this "rapidly" concept, only "no" can be the answer. It means that either yes or no, the BBT cannot escape from a self-refuted destination.

Stone wall three: accelerated expansion.

Acceleration means force. A continuous acceleration requires a continuous force. How has a continuous force acting today not destroyed the concept of *completion* for an explosion that the BBT claimed happening 13.5B years ago? Will this force, like the CMB, be also considered a remnant of something by the BBT supporters?

Stone wall four: no huge space void found.

According to the BBT, at the completion of the explosion, everything flies away from each other in an isotropic manner. The concept of completion inevitably suggests the existence of some final patches of materials out of the explosion. Trailing behind such final patches of whatever can only be absolute emptiness. Subsequently, the isotropic movement of the final patch coming together must embrace a void, in which nothing but an absolute vacuum is found. The void must expand as fast as the final patch of material can fly. After the expansion of 13.5B years of the universe, this void must be unfathomably huge in the heavens. Do people ever by any chance see such a void in the sky? None! Such a void is so logically unavoidable if the BBT must insist the existence of a onetime explosion for the birth of the universe. The absence of such a void therefore inevitably witnesses the birth defect of the BBT.

Being aware of the dire birth defect, to salvage, some BBT supporters suggest that materials and energy somehow continue springing up from somewhere in the universe even today. This suggestion directly removes the idea of *completion* of a single explosion of the Singularity. Besides, in order to survive, this suggestion has to remove the conservation laws of energy and mass. The BBT cannot have it both ways: The explosion completed 13.5B years ago has not yet completed today.

Stone wall five: the self-refuted mathematical nature of Relativity.

It has been commonly known that the main frame work of the cosmic model conceived by the BBT relies on Einstein's general relativity. But general relativity is a work generalizing special relativity, providing a unified description of gravity as a geometric property of space and time. Consequently, if special relativity is found to be a failing theory, the concept of "spacetime" will be falsified, and so will the concept "gravity as a geometric property" (other than a physical property of something). Unfortunately to the BBT, special relativity *is* a mathematically self-refuted theory [4].

Stone wall six: gravity.

No matter how powerful the onetime explosion of the Singularity could be, the omnipresent gravity produced by the materials must continuously impede the materials' movement leaving the collective center of mass of all these materials. If the BBT is valid, there are only two consequences for the movement to end up with: (1) all the materials will eventually contract back to their collective mass center, or (2) the exploding force outcompetes the overall gravitational force produced by the materials as an entirety, and the materials continue to move away from the mass center. However, they must then show deceleration in the movement.

What is cruel to both of the above hypothetical consequences is that the universe is currently found expanding with *acceleration*. Based on the idea that an explosion already completed long ago according to the BBT, the continuous but accelerating expansion of the universe must lead to the denial of the existence of a collective mass center for the universe. The reason is this: if what the BBT conceives is true, the universe must have only limited quantity of materials and therefore a collective mass center can exist and must exist for the universe. On the contrary, a collective mass center can find no place in an unlimited space and if in it the materials has a homogenous distribution. If the BBT must end up rejecting the existence of a mass center for the universe, its preaching must surrender to the concept of an unlimited universe.

Stone wall seven: coincidence of time window.

When the BBT claims that the youngest stars from the most remote "edge" in our observation are the earliest creation of the Big Bang explosion, can it explain how it has legitimately established a coincidence of time window for the observation? Had our skill of observation been born later than this time window, we could see nothing but older stars at the same distance that the newly born stars are seen today. If we keep staring at the same direction, no matter how long into the future, we cannot expect to see more stars debut, because, according to the BBT, we have seen "the earliest creation", and no more another "earliest" is logically possible. Had our skill of observation been born earlier than this time window, we can see absolutely nothing at the same distance we found the earliest creation, because these youngest stars have not had enough time to have their portraits transmitted to our observation instruments. Instead, we can only see older stars at distance closer to us.

Not only all the seven stone walls coming together decline the idea of a limited universe from gaining validity, but they literally divert our reasoning to accept an unlimited universe. Let's go over them once more and see how they would serve as pillars supporting the idea of an unlimited universe.

Pillar one: edge of the universe.

While a physical edge encircling the universe cannot exist, we find no reason to reject the existence of an edge that is restrictively in the sense of geometry. Such a geometry edge will enable us to realize that space is one continuous entity straddling across this edge. There can be two different worlds bordering this edge, but both worlds are owned by one continuous space, and therefore each world is one portion of the one single continuous universe signified by the single continuous space.

Our experience tells us that we live in a space in which materials have been detectable to us. Then we can assume that the space with detectable materials would all belong to one side of the space bordering the geometrical edge. But on the other side, the world has not been detectable to us, but logic and reality decline us from claiming it nonexistent—this is what a geometrical edge about. The most we can do regarding these two worlds separated by the geometry edge is to regard the world we live in as the visible portion of the universe, the other world is not yet visible. As the visible portion can expand and even expand with acceleration in an isotropic manner, we have to say that it is the invisible portion offers the space for the expansion of the visible portion to go on.

Only a geometry edge can infinitely stretch in accommodation with the unlimited expansion of anything for 13.5B years. The expansion of the visible portion of the universe is still going on with acceleration, now; no physical boundary can go along with it.

Pillar two: cosmic microwave background (CMB). We

see young stars debut in remotely deep space in every direction. If we see the light they produce, we can be rest assured that the nuclear reactions fiercely going on there also profusely produce all kinds of electromagnetic waves, among which microwaves must present.

While visible light has far higher collimation in propagation, microwaves is far more diffusively spreading in their propagation. When we aim our astronomical telescope at two stars in deep space, even if they are close in distance from each other, the light they emit can help us to discern their separation pretty well in most of the cases. However, if we use antenna to catch the microwaves emitted by them, we may most likely fail to discern which wave has been sent by which star. Therefore when we look into a big area in the night sky, even though we can count the number of the shining stars with pin-point accuracy, we cannot expect to have the same accuracy to count the microwave sources.

When we count the shining stars in deep space, we can tell the age of an individual star by the light it emits, but we cannot do the same thing to the microwave source relying on the information carried by the microwaves. We can only tell the overall intensity of the microwaves from the same area we found the stars. The sources contributing to our measurement may include sources having extensively different distances from us and individually invisible to our naked eyes or even instruments. In addition, a great deal of microwaves falling into our observation may be just some invaders that have diffused into the area aimed at by our observation; they are actually from other radiating bodies neighboring to the area we observe. All these microwaves share one thing in common in their propagation: except the tiny bundle caught by our observation, they would all pass us and distance away from their sources father and farther away. Completely disappearing in the endless deep space is their only destination. Nature has no mechanism to send them back to strike at our observation instrument again. In other words, whatever microwaves we detect from the outer space are all "first born", but not anything as secondary returning, or some "coming-back-kids".

To our amazement, the BBT conceives all microwaves that already passed away to be able to return to the space they left behind for an unexplained reason, and calls these "coming-back-kids" the *cosmic background radiation*. Even more amazingly, according to the BBT, they are able to come back after an almost eternal survivorship—13.5B years after the vanishing of the supposed explosion of the Singularity pet fantasized by the BBT. What the BBT is not aware of is that the microwaves named as cosmic background radiation exactly reveals our universe to be infinite.

We mentioned before that in any one direction of our observation regarding microwaves, the overall intensity is a sum contributed by sources from various distance. If we set our distance short, for example, focusing on the sun, we may see very strong microwave bursting from it. However, if we move our observation sideways by a certain angle,

we may see near zero intensity from the **same distance**, because there is no source there. Let's imagine a shell that has a radius equal to the distance between the sun and us, and add all microwave radiation intensity from the sources found on this shell. If we averaged out what we have added up over the areas of this shell, we will have an average intensity per unit area for this shell. Let's call this value A_1. Then, next, we extend our measurement to a shell of bigger radius but still centered at us and repeat what we do in obtaining A_1. Let's call this new figure A_2. After many repetitions with bigger and bigger shells, we will get A_1, A_2, A_3...$A_{(n-2)}$, $A_{(n-1)}$ ...$A_{(q-2)}$, $A_{(q-1)}$, A_q . Regarding these figures, we will find the following relationship:

(1). Generally, we have $A_1<A_2<A_3<...<A_{(n-2)}<A_{(n-1)}<...<A_{(q-2)}<A_{(q-1)}<A_q$. However, interruption such as $A_{(n-2)}>A_{(n-1)}$ may occasionally appear here and there.

(2). Adding all the values of A's together, we will find that $A_1+A_2+A_3+...+A_{(n-2)}+A_{(n-1)}+...+A_{(q-2)}+A_{(q-1)}+A_q$ would end up with a constant value so long as value q is large enough.

The constant value we mention above should be a match in the sense of mathematics to what the BBT calls *cosmic microwave background*. Unfortunately, the microwaves are misinterpreted as something secondarily coming back by the BBT. The constant has an upper limit regardless of how large the value q maybe. If a reader is interested in the mathematical derivation of this constant, he is invited to visit *www.huntune.net*. The derivation is found in the Section of "5-IV. Distribution of Radiating Energy" in the PDF copy (and **PDF copy only**) of the article Hubble's Law—*How Nature Has Formulated It*, led to by clicking the box "Birth of Hubble's Law" on the menu bar. One note must be given here, though. After a certain value A_q, the radiation intensity per unit area for the even bigger shells will decrease, because newer burning bodies are yet waiting in line to be debut—a typical and inevitable phenomenon for an infinite universe.

Pillar three: accelerated expansion.

As suggested by the argument of gravity shown in stonewall-six, the observation of an accelerating expansion of the universe cannot support a limited universe. If not supporting a limited universe, it must be a fact to be made possible by an infinite universe. Of course, for this idea to be addressed, we need to go back to the idea mentioned in pillar one: the unlimited universe has two portions. One portion is visible to us, which is forever engulfed by the invisible potion. There is no doubt that whatever we can detect belongs to the visible portion. Naturally, when someone says the universe is expanding, he can only mean that it is the visible portion of the universe that expands.

As far as the perspective of expansion is concerned, the acceleration rendered by our observation is concluded based on the speed comparison between moving objects with respect to distance from us, but not on the movement of any individual object with respect to our clock. Matching with such a movement distribution with respect to distance is a scene of age distribution among these moving objects: the faster they move and farther away from us the younger they become. Logic then must potentially lead us to believe that ahead of the youngest moving cluster we can ever detect, some even newer generation of heavenly bodies are yet to spring up from the dark. Upon the debut of this newer generation, the so called "youngest moving cluster" a while ago would then look older, because the newly debut generation must have been showing even younger burning light in their "portraits" while running ahead with speed that the originally "youngest moving cluster" cannot catch up. The regeneration of newer and faster running heavenly bodies as distance increases from us must require the following two criteria to be satisfied:

(1) Materials of high internal power but having been idle all the time are lurking in the path of some running heavenly bodies. Their internal energy, when released through certain conversion reaction, has a finite upper limit per unit mass quantity.

(2) If some big quantity of gathering of these materials is landed on by some burning heavenly bodies, the aforementioned conversion reaction must happen, resulting in a new generation of heavenly bodies that run even faster away from us. Soon, the new generation of burning bodies will relay the reaction to materials laying even further ahead.

The landing-on is not some event that must absolutely happen at every instant in every location to all material gathering in space. It is some events that inevitably happen sooner or later, here and there due to probability but also further and further away from us. Once happened, a chain reaction to have (1) and (2) above repeated in space forever becomes unstoppable.

When the landing happens, the new and yet to burn and explode materials inherit the momentum from the incoming body. The new born and burning fragments ejected out of the explosion then have extra momentum added to their traveling capability with what their internal energy bestows them. With the extra momentum, the newborns must run faster than the incoming body. Generation after generation, the repetitive momentum accumulation propels the newer and newer generation to run faster and faster. Again, only an unlimited universe can provide the arena for such a show to demonstrate; a limited universe is by no means able to be so generous.

The generous space offering displayed by an infinite universe further compels us to accept a scene that the visible portion of the universe is forever a tiny part in the unlimited universe, no matter how the visible portion would have expanded. In the invisible portion, highly explosive materials are homogeneously stocked everywhere, but the homogeneity in large scale is not absolute. It is locally interrupted allover in the entire universe. Given that 74% of

the materials spread in the observable portion of the universe is still hydrogen after 13.5B years of all kind of nuclear and chemical reactions, we have reason to believe that the most primitive materials that our universe originally had is hydrogen all the time.

Pillar four: no huge space void found.

A space void should be absolutely natural and thus imperative to entitle the BBT with validity. The absence of such a void then must serve rejecting the validity of the BBT. Given how an accelerating expansion scene is made possible due to the materials' original distribution, the absence of the space void is some forceful evidence retrospectively witnessing the originally homogeneous characteristic in material distribution for the universe before its visible portion appeared.

Pillar five: special Relativity being self-refuted.

If the BBT needs relativity theory as its frame work, it would not stand well when special relativity must show being refuted by itself. If the "limited" is gone, what is left for choice? Needless to say, the "unlimited", or infinite.

Pillar six: gravity.

We have experiment showing that gravity is a physical behavior highly accurately resembling what is shown by objects immersed in fluid. From this comparison, we have reason to believe that everything in the universe is embraced by a fluid and therefore the existence of the omnipresence of gravity. Calculation shows that, to cause the gravity with the magnitude we have been familiar with between heavenly objects, such a fluid must have an intrinsic pressure of no less than $1x10^{17}$ newton/m^2 [5] . To hold this fluid of insanely high intrinsic pressure in bay, we need a physical boundary for the universe. However, no materials in human's knowledge can do the job if nature is ever to provide a physical boundary for the universe. The only solution is to let this fluid existing in a universe that has unlimited space.

An unlimited universe prevents the existence of a unique mass center for the entire universe. Without the presence of such a center, there would never be any possibility that the universe would eventually contract to one ultimate single point like what many versions of Big Crunch have speculated and preached. In an unlimited universe, gravitational balance between material bodies is so achieved: with respect to any free material body, the entire universe encircling it acts like a hollow dome but with a homogeneous shell, which is the entire material content of the universe. Inside this hollow dome, any material body will not have gravitational interaction with any gravity body outside of the shell. This phenomenon regarding an object inside a hollow dome of homogeneous wall is well known to students studying physics.

Unfortunately, to any individual body inside the "hollow" dome of the universe, the local wall of the doom is "patched" with loose material clouds. Over times, The materials may shed piece by piece because of local gravity and more and more pile up on this body. The piling up may have started as a very slow process but someday very rapidly as the mass of piling up gradually increases. Various local conditions may push the appearance of various sizes of aggregate of such piling up in the entire universe, from small chunks of cloud all the way up to what is called black holes today. The prolonged process of material accretion produces heat, which can escape from any of the piling up, of course. Finally, however, by one extremely rare chance, heat cannot sufficiently escape from one of the black hole candidates but reaches a threshold temperature at which thermonuclear reaction is to be induced. A first ever light out of material explosion appears in the universe. An evolution phase of no return begins for our universe since then.

Pillar seven: coincidence of a time window

Directly, only if we extend this time window of observation to forever can we permanently see the unexhausted pouring in of the images of new stars from more and more remote space into our observation instruments. But to have the infinite extension of such a time window made possible must require the existence of an infinite universe.

Conclusion: Human beings have never been able to see the "out-most" rim of the universe, and there never be such a thing for them to see. Given how ever younger stars gain their ever higher speed at ever more remotely deep space through momentum accumulation (see pillar three argument), there must be someday in which some heavenly objects fly away from us at speed beyond what our observation can ever catch (maybe it already happens).

REFERENCES

1. Olbers' Paradox, https://en.wikipedia.org/wiki/Olbers%27_paradox
2. Cosmic Microwave Background, wikipedia
3. Timeline of the Metric Expansion of Space, wikipedia
4. Special Relativity Is Self-refuted, by Cameorn Rebigsol, p148, 2016 Proceedings, CNPS, or *The Self-refuted Relativity* in *www.huntune.net*
5. Aether, the Mother of All Forces in Nature, by Cameron Rebigsol, p61, 2018 Proceedings, CNPS , or "An All-Force-Unifier" in www.huntune.net

Aether Based Gravity, Electromagnetism, Quantum Mechanics and Entanglement

Duncan Shaw

1517 Angus Drive, Vancouver, BC, Canada, V6J 4H2, duncanshaw@shaw.ca

This paper ties together my articles and papers that propose a physical model of the cause of gravity and a physical base of the phenomena of electromagnetism, quantum mechanics and entanglement. The paper proposes that the medium of aether is the common element that underlies gravity, electromagnetism, quantum mechanics and entanglement.

Keywords: aether, ether, medium, gravity, electromagnetism, quantum mechanics, entanglement, fluid, condensation, diffusion

A. Introduction

The search for a physical concept that unifies gravity and electromagnetism is longstanding. This paper pursues that quest. It suggests that the Scottish physicist, James Clerk Maxwell, provided groundwork for unification in his seminal work, The Dynamical Theory of the Electromagnetic Field[1], published in 1865, in which he proposed a physical theory of aether upon which he based his fundamental equations of electromagnetism that are still in use today, over a century and a half later.

My interest in Maxwell's Dynamical Theory arose when I was considering and developing ideas for a physical concept of the cause of gravity. When I read his treatise it occurred to me that if his form of aether is viewed as a medium that has the capacity to flow, it might serve as a candidate for the cause of gravity. In result, the articles cited below in the CAUSE OF GRAVITY section set out my concept of the cause of gravity, in large part based upon Maxwell's theory of aether. The proposed gravity model involves the collisional force of aether flowing into cosmic bodies, driven by the intrinsic energy of the medium of aether, much like the intrinsic energy of the medium of air drives the flow of air into an ordinary household vacuum cleaner, and drives the flows of our atmosphere from high pressure areas to low pressure areas.

My research moved from the cause of gravity to the underpinnings of electromagnetism. It appeared to me that Maxwell's aether theory, though little used today, is in fact the best available physical cause-and-effect approach to electromagnetism. See the section below, **ELECTROMAGNETISM**.

I turned next to the apparently inexplicable phenomenon of entanglement. It, too, appeared to me to lend itself to an explanation based upon Maxwell's concept of aether. While I was preparing my paper on entanglement, it occurred to me that the explanation I was proposing for entanglement could in fact be the long sought-after physical foundation of the quantum mechanics theory. So, I expanded the scope of the entanglement paper to include the proposed explanation to the quantum mechanics theory. See the section below, **QUANTUM MECHANICS AND ENTANGLEMENT**.

In the present climate of theoretical physics, there is a significant problem in proposing concepts based upon the medium of aether. Maxwell's theory of aether, while initially having received a significant measure of acceptance, subsequently fell into disuse and even outright rejection. The Michelson-Morley experiment in 1881 and similar experiments, Einstein's Special Theory of Relativity in 1905, and the advent of the quantum mechanics theory in the 1920s, have been interpreted by many in the science community as establishing that aether does not exist

Yet, it seems to me that some form of aether is necessary to base physical explanations of gravity, electromagnetism, quantum mechanics and entanglement. My articles cited below argue that a medium of aether as theorized by Maxwell in fact exists and is likely the common physical underpinning of all these phenomena. See the **AETHER** section below.

Taken as a whole, my articles propose that the medium of aether, substantially as theorized by Maxwell, unify gravity with electromagnetism, quantum mechanics and entanglement. All these phenomena are related to the same substance – aether. In regard to gravity, inflow of condensed aether provides collisional momentum that is the direct cause of gravity, and outflow of gaseous aether replenishes aether in space. Outflowing aether also removes heat from cosmic bodies that is caused by the collisional force of inflowing aether. Interactions of aether cells within the medium cause the phenomena of electromagnetism, quantum mechanics and entanglement. Interactions of aether cells also provide the energy the driving force – that propels the inflow of aether that causes gravity and the outflow that replenishes aetherin space.

My articles that support these propositions are discussed below.

B. Aether

A proposition runs through my articles and papers cited below is that a medium of aether permeates space and cosmic bodies. The medium consists of sub-atomic cells that are real substance, not mathematical constructs.

The posited aether is modeled substantially on the form of aether proposed by James Clerk Maxwell in 1865 in his treatise, The Dynamical Theory of the Electromagnetic Field1. In this work Maxwell set out his theory of electromagnetic fields and his equations of electromagnetism that are still in use today. His equations were based upon his posited form of aether. Here are some passages from Maxwell's treatise that describe his proposed form of aether:

- We have therefore some reason to believe, from the phenomena of light and heat, that there is an ethereal medium filling space and permeating bodies, capable of being set in motion and of transmitting that motion from one part to another, and of communicating that motion to gross matter so as to heat it and affect it in various ways. [section 4]

- We may therefore receive, as a datum derived from a branch of science independent of that with which we have to deal, the existence of a pervading medium, of small but real density, capable of being set in motion, and of transmitting motion from one part to another with great, but not infinite, velocity. [section 6]

- But when electromotive force acts on a dielectric it produces a state of polarization of its parts similar in distribution to the polarity of the parts of a mass of iron under the influence of a magnet, and like the magnetic polarization, capable of being described as a state in which every particle has its opposite poles in opposite conditions [section 11]

- Here, then, we perceive another effect of electromotive force, namely, electric displacement, which according to our theory is a kind of elastic yielding to the action of the force, similar to that which takes place in structures and machines owing to the want of perfect rigidity of the connections. [section 12]

- The energy in electromagnetic phenomena is mechanical energy. The only question is, Where does it reside? On our theory it resides in the electromagnetic field, in the space surrounding the electrified and magnetic bodies, as well as in those bodies themselves, and is in two different forms, which may be described without hypothesis as magnetic polarization and electric polarization, or, according to a very probable hypothesis, as the motion and the strain of one and the same medium. [section 74]

- It appears therefore that certain phenomena in electricity and magnetism lead to the same conclusion as those of optics, namely, that there is an ethereal medium pervading all bodies, and modified only in degree by their presence; that the parts of this medium are capable of being set in motion by electric currents and magnets; that this motion is communicated from one part of the medium to another by forces arising from the connections of those parts; that under the action of these forces there is a certain yielding depending on the elasticity of these connections; and that therefore energy in two different forms may exist in the medium, the one form being the actual energy of motion of its parts, and the other being the potential energy stored up in the connections, in virtue of their elasticity. [section 15]

- Thus, then, we are led to the conception of a complicated mechanism capable of a vast variety of motion, but at the same time so connected that the motion of one part depends, according to definite relations, on the motion of other parts, these motions being communicated by forces arising from the relative displacement of the connected parts, in virtue of their elasticity. [section 16]

My papers and articles treat the "parts and connections" of Maxwell's aether as structured cells. My reasoning is that flexible structures are necessary to permit Maxwell's parts and connections to possess the key property of aether proposed by Maxwell, that being elasticity.

Based essentially on Maxwell's descriptions of his form of aether, I infer that aether cells have the capacity to:

- expand and shrink, twist and untwist, vibrate and rotate;
- collide and rebound;
- attach and detach;
- store and transmit energy;
- form a medium that fills space and permeates bodies;
- form a medium that transmits motions and waves;
- collectively form patterns; and
- interact with each other and with atomic matter.

Also, based on physics applicable to ordinary atoms and molecules, I infer that aether cells have the capacity to:

- collectively flow as a fluid, and
- exist in separate and distinct states – like atomic matter – including a gaseous state and a condensed state, probably liquid.

Maxwell's aether theory initially met with general acceptance. However, it subsequently fell into disuse. This happened mainly as a result of the Michelson-Morley experiment in 1881 and other experiments, the advent of Einstein's Special Theory of Relativity in 1905, and the development of the quantum mechanics theory in the 1920s.

My articles contend that a medium of aether does in fact exist, substantially as theorized by Maxwell. Experimental physics, particularly in regard to entanglement, has been based upon the premise that particle-waves called quanta or photons transmit electromagnetic radiation by physically travelling from source to destination, as distinct from the aether approach of Maxwell that electromagnetic radiation is transmitted by waves through the medium of aether. Entanglement experiments have been unable to establish any underlying physical explanation for entanglement and for the quantum mechanics theory. I propose that the likely physical explanation lies in plain sight – in the aether theory that Maxwell developed in 1865.

My article, Reconsidering Maxwell's Aether [2], contends that the medium of aether, substantially as theorized by Maxwell, underlies electromagnetism. The article sets out evidence that aether in fact exists, and provides reasons why aether should be reconsidered as fundamental to electromagnetism. In addition, the article counters the arguments that led to the general disuse of the concept of aether in the science community. See the ELECTROMAGNETISM section below.

My article, Aether Explanation of Entanglement3, proposes that the medium of aether provides the missing physical foundation of the quantum mechanics theory and the physical setting that explains entanglement. The article provides reasons that support resuscitation of Maxwell's aether theory (see p.37). See the QUANTUM MECHANICS AND ENTANGLEMENT section below.

C. Cause of Gravity

The age-old question of whether there is a mechanical cause of gravity has not yet been answered with a theory that has gained general acceptance in the scientific community. In the words of Richard Feynman in The Feynman Lectures on Physics:

What about the machinery of it? All we have done is to describe how the earth moves around the sun, but we have not said what makes it go. Newton made no hypotheses about this; he was satisfied to find out what it did without getting into the machinery of it. No one has since given any machinery.

In the articles cited below5,6,7,8, I propose a conceptual model of flowing aether as the physical cause of gravity. Here is a brief summary:

- The gravity process is cyclic. It involves flows of aether from space into cosmic bodies and from cosmic bodies back into space.
- The Inflowing aether and the outflowing aether are different states of aether. Outflowing aether consists of separate aether cells in a gaseous state. Inflowing aether consists of groups of aether cells that have condensed into liquid-state droplets, each of which is comprised of numerous cells.
- Inflowing aether collides with matter that is in its path. The collisions push matter toward cosmic bodies. THE INFLOW COLLISIONS ARE THE DIRECT CAUSE OF GRAVITY.
- Outflowing aether also collides with matter in its path. However, because outgoing cells are considerably smaller than incoming droplets, outflowing cells tend to pass by or through the matter of cosmic bodies. Thus, the collisional force of inflowing aether on

cosmic bodies is considerably greater than the collisional force exerted by outflowing aether.

- The predominance of the collisional force of inflowing aether over the collisional force of outflowing aether explains why gravity is a one-way force.
- As aether flows from the expanse of space into the relatively small target of a cosmic body, the flow converges. The convergence causes the flow to accelerate – Bernoulli's principle and the Venturi effect. This explains why gravity is an accelerating force.
- As gaseous-state aether flows through space, it condenses into liquid state aether. An analog is gaseous water molecules that evaporate from the surface of the Earth, rise into the Earth's atmosphere and condense into liquid droplets.
- As inflowing liquid-state aether approaches and collides with cosmic bodies, heat generated by the collisions causes the inflowing aether to vaporize into gaseous-state aether.
- What causes inflow and outflow? The answer lies in the science of fluid mechanics. Substances that comprise fluids seek equilibrium of concentration. This occurs by way of diffusion, that is, the random movement of gases and liquids from areas of higher concentration to areas of lower concentration. The phenomenon of two-way diffusion of fluids is described by G. K. Batchelor in his textbook, An Introduction to Fluid Mechanics[9]. See also Landau and Lifshitz, Fluid Mechanics, 2nd edition[10].
- In regard to inflowing aether, its level of concentration of droplets in the vicinity of cosmic bodies is constantly reduced below its level in space by vaporization of droplets caused by collisions with cosmic bodies. In regard to outflowing aether, its level of concentration of gaseous aether cells in space is constantly reduced by condensation of its aether cells into droplets of liquid aether. Each state of aether seeks its own equilibrium of concentration, with gaseous aether flowing into space and liquid aether flowing toward cosmic bodies. They flow through each other by diffusion and perhaps by convection, each seeking –but never reaching – its own equilibrium of concentration.
- Where is the energy that drives the flows? It lies in the constant movements of aether cells and droplets – their collisions and rebounding – their elasticity – their vibrations – within the medium of aether. This is like the energy of interacting molecules that push air towards the intake of a vacuum cleaner, and cause winds in our atmosphere to flow from areas of high pressure to areas of low pressure.
- Does this energy diminish and run out? Not according to the law of conservation of energy. The energy may change its form, but with the various processes and events occurring in the universe, it is reasonable to assume that the aether medium that pervades the

universe will both lose and gain energy, but will remain in overall energy equilibrium.

The following articles develop and describe the proposed cause-of-gravity model:

The Cause of Gravity: A Concept5 proposes the concept of gravity being caused by the ram (pushing) force of aether cells that flow into cosmic bodies and collide with atomic matter, less the pushing force of constituent particles that flow back into space. The one-way-force aspect of gravity is explained by inflowing aether cells being larger than their constituent outflowing particles and therefore more likely to collide with the structure of atomic matter. The accelerating-force aspect of gravity is explained by convergence of inflow aether from the wide expanse of space into the relatively small areas occupied by cosmic bodies. The fact that gravity between the Sun and the Earth appears to be instantaneous action-at-a-distance is explained by the flow of aether from space into the solar system moving directly toward the Sun at the instant when it encounters and collides with the Earth.

Flowing Aether: A Concept 6 introduces the concept of aether having gaseous and liquid states. The size difference between inflow droplets and outflow cells explains why gravity is a one-way force. This replaces the previous explanation based upon the size difference between aether cells and their constituent particles.

Outflowing Aether [7] deals with the outflow of aether into space. It proposes that gaseous aether is produced by vaporization of incoming liquid aether and that the gaseous aether travels into space by way of convection and diffusion. The idea is drawn from the rain cycle on Earth, namely: evaporation of water molecules from the surface of the Earth, flow of the water molecules into the atmosphere by diffusion and convection, condensation of the molecules into droplets, and their return to the Earth as rain.

Aether Concept of Gravity [8] provides a summary of the points made in the above papers and sets out, step-by-step, the various interrelated factors that comprise the proposed model of the cause of gravity.

D. Electromagnetism

As stated in the INTRODUCTION section above, James Clerk Maxwell, in his treatise, The Dynamical Theory of the Electromagnetic Field1, theorized a form of aether as the physical context for his equations of electromagnetism that are still in use today. Subsequently, with the advent of the Michelson-Morley experiments, Einstein's Special Theory of Relativity and the Quantum Mechanics theory, Maxwell's aether theory has generally fallen into disuse.

My article, Reconsidering Maxwell's Aether2, contends that the medium of aether, substantially as theorized by Maxwell, underlies electromagnetism. The article counters the arguments that have led to the disuse of aether. It cites evidence that aether in fact exists, and provides reasons why aether should be reconsidered as fundamental to electromagnetism.

The article provides a brief summary of Maxwell's aether theory:

- As a fundamental proposition, the concept of action-at-distance is rejected; rather, there must be a substance within which electromagnetic phenomena occur.
- Electromagnetic fields are composed of matter in motion. The matter in motion is an aetherial medium of small but real density that fills space and permeates bodies, and is capable of transmitting motion.
- The medium consists of parts and connections that are capable of elastic yielding. It can store energy by elastic displacement of its parts and from the motion of its parts.
- The medium has the capacity to propagate waves.
- Rotation in a magnetic field arises from rotational movement of the aetherial medium.
- Electromotive force causes electric current. Electric current is variations of electric displacement.
- The elasticity of electric displacement causes a back-flow of current when the electromotive force is removed.
- Electric current has momentum which it transfers to the surrounding electromagnetic field through its connection to the field; and the transfer of momentum operates in reverse from the electromagnetic field to the current, the direction depending upon the relative levels of energy in the current and in the surrounding electromagnetic field.
- Polarization is a "forced" state of aether that is placed under stress by electromotive force. Polarization disappears when the electromotive force is removed.

The paper sets out potential implications of returning to Maxwell's aether. If the concept of Maxwell's aether is resurrected, this opens up a mechanical concept of electromagnetism. The electromagnetic phenomena the article considers include: electric current, back surge of electricity, magnetic fields that surround conductors, polarization, magnetism, electromagnetic radiation, electromagnetic fields, wave lengths, interference, refraction, wave/particle duality, and quantization.

E. Quantum Mechanics and Entanglement

I recommend that before considering this section, the reader re-read the passages from Maxwell's The Dynamical Theory of the Electromagnetic Field that are quoted in section 2. AETHER.

The quantum mechanics theory was developed in the 1920s and is generally accepted by present-day physics for its mathematics. While the mathematics of the quantum mechanics theory have been experimentally verified, there is still no accepted concept of the physical mechanics that underlie the quantum mechanics theory. Finding or developing a concept to fill this gap is a challenge to present-day science. My article, Aether Explanation of

Entanglement[3], proposes that this may be accomplished by reviving Maxwell's theory of aether.

Entanglement is a phenomenon that produces seemingly instantaneous communication of electromagnetic characteristics at sites situated at appreciable distances from each other. Entanglement has been thoroughly explored by numerous experiments. The experiments have failed to discover the underlying physical cause of entanglement. It is significant that the entanglement experiments do not appear to have addressed the possibility that the medium of aether as conceived by Maxwell might provide a setting in which entanglement makes sense.

The article proposes that the medium of aether, essentially as described by Maxwell, is (1) the missing physical foundation of the quantum mechanics theory, and (2) the physical setting that explains entanglement and eliminates the problem of instantaneous action-at-a-distance.

The article considers correlations of electromagnetic characteristics recorded by sensors used in entanglement experiments. The correlated characteristics include levels of energy, momentum, angles of momentum, spin, vibrations, frequencies and wavelengths, patterns of polarization, rotations and torque. The article ties correlations into the use of Maxwell's form of aether as the physical base of quantum mechanics and entanglement.

The proposal relies on Maxwell's proposition that aether permeates space and cosmic bodies. From this, it is reasoned that aether must permeate the areas in which entanglement experiments have been carried out. It is proposed that the readings of electromagnetic characteristics at the sensors in the entanglement experiments are derived from the surrounding aether medium, rather than from emitted photons. The characteristics in the aether medium are a combination of those already in the medium before the power sources used in the experiments are engaged, plus those that are added by emissions from the power sources once they are turned on. This reasoning invokes the known phenomenon of superposition. The resulting characteristics are spread throughout the aether medium (in other words, correlated) by way of interactions of the aether cells that comprise the medium.

On this approach to entanglement, the characteristics recorded by the sensors are provided by medium itself, not by travelling photons or quanta. The characteristics are correlated by interactions within the medium. As a result, the characteristics recorded by the sensors are those in place in the medium at the moment the sensors record them. This eliminates communication between the sensors as the cause of correlations. Importantly, this eliminates the instantaneous action-at-a-distance problem that is associated with the present approach to entanglement.

F. Aether Medium Concept Versus Travelling Photons Concept

Conceptually, both aether cells and photons have the capacity to carry and transmit the various characteristics of electromagnetic radiation. These characteristics include energy, momentum, angles of momentum, spin, vibrations, waves, polarization, rotation and torque, and various levels and variations of the characteristics. It may fairly be assumed that in order to carry and transmit these characteristics, aether cells and photons must be entities that are structured in a manner that provides the capacity – the elasticity – that enables them to carry and transmit the characteristics.

Conceptually, aether cells and photons also differ from each other. Aether cells form a medium of aether cells that interact with each other by collisions and rebounds, and by this means transmit electromagnetic radiation. The distance that aether cells travel in the aether medium is limited to the mean free paths between the constituent cells. In contrast, photons transmit electromagnetic radiation by travelling intact from the source of radiation to the point of reception. The trajectories of photons are theoretically unlimited. They may travel short distances, and they may travel vast distances, including from far away galaxies that are billions of light years from the Earth. Both aether cells and photons collide with matter at the end of their respective trajectories and transmit electromagnetic characteristics to the matter they collide with.

What concept is preferable, the aether medium or the travelling photons?

In my view, the aether medium approach is preferable. Put simply, the concept that photons can travel from far away galaxies through light-years of distance to the retinas of our eyes without collisions that impede their travel is problematic, given the trillions of cosmic bodies and the immense amount of other matter that logically must block the paths of the travelling photons.

The aether medium concept has certain powerful advantages. It brings elements of closeness and interactions of the aether cells that constitute the medium. This permits aether cells to act in unison and interchange their energy and characteristics. Thus, the medium of aether can flow like the medium of air, and by its flows cause the force of gravity. Movements and interactions of aether cells within the medium can provide the energy that propels the flows of the medium in the gravity process. The medium provides a setting within which its constituent cells can interact with each other and thereby produce electromagnetic phenomena. The medium permits light to be transmitted by series of interactions (collisions) of its cells. The collisions and rebounds of the cells can propel the cells to the speed of light and thus permits transmission of radiation through the medium at the speed of light. The congregation of cells within the medium permits transmission of waves of unlimited variety of wavelengths, set by groups of cells within the medium vibrating in rhythmic unison with each other. The medium permits characteristics such as momentum, spin, vibrations, frequencies, patterns of polarization and torque to be spread throughout the medium, and to the sensors used in the entanglement experiments. The medium permits physical correlation of those characteristics within the medium.

And, the medium permits polarization of the aether cells that surround the Earth and thus form the Earth's magnetic field.

This is by no means a complete list of the phenomena that are consistent with there being a medium of aether, essentially in the form conceived by Maxwell.

In contrast, the travelling photon approach is encumbered with some difficult problems. As seen in the entanglement experiments, the use of the travelling photons concept has failed to find any logical cause and effect explanation for the quantum mechanics theory and for entanglement. The travelling photons concept has failed to explain Bell's inequalities, and has failed to provide the element of physical reality that the Einstein-Podolsky-Rosen paper, Can Quantum-Mechanical Description of Physical Reality be Considered Complete? [11], says is missing from the quantum mechanics theory. These problems suggest that a conceptual approach that is fundamentally different from that of travelling photons may be called for.

It is significant that the entanglement experiments have not been based upon Maxwell's concept of aether. Have we made a mistake in overlooking Maxwell's wisdom in our quest for physical explanations for electromagnetism, quantum mechanics and entanglement? I think it is likely that we have.

I contend that Maxwell's physical theory of aether provides a rational explanation for the correlations that are observed in the entanglement experiments. Maxwell was one of the world's most gifted physicists. His aether theory was developed as the underpinning of his electromagnetic field equations, one of the most important breakthroughs in theoretical physics. And, his equations remain valid to this day.

Can the data obtained from the entanglement experiments be put to use in determining whether the Maxwell's aether approach is valid? I expect that an analysis of existing data from the entanglement experiments would shed light on this question, and I recommend that this task be undertaken. However, this is not a challenge that I am equipped to undertake. That is for others who have the requisite mathematics, should they wish to do so.

In this regard, I note that Richard Feynman, in The Feynman Lectures on Physics 12, compared the mathematics of interference of electrons with the mathematics of interference of water waves in one-slit and two-slit experiments. He found the mathematics to be the same for both water waves and electrons. He said:

"Yet, surprisingly enough, the mathematics for relating P_1 and P_2 to P_{12} (the electron experiment) is extremely simple. For P_{12} is just like the curve I_{12} of Fig. 1-2 [the water experiment], and that was simple. What is going on at the backstop can be described by two complex numbers that we can call ϕ_1 and ϕ_2 (they arc functions of x, of course). The absolute square of ϕ_1 gives the effect with only hole 1 open. That is, $P1 = |\phi_1|^2$. The effect with only hole 2 open is given by ϕ_2 in the same way. That is, $P_2 = |\phi_2|^2$. And the combined effect of the two holes is just $P_{12} = |\phi_1 + \phi_2|^2$. The mathematics is the same as that we had for the water waves! (It is hard to see how one could get such a simple result from a complicated game of electrons going back and forth through the plate on some strange trajectory). [Emphasis added]

A propos Feynman's last observation – that it is hard to see how one gets such a simple result from a complicated game of electrons I suggest that the result becomes simple if one starts from the premise that the interference of electrons occurs within the medium of aether, just like the interference of waves occurs within the medium of the water.

G. Conclusions

The articles reviewed in this paper propose and support physical cause-and-effect concepts of gravity, electromagnetism, quantum mechanics and entanglement. The proposals are based upon the proposition that there exists a medium of aether, basically as theorized by James Clerk Maxwell in 1865 in his work, The Dynamical Theory of the Electromagnetic Field.

The articles indicate significant conceptual ties between the phenomenon of gravity and the phenomena of electromagnetism, quantum mechanics and entanglement. The dominant conceptual tie is that all these phenomena arise from the same substance – aether – flowing aether as the cause of gravity, and the medium of aether within which the phenomena of electromagnetism, quantum mechanics and entanglement occur. A further tie is that the source of energy that propels the flows of aether in the gravity process is the same source of energy that causes the phenomena of electromagnetism, quantum mechanics and entanglement, that being the movements and interactions of aether cells within the medium of aether.

The present paper provides reasons why the aether medium concept is preferable to the travelling photon concept.

The present article proposes that the data obtained in the entanglement experiments be analyzed to determine whether or not it accords with the Maxwell's aether concept.

REFERENCES

1. J. C. Maxwell, The Dynamical Theory of the Electromagnetic Field, (Wipf and Stock, Eugene, OR, 1996).
2. D. W. Shaw, Phys. Essays 27, 601 (2014).
3. D. W. Shaw, Phys. Essays 31, 29 (2018).
4. R. Feynman, The Feynman Lectures on Physics, The Definitive Edition, Vol. 1 (Addison Wesley, Reading, MA, 2006), pp. 7-9.
5. D. W. Shaw, Phys. Essays 25, 66 (2012).
6. D. W. Shaw, Phys. Essays 26, 523 (2013).
7. D. W. Shaw, Phys. Essays 29, 4 (2016).
8. D. W. Shaw, Proceedings of John Chappell Natural Philosophy Society, Vol. 3, p. 180 (2017).
9. G. K. Batchelor, An Introduction to Fluid Mechanics (Oxford University Press, New York, NY, 2000) at pp. 28-29.
10. L. D. Landau and E. M. Lifshitz, Fluid Mechanics, 2nd

edition (Elsevier Butterworth Heinemann, Oxford, UK, 2004).

11. A. Einstein, D. Podolsky and N. Rosen, Phys. Rev. 47, 777 (1935).

12. R. Feynman, The Feynman Lectures on Physics, The Definitive Edition, Vol. 3, p. 1-5.

Author Index